MY FIRST 500 KOREAN WORDS

MY FIRST 500 KOREAN WORDS

초판발행	1st Edition published	2017. 5. 15
지은이	Written by	TalkToMeInKorean
책임편집	Edited by	선경화 Kyung-hwa Sun, 스테파니 베이츠 Stephanie Bates,
		에밀리 프리즈러키 Emily Przylucki
디자인	Designed by	한보람 Bo Ram Han
녹음	Voice Recording by	TalkToMeInKorean
펴낸곳	Published by	롱테일북스 Longtail Books
펴낸이	Publisher	이수영 Su Young Lee
편집	Copy-edited by	김보경 Florence Kim
주소	Address	서울 마포구 양화로 12길 16-9(서교동) 북앤드빌딩 3층
		3rd Floor Book-And Bldg. 16-9 Yanghwa-ro 12-gil, Mapo-gu, Seoul, KOREA
전화	Telephone	+82-2-3144-2708
팩스	Fax	+82-2-3144-2597
이메일	E-mail	TTMIK@longtailbooks.co.kr
ISBN	979-11-86701-61-4	13710

MY FIRST
500
KOREAN WORDS

이야기로 배우는
한국어 기본 단어 500

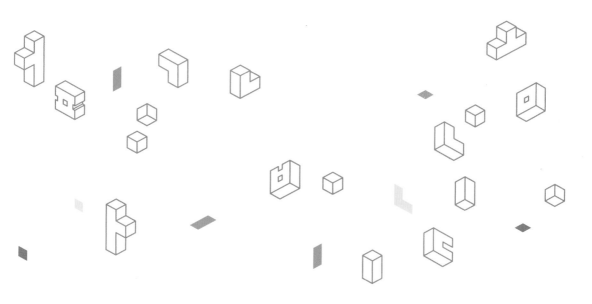

CONTENTS

Day 01 ⋮ 041	Day 02 ⋮ 049	Day 03 ⋮ 057
나	매일	시험
회사원	일찍	의자
너무	일어나다	책상
바쁘다	물	더럽다
우리	마시다	위
보통	세수	청소
주말	옷	깨끗하다
만나다	입다	공책
영화	화장	필통
카페	회사	시작하다

Day 04 ⋮ 065	Day 05 ⋮ 073	Day 06 ⋮ 081
배고프다	어린이	겨울
아까	학교	방학
빵	가족	할머니
음료수	공원	가다
주다	많다	버스
지금	어른	지하철
배부르다	아기	타다
좋다	적다	고양이
선생님	신기하다	동물
무섭다	어떻게	놀다

My First 500 Korean Words is a vocabulary book designed for beginner learners of the Korean language. This book introduces 500 essential Korean words in context to make them more meaningful for you and easier to memorize. Learning vocabulary in this fashion provides you with an opportunity to substantially increase your ability to understand, retain, and use Korean words without having to solely rely on the standard rote memorization method.

Along with the 500 words in this book which are used on a daily basis by native speakers, related words and expressions are included to give you access to a broader understanding of the Korean language. Each chapter also provides you with some creative opportunities to review what you have learned through word matching, crossword puzzles, and fill-in-the-blank questions. It is recommended that you study one chapter per day in this book, but if you are busy and need to take two or three days to complete one chapter, the results will be great as long as you stay consistent and don't give up!

If you are ready to learn,
let's get started!

HOW TO USE THIS BOOK

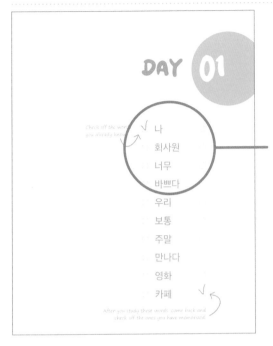

Each "Day" introduces 10 words. Place a check next to the words you already knew prior to this chapter, and then come back to this page to see how many words you memorized at the end of the Day.

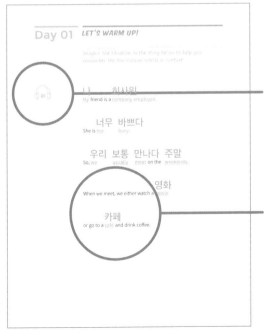

Listen to the words of the "Day" pronounced by native Korean speakers by downloading the MP3 audio files at **TalkToMeInKorean.com/audio.**

Before diving into the vocabulary, read the short story in English with the Korean translation of the 10 words written above. This will help put the words, which will be introduced on the following pages, into context.

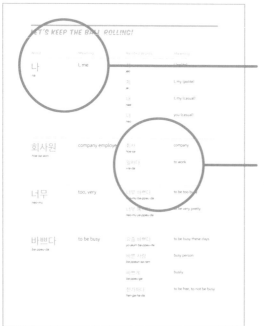

The main words are listed here with their meaning in English.

Words in this section are related to the main vocabulary word. You can find plural forms, synonyms, antonyms, common collocations, conjugated forms, derivative forms, or casual/honorific forms.

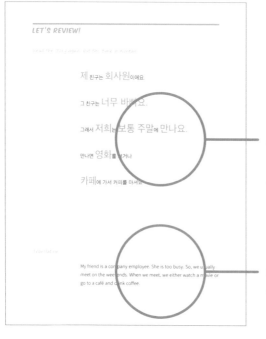

After committing the 10 words to memory, read the same story from Section 1, only this time entirely in Korean.

Check your understanding of the story with this English translation.

Review what you have studied with a few exercises.

주말	I, me
만나다	to meet
보통	movie
카페	to be busy
너무	café
바쁘다	we, our
나	usually, usual, regular
회사원	weekend
영화	company employee
우리	too, very

Crossword Puzzle

01 to meet
02 weekend
03 to be busy
04 I, me
05 company employee
06 we, our
07 usually, usual, regular

Complete the story by filling in each blank with a word you have learned, but in its correct conjugated form.

Fill in the blanks using one of the words that you learned in Day 03. Please refer to page 132, review how to conjugate verbs/adjectives.

1. ___ (친구는 회사원이에요.)   My friend is a company employee.

2. 제 친구는 ___ 이에요.   My friend is a company employee.

3. 그 친구는 ___ 이에요.   She is too busy.

4. 그 친구는 너무 ___ .   She is too busy.

5. 그래서 ___ 는 보통 주말에 만나요.   So, we usually meet on the weekends.

6. 그래서 저희는 ___ 주말에 만나요.   So, we usually meet on the weekends.

7. 그래서 저희는 보통 ___ 에 만나요.   So, we usually meet on the weekends.

8. 그래서 저희는 보통 주말에 ___ .   So, we usually meet on the weekends.

9. 만나면 ___ 를 보거나 카페에 가서 커피를 마셔요.   When we meet, we either watch a movie or go to a café and drink coffee.

10. 만나면 영화를 보거나 ___ 에 가서 커피를 마셔요.   When we meet, we either watch a movie or go to a café and drink coffee.

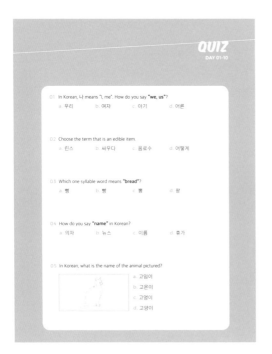

01 In Korean, 나 means "I, me". How do you say **"we, us"**?
   a. 우리   b. 여자   c. 아기   d. 어른

02 Choose the term that is an edible item.
   a. 린스   b. 싸우다   c. 음료수   d. 어떻게

03 Which one syllable word means **"bread"**?
   a. 뼝   b. 빵   c. 뿡   d. 팡

04 How do you say **"name"** in Korean?
   a. 의자   b. 뉴스   c. 이름   d. 휴가

05 In Korean, what is the name of the animal pictured?
   a. 고엄이
   b. 고온이
   c. 고엉이
   d. 고양이

After studying 10 "Days" worth of words (or 100 words), there is a multiple choice quiz covering all of the vocabulary so that you can check your progress and create new goals.

Honorific Speech in Korean

In Korean, the relationship between the speaker/writer and the audience or listener is reflected in speech to or about someone. There are three main honorific speech types in Korean: subject, object, and relative.

Relative-honorific speech is most commonly known as "speech levels," where a speaker uses either high or low forms of speech to the person being spoken to, regardless of the topic being discussed. The level of relative-honorific speech is usually determined based on the age of the speaker versus the listener. This explains why Korean people will often ask you about your age when first meeting you - they want to know what level of speech to use. Subject-honorific speech uses honorifics toward the subject of a sentence (not directly speaking to someone, but rather ABOUT someone who is older or in a higher position), while object-honorific speech is speaking to the object of a sentence using honorifics.

As a beginner level learner, you will focus mainly on relative-honorific speech.

When it comes to relative-honorific speech, there are two main speech levels: formal and informal.

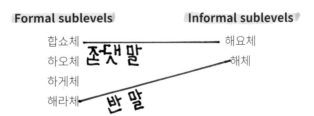

Formal sublevels	Informal sublevels
합쇼체 ——————————————— 해요체	
하오체 존댓말	해체
하게체	
해라체 반말	

합쇼체 and 해요체 are polite forms which are used to speak to someone who is older or in a higher position than you, and these forms belong to a category of polite language called 존댓말 (존대 means "to treat with respect"). Even when speaking to someone who is younger or in a lower position than you, it is polite to use 존댓말 until you get permission to use casual language from him/her.

Casual forms such as 해라체 and 해체 belong to the 반말, or casual language, category. You can use 반말 to someone who is much younger or in a lower position than you. Between adults, 반말 is not used right away, even after finding out each other's ages, as the younger person may feel offended. Instead, 반말 is generally used between close friends and with children.

In contemporary Korean language, typically only the following four sublevels are used: 합쇼체, 해라체, 해요체, and 해체.

Endings used for each sublevel in declarative sentences:
　　합쇼체: -(스)ㅂ니다
　　해라체: -(ㄴ)다
　　해요체: -아/어/여요
　　해체: -아/어/여

If conjugating these endings with a verb, the ending changes slightly based on the verb stem. The verb 가다 (to go) is used in the following example:
　　합쇼체: 가다 + -(스)ㅂ니다 = 갑니다
　　해라체: 가다 + -(ㄴ)다 = 간다
　　해요체: 가다 + -아/어/여요 = 가요
　　해체: 가다 + -아/어/여 = 가

Since 합쇼체 is too formal to use every day, only 해요체 is used in this book.

Aside from endings, speakers sometimes use lower forms of certain words to sound humble or polite when speaking to someone in a higher position. For example, "I" is 나 in Korean, but 저 is the lower form of 나 in 존댓말. "We" is 우리, but 저희 is used to express humility or politeness.

Conjugation of Regular Verbs

The infinitive form (also known as "dictionary form") of Korean verbs always ends with -다, but for most verb conjugations in Korean, you use the "verb stem" of a verb and add various endings to it. The verb stem is formed by simply dropping the -다 from the infinitive form of a verb. All verbs in Korean end with -다 (e.g. 가다, 보다, 하다, etc.), so if you remove -다 from the end, you are left with the verb stem (e.g. 가, 보, 하, etc.).

Present Tense = -아/어/여요

Present tense verbs in Korean cover a wider range of tenses than in English; therefore, a sentence in the present tense in Korean can be translated to many different things in English. For example, 가요 can be translated as "I go", "I'm going", "I'm going to go", or even "I will go".

To create a present tense sentence, add -아요, -어요, or -여요 after the verb stem. If the verb stem's last vowel is ㅏ or ㅗ, it is followed by -아요. If the last vowel is NOT ㅏ or ㅗ, it is followed by -어요. Only one verb stem, 하, is followed by -여요. However, 하여요 is always shortened to 해요.

Examples

만나다 = to meet

만나 + -아요 → 만나아요 → 만나요. (I meet. / I'm meeting. / etc.)
- When ㅏ meets -아요, 아 is omitted to become 만나요, not 만나아요.

마시다 = to drink

마시 + -어요 → 마시어요 → 마셔요. (I drink. / I'm drinking. / etc.)
- When ㅣ and -어 are combined, it becomes ㅕ.

보내다 = to send

보내 + -어요 → 보내어요 → 보내요. (I send. / I'm sending. / etc.)
- When ㅐ meets -어요, 어 is omitted to become 보내요, not 보내어요.

시작하다 = to start, to begin

시작하 + -여요 → 시작하여요 → 시작해요. (I start. / I will start. / etc.)
- When 하 and -여 are combined, 하여 is always shortened to 해.

Past Tense
= -았/었/였어요

Add -았어요, -었어요, or -였어요 after the verb stem to form a past tense statement. If the last vowel of the verb stem is ㅏ or ㅗ, it is followed by -았어요. If the last vowel is NOT ㅏ or ㅗ, it is followed by -었어요. Only one verb stem, 하, is followed by -였어요. However, 하였어요 is usually shortened to 했어요.

Examples

만나다 = to meet

만나 + -았어요 = 만났어요. (I met.)

- When ㅏ meets -았, 아 is omitted to become 만났어요, not 만나았어요.

마시다 = to drink

마시 + -었어요 = 마셨어요. (I drank.)

- When ㅣ and -어 are combined, it becomes ㅕ.

보내다 = to send

보내 + -었어요 → 보내었어요 → 보냈어요. (I sent.)

- When ㅐ meets -었, 어 is omitted to become 보냈어요, not 보내었어요.

시작하다 = to start, to begin

시작하 + -였어요 = 시작했어요. (I started.)

- When 하 and -였 are combined, 하였 is usually shortened to 했.

Future Tense
= -(으)ㄹ 거예요

To create a future tense sentence, add either -을 거예요 or -ㄹ 거예요. If the last syllable of the verb stem is a consonant, add -을 거예요, and if the verb stem ends with a vowel, add -ㄹ 거예요. Although -(으)ㄹ 거예요 is basically a future tense sentence ending, you can also use this to express your assumption about something. Depending on the context, -(으)ㄹ 거예요 can be translated as either "it will/I will/they are going to" or "I think/I assume".

Examples

일어나다 = to get up, to wake up

일어나 + -ㄹ 거예요 = 일어날 거예요. = I will get up. / I think he (she) will get up.

입다 = to wear, to put on

입 + -을 거예요 = 입을 거예요. = I will wear. / I think she (he) will wear.

Modifier (1)
= -(으)ㄴ

Used after a verb stem, this suffix changes a verb into a modifying adjective (in the past tense) to be used in front of a noun. This is similar to the role of a clause such as "that I found" or "that I bought yesterday" that is typically used after a noun in English.

Examples

찾다 = to find

찾은 = that I found, that they found

어제 찾은 책 = the book that she found yesterday

Modifier (2)
= -는

Used after a verb stem, this suffix changes a verb into a modifying adjective (in the present tense) to be used in front of a noun. This is similar to the role of a clause such as "that I like" or "that I use everyday" that is typically used after a noun in English.

Examples

가다 = to go

가는 = that I go to

매일 가는 곳 = a place that I go to every day

Modifier (3)
= -(으)ㄹ

Used after a verb stem, this suffix changes a verb into a modifying adjective (in the future tense) to be used in front of a noun. This is similar to the role of a clause such as "that will start tomorrow" or "that you will see there" that is typically used after a noun in English.

Examples
연습하다 = to practice
연습할 = that I will practice
연습할 계획 = a plan that I will practice, a plan to practice

Passive Voice =
-이/히/리/기- & -되다

Although there is no set-in-stone rule when it comes to passive voice, the general rules are as follows:

(1) 이
When the dictionary form of the verb ends in -ㅎ다, 이 is added to the verb stem ending and changes to -ㅎ이다.

Examples
놓다 (to put down) → 놓이다 (to be put down)
쌓다 (to pile up) → 쌓이다 (to be piled up)

(2) 히
When the dictionary form of the verb ends in -ㄱ다, -ㄷ다 or ㅂ다, 히 is added to the verb stem ending and changes to -ㄱ히다, ㄷ히다 or ㅂ히다.

Examples
막다 (to block) → 막히다 (to be blocked)
닫다 (to close) → 닫히다 (to be closed)

(3) 리

When the dictionary form of the verb ends in -ㄹ다, -리 is added to the verb stem ending and changes to -ㄹ리다.

Examples

열다 (to open) → 열리다 (to be opened)

팔다 (to sell) → 팔리다 (to be sold)

(4) 기

When the dictionary form of the verb ends in -ㄴ다, ㅁ다, ㅅ다 or ㅊ다, -기 is added to the verb stem ending and changes to -ㄴ기다, -ㅁ기다, -ㅅ기다 or -ㅊ기다.

Examples

안다 (to hug) → 안기다 (to be hugged)

담다 (to put something in a basket/bag) → 담기다 (to be put into a basket/bag)

Passive Voice of 하다 Verbs

하다 verbs are combinations of nouns + 하다. For example:

시작 (start, begin) + 하다 = to start, to begin

걱정(worry) + (하다) = to worry

To change these 하다 verbs into passive voice, change 하다 to 되다.

Examples

시작하다 → 시작되다 (to be started)

걱정하다 → 걱정되다 (to be worried)

Conjugation of Adjectives

In English, adjectives such as "pretty", "big", and "tall" are already in the correct format to be used in a sentence. In Korean, however, adjectives must be conjugated because they are in the infinitive form. For example:

예쁘다 = to be pretty
크다 = to be big
높다 = to be tall

To use these to modify a noun (pretty girl, big dog, tall mountain), you must conjugate the word into the modifier format: drop the -다 to get the adjective stem by itself, and if the stem ends with a vowel, add -ㄴ as the final consonant. If the stem ends with a consonant, add -은.

Examples
크다 = to be big (adjective in the infinitive form)
큰 = big (base adjective form)

높다 = to be high (adjective in the infinitive form)
높은 = high (base adjective form)

When adjectives are used as predicate adjectives rather than as modifiers, such as in "OOO is pretty", "OOO is big", and "OOO is important", you can conjugate the adjectives just as you would verbs depending on the tense.

Examples
바쁘다

Present Tense 바쁘 + -아요 → 바쁘아요 → 바빠요. (OOO is busy.)

• When ― meets another vowel, ― is omitted to become 바빠요, not 바쁘아요.

바쁘 + -았어요 → 바쁘았어요 → 바빴어요. (OOO was busy.)

Past Tense:
• When ― meets another vowel, ― is omitted to become 바빴어요, not 바쁘았어요.

바쁘 + -(으)ㄹ 거예요 → 바쁠 거예요. (OOO will be busy.)

Future Tense:

Adverbs = -게

If you add -게 to an adjective stem, it become an adverb.

Examples

조용하다 = to be quiet

조용하게 = quietly

싸다 = to be cheap

싸게 = cheaply

Conjugation of Irregular Verbs/Adjectives

Irregulars: ㅂ

When the following verbs or adjectives are followed by a suffix which starts with a vowel, the ㅂ is eliminated and becomes 우.

더럽다 = to be dirty

무섭다 = to be scary

차갑다 = to be cold

덥다 = to be hot (weather)

눕다 = to lie down

뜨겁다 = to be hot

시끄럽다 = to be noisy

어둡다 = to be dark
귀엽다 = to be cute
무겁다 = to be heavy
춥다 = to be cold (weather)
어렵다 = to be difficult
가깝다 = to be close
쉽다 = to be easy
가볍다 = to be light

Example
더럽다

Present Tense: 더럽 + -어요 → 더러우 + -어요 → 더러우어요 → 더러워요
Past Tense: 더럽 + -었어요 → 더러우 + -었어요 → 더러우었어요 → 더러웠어요
Future Tense: 더럽 + -(으)ㄹ 거예요 → 더러우 + -(으)ㄹ 거예요 → 더러울 거예요

Irregulars: 르

When the following verbs or adjectives are followed by -아/어/여요 (present tense) or -았/었/였어요 (past tense), 르 is changed to ㄹ and placed at the end of the previous syllable, while one more ㄹ is added to the verb/adjective ending.

배부르다 = to be full
바르다 = to apply
부르다 = to call
모르다 = to not know
다르다 = to be different
고르다 = to pick, to choose

Example
배부르다

Present Tense
배부르 + -어요 → 배불ㄹ + -어요 → 배불러요

Present Tense: 배부르 + -었어요 → 배불ㄹ + -었어요 → 배불렀어요

Past Tense:

Irregulars: ㄷ

When the following verbs are followed by a suffix which starts with a vowel, ㄷ is changed to ㄹ.

듣다 = to hear
걷다 = to walk
알아듣다 = to understand

Example
듣다

Present Tense: 듣 + -어요 → 들 + -어요 → 들어요

Past Tense: 듣 + -었어요 → 들 + -었어요 → 들었어요

Future Tense: 듣 + -(으)ㄹ 거예요 → 들 + -(으)ㄹ 거예요 → 들을 거예요

To be + Noun

Present Tense = NOUN + -이에요/예요

Add -이에요/예요 after the noun. If the noun has a final consonant in the last letter, add -이에요, and if it does not have a final consonant and ends in a vowel, add -예요.

Examples
주말 = weekend
주말 + -이에요 = 주말이에요. (It is the weekend.)

의자 = chair
의자 + -예요 = 의자예요. (It is a chair.)

Past Tense = NOUN + -이었어요/였어요

Add -이었어요/였어요 after the noun. If the noun has a final consonant in the last letter, add -이었어요, and if it does not have a final consonant and ends in a vowel, add -였어요.

Examples

주말 = weekend

주말 + -이었어요 = 주말이었어요. (It was the weekend.)

의자 = chair

의자 + -였어요 = 의자였어요. (It was a chair.)

Future Tense = NOUN + -일 거예요

Add -일 거예요 after the noun.

Examples

주말 = weekend

주말 + -일 거예요 = 주말일 거예요. (It will be the weekend.)

의자 = chair

의자 + -일 거예요 = 의자일 거예요. (It will be a chair.)

Conjunctions

Conjunctions connect two sentences together and are used at the beginning of the second sentence in Korean. Listed below are the conjunctions used in this book.

그래서	so, therefore
그리고	and
하지만	but, however (used when the second sentence is in direct contradiction to the first sentence)
그런데	but, however, by the way (used when the second sentence is in contradiction to the first sentence, or when the second sentence is slightly changing the direction of the topic)
그래도	but, still

Numbers

In Korean, there are two number systems: sino-Korean numbers (based on the Chinese number system) and native Korean numbers.

	sino-Korean	native Korean
0	영/공	-
1	일	하나
2	이	둘
3	삼	셋
4	사	넷
5	오	다섯
6	육/륙	여섯
7	칠	일곱

8	팔	여덟
9	구	아홉
10	십	열

Telling Time

Both sino-Korean numbers and native Korean numbers are used when telling time. When you say the hour (시), native Korean numbers (하나, 둘, 셋, 넷, etc.) are used, but when you say the minute (분), sino-Korean numbers (일, 이, 삼, 사, etc.) are used.

1 o'clock	1시	한 시
2 o'clock	2시	두 시
3 o'clock	3시	세 시
4 o'clock	4시	네 시
5 o'clock	5시	다섯 시
6 o'clock	6시	여섯 시
7 o'clock	7시	일곱 시
8 o'clock	8시	여덟 시
9 o'clock	9시	아홉 시
10 o'clock	10시	열 시
11 o'clock	11시	열한 시
12 o'clock	12시	열두 시

1 minute	1분	일 분		**31 minutes**	31분	삼십일 분
2 minutes	2분	이 분		**32 minutes**	32분	삼십이 분
3 minutes	3분	삼 분		**33 minutes**	33분	삼십삼 분
4 minutes	4분	사 분		**34 minutes**	34분	삼십사 분
5 minutes	5분	오 분		**35 minutes**	35분	삼십오 분
6 minutes	6분	육 분		**36 minutes**	36분	삼십육 분
7 minutes	7분	칠 분		**37 minutes**	37분	삼십칠 분
8 minutes	8분	팔 분		**38 minutes**	38분	삼십팔 분
9 minutes	9분	구 분		**39 minutes**	39분	삼십구 분
10 minutes	10분	십 분		**40 minutes**	40분	사십 분
11 minutes	11분	십일 분		**41 minutes**	41분	사십일 분
12 minutes	12분	십이 분		**42 minutes**	42분	사십이 분
13 minutes	13분	십삼 분		**43 minutes**	43분	사십삼 분
14 minutes	14분	십사 분		**44 minutes**	44분	사십사 분
15 minutes	15분	십오 분		**45 minutes**	45분	사십오 분
16 minutes	16분	십육 분		**46 minutes**	46분	사십육 분
17 minutes	17분	십칠 분		**47 minutes**	47분	사십칠 분
18 minutes	18분	십팔 분		**48 minutes**	48분	사십팔 분
19 minutes	19분	십구 분		**49 minutes**	49분	사십구 분
20 minutes	20분	이십 분		**50 minutes**	50분	오십 분
21 minutes	21분	이십일 분		**51 minutes**	51분	오십일 분
22 minutes	22분	이십이 분		**52 minutes**	52분	오십이 분
23 minutes	23분	이십삼 분		**53 minutes**	53분	오십삼 분
24 minutes	24분	이십사 분		**54 minutes**	54분	오십사 분
25 minutes	25분	이십오 분		**55 minutes**	55분	오십오 분
26 minutes	26분	이십육 분		**56 minutes**	56분	오십육 분
27 minutes	27분	이십칠 분		**57 minutes**	57분	오십칠 분
28 minutes	28분	이십팔 분		**58 minutes**	58분	오십팔 분
29 minutes	29분	이십구 분		**59 minutes**	59분	오십구 분
30 minutes	30분	삼십 분		**60 minutes**	60분	육십 분

Counters

When counting things or people in Korean, you often need to use what is called a "counter" or a "counter unit". In English, if you want to talk about books, and there happen to be three of them, you can simply say "three books"; however in Korean, you need to use the format of "book + three + counter". Listed below are the counters used in this book.

Counter	Used with
개	things in general
명	people
마리	animals

Grammar Points Introduced in This Book

All of the examples in this section appear in this book.

NOUN + -은/는 (Day 1)	**(topic marking particles)** Ex) 저희 집에는 = at our house
NOUN + -에 (Day 1)	**at** Ex) 회사에 있다 = to be at work
	on Ex) 의자에 앉다 = to sit on a chair
	in Ex) 쓰레기통에 버리다 = to throw away in a trash bin

into
Ex) 서점에 들어가다 = to go into a bookstore

to
Ex) 시장에 가다 = to go to the market

NOUN + -을/를 **(Day 1)**	**(object marking particles)** Ex) 종이를 찢어요. = I tear some paper.
NOUN + -도 **(Day 2)**	**also, too** Ex) 지하철도 = the subway, too
NOUN + -이/가 **(Day 3)**	**(subject marking particles)** Ex) 해가 떠요. = The sun rises.

NOUN + -에서
(Day 3)

at
Ex) 시장에서 사다 = at the market

from
Ex) 필통에서 = from a pencil case

in
Ex) 사전에서 = in a dictionary

out of
Ex) 세 개 중에서 = out of three

NOUN + -와/과
(Day 3)

with
Ex) 저희와 = with us

and
Ex) 때와 장소 = time and place

NOUN + -(으)로 **(Day 3)**	**to, into** Ex) 방으로 = into a room **with** Ex) 칼로 = with a knife **through/via** Ex) 인터넷으로 = via the Internet **for** Ex) 아침으로 = for breakfast **as** Ex) 생일 선물로 = as a birthday present
NOUN + -부터 **(Day 4)**	**since, from** Ex) 언제부터 = since when
NOUN + -까지 **(Day 4)**	**until, up to** Ex) 지금까지 = until now 여기까지 = up to here
NOUN + -(이)랑 **(Day 4)**	**NOUN and NOUN** Ex) 빵이랑 음료수 = bread and a drink/beverage **with** Ex) 가족이랑 = with my family
NOUN + -한테 **(Day 4)**	**to** Ex) 엄마한테 = to (my) mom **by** Ex) 선생님한테 = by (my) teacher

from

Ex) 친구한테 돈을 빌렸어요. = I borrowed money from a friend.

NOUN + -보다 **(Day 5)**	**than** Ex) 가수들보다 = than singers
NOUN + -들 **(Day 5)**	**(a plural suffix)** Ex) 남자들 = men
NOUN + -만 **(Day 7)**	**only** Ex) 바지만 = only pants
NOUN + -의 **(Day 17)**	**of** Ex) 옆집 부부의 딸 = the daughter of the next door couple
NOUN + -에게 **(Day 23)**	**to** Ex) 나에게 = to me
NOUN + -을/를 위해 **(서)** **(Day 29)**	**in order for, for** Ex) 엄마를 위해서 = for (my) mom
NOUN + -이나 **(Day 46)**	**or** Ex) 신문이나 종이 = newspapers or paper
VERB + -(으)면 **(Day 1)**	**if** Ex) 졸면 = if I doze off
VERB/ADJECTIVE + **-아/어/여서** **(Day 1)**	**(connecting reason and result)** Ex) 공항이 너무 넓어서 길을 잃어버렸어요. = The airport is so spacious that I lost my way.

(connecting an action and another action which takes place after the first action)

Ex) 카페에 가서 커피를 마셔요. = I go to a café and drink coffee.

(connecting an action and the purpose or the plan after the action)

Ex) 지구를 떠나서 우주로 갔어요.
= He left Earth and went to outer space.

VERB + -거나 **(Day 1)**	**or** Ex) 영화를 보거나 = watch a movie or
VERB + -고 **(Day 2)**	**VERB and VERB** Ex) 물을 마시고 세수를 해요. = I drink water and wash my face.
ADJECTIVE + -아/어/여지다 **(Day 3)**	**to become ADJECTIVE** Ex) 건강해지다 = to become healthy 건강해져요. = I become healthy.
VERB + -고 싶다 **(Day 6)**	**to want to VERB** Ex) 놀고 싶다 = to want to hang out 놀고 싶어요 = I want to hang out.
VERB/ADJECTIVE + **-지 않다** **(Day 9)**	**not** Ex) 먹지 않다 = to not eat 먹지 않아요. = I don't eat. / One doesn't eat.
VERB + -(으)ㄹ 수 **있다** **(Day 10)**	**can, be able to** Ex) 구별할 수 있다 = to be able to distinguish 구별할 수 있어요. = You can distinguish them.

VERB + -아/어/여 주다 **(Day 10)**	**to VERB for someone** Ex) 가르쳐 주다 = to teach 가르쳐 줘요. = I teach.
VERB (passive voice) + -어 있다 **(Day 10)**	**to be put into a certain state (by someone) and stay that way** Ex) 열려 있다 = to be open (and remain open) 열려 있어요. = It is open.
VERB + -아/어/여하다 **(Day 11)**	**(making intransitive verbs into transitive verbs)** Ex) 궁금해하다 = to feel curious 궁금해해요. = One feels curious.
VERB + -(으)ㄹ까요? **(Day 11)**	**I wonder** Ex) 기뻐할까요? = I wonder if she will be happy.
VERB + -는 것 **(Day 14)**	**VERB-ing** Ex) 집에 있는 것 = staying at home **something that one VERB** Ex) 못하는 것 = something that one is not good at
VERB + -기 전에 **(Day 20)**	**before VERB-ing** Ex) 해가 지기 전에 = before the sun sets
VERB + -고 있다 **(Day 26)**	**to be VERB-ing** Ex) 배우고 있다 = to be learning 배우고 있어요. = I am learning.

VERB + -(으)ㄴ/는/ (으)ㄹ 것 같다 (Day 32)	**to think (SUBJECT) VERB** Ex) 다친 것 같다 = to think (someone) hurt 다친 것 같아요. = I think I am hurt.
VERB + -는데 (Day 32)	**but** Ex) 약속이 있는데 늦었어요. = I had plans, but I was late. **(explaining the situation first before explaining what happened)** Ex) 집에 가는데 비가 왔어요. = On my way home, it rained.
VERB + -기 위해서 (Day 33)	**in order to VERB** Ex) 듣기 위해서 = in order to listen
VERB + -아/어/여 보다 (Day 33)	**to try VERB-ing** Ex) 입어 보다 = to try putting on, to try on (clothes) 입어 봐요. = I try it on.
VERB + -다가 (Day 36)	**while VERB-ing** Ex) 운동을 하다가 = while working out
VERB + -기 힘들다 (Day 36)	**to be hard to VERB** Ex) 먹기 힘들다 = to be hard to eat 먹기 힘들어요. = It's hard to eat.
VERB + -자마자 (Day 37)	**as soon as** Ex) 집에 오자마자 = as soon as I come home
SUBJECT + VERB + -다고 (Day 38)	**(to say/believe/hear) that SUBJECT VERB** Ex) 벌레가 있다고 했어요. = He said that there was a bug.

VERB + -아/어/여야 하다 (**Day 39**)	**must** Ex) 먹어야 하다 = must eat 먹어야 해요. = I must eat.
VERB + -(으)ㄴ/는지 (**Day 41**)	**(marking the end of a question inside a compound sentence)** Ex) 언제부터 좋아했는지 몰라요. = I don't know since when I have liked it.
VERB + -(으)ㄴ 다음에 (**Day 45**)	**after VERB-ing** Ex) 결혼한 다음에 = after getting married
VERB + -기로 정하다 (**Day 45**)	**to decide to VERB** Ex) 하기로 정하다 = to decide to do 하기로 정해요. = I decide to do.
VERB + -기도 하다 (**Day 46**)	**also VERB** Ex) 유리창을 닦기도 하다 = to also wipe the glass window 유리창을 닦기도 해요. = I also wipe the glass window.
SUBJECT + VERB/ ADJECTIVE + -(으)ㄹ 때 (**Day 46**)	**when SUBJECT VERB/ADJECTIVE** Ex) 손님이 없을 때 = when there are no customers
VERB + -(으)ㄹ 수도 있다 (**Day 47**)	**might, maybe** Ex) 실수할 수도 있다 = to maybe make a mistake 실수할 수도 있어요. = You might make a mistake.

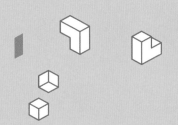

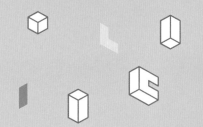

LET'S BEGIN!

제 ~I/My in polite form

저 ~I in polite form

저희 ~ We/our, polite, excluding the listener

Check off the words you already know.

✓ 나 I/me ✓

① 회사원 company employee ✓

✓ 너무 ✓ too/very

② 바쁘다 ✓ to be busy

✓ 우리 ✓ our/we

③ 보통 ✓ usual/usually/regular

✓ 주말 ✓ weekend

⑤ 만나다 ✓ to meet

○ 영화 ✓ movie

✓ 카페 ✓ café

After you study these words, come back and check off the ones you have memorized.

Day 01

Imagine the situation in the story below to help you
remember the ten Korean words in context.

나   회사원

<u>My</u> friend is a <u>company employee.</u>

너무 바쁘다

She is <u>too</u>   <u>busy.</u>

우리 보통 만나다 주말

So, <u>we</u>   <u>usually</u>   <u>meet</u> on the   <u>weekends.</u>

영화

When we meet, we either watch a <u>movie</u>

카페

or go to a <u>café</u> and drink coffee.

LET'S KEEP THE BALL ROLLING!

Word	Meaning	Related Words	Meaning
나 na 나	I, me	저 **저** jeo	I (polite)
		제 **제** je	I, my (polite)
		내 **내** nae	I, my (casual)
		너 **너** neo	you (casual)
회사원 hoe-sa-won 회사원	company employee	회사 **회사** hoe-sa	company
		일하다 **일하다** i-ra-da	to work
너무 neo-mu 너무	too, very	너무 바쁘다 **너무바쁘다** neo-mu ba-ppeu-da	to be too busy
		너무 예쁘다 **너무 예쁘다** neo-mu ye-ppeu-da	to be very pretty
바쁘다 ba-ppeu-da 바쁘다	to be busy	요즘 바쁘다 **요즘바쁘다** yo-jeum ba-ppeu-da	to be busy these days
		바쁜 사람 ba-ppeun sa-ram	busy person **바쁜 사람**
		바쁘게 ba-ppeu-ge	busily **바쁘게**
		한가하다 han-ga-ha-da	to be free, to not be busy **한가하다**

우리
u-ri

we, our

우리

우리 나라 *u-ri na-ra*	우리 나라	our country, my country
우리 집 *u-ri jip*	우리 집	our house, my house
우리 학교 *u-ri hak-kkyo*	우리 학교	our school, my school
저희 *jeo-hui*	저희	we, our (polite, excluding the listener)

보통
bo-tong

usually, usual, regular

보통

| 보통 때 *bo-tong ttae* | 보통 때 | usually, normally |
| 보통 사람 *bo-tong sa-ram* | 보통 사람 | regular person |

주말
ju-mal

weekend

주말

이번 주말 *i-beon ju-mal*	이번 주말	this weekend
주말에 *ju-ma-re*	주말에	on the weekend
주말마다 *ju-mal-ma-da*	주말마다	every weekend
쉬다 *swi-da*	쉬다	to rest
평일 *pyeong-il*	평일	weekday

만나다
man-na-da

to meet

만나 다

우연히 만나다
u-yeo-ni man-na-da

to bump into

우연히 만나다

못 만나다
mot man-na-da

to not be able to meet

못 만나 다

안 만나다
an man-na-da

to not meet

안 만나 다

헤어지다
he-eo-ji-da

to say good-bye, to part

헤 어지 다

영화
yeong-hwa

movie

영화

영화를 보다
yeong-hwa-reul bo-da

to watch a movie

영화를 보다

영화관
yeong-~~hwa~~ gwan
hwa

movie theater

영화관

주인공
ju-in-gong

main character

주인 공

영화배우
yeong-hwa-bae-u

movie actor/actress

영화 배우

카페
ka-pe

café

카페

카페에 가다
ka-pe-e ga-da

to go to a café

카페에 가 다

커피
keo-pi

coffee

키피

차
cha

tea

차

LET'S REVIEW!

Read the story again, but this time in Korean!

제 친구는 회사원이에요.

그 친구는 너무 바빠요.

(그래서)저희는 보통 주말에 만나요.
  ↑
  So

만나면 영화를 보(거나)
          ↑
          or

카페에 가서 커피를 마셔요.

Translation

My friend is a company employee. She is too busy. So, we usually meet on the weekends. When we meet, we either watch a movie or go to a café and drink coffee.

Match each Korean word to its English translation.

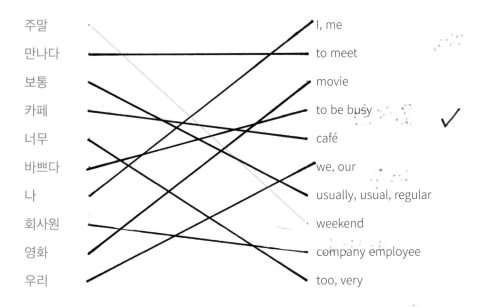

주말	I, me
만나다	to meet
보통	movie
카페	to be busy
너무	café
바쁘다	we, our
나	usually, usual, regular
회사원	weekend
영화	company employee
우리	too, very

Crossword Puzzle

01 to meet ✔
02 weekend ✔
03 to be busy ✗ 바쁘다
04 I, me ✔
05 company employee ✗ 회사원
06 we, our ✔
07 usually, usual, regular ✔

Fill in the blanks using one of the words that you learned in Day 01.
(Please refer to page 017 to review how to conjugate verbs/adjectives.)

✔ 1. (**제**) 친구는 회사원이에요.   My friend is a company employee.

✔ 2. 제 친구는 (**회사원**)이에요.   My friend is a company employee.

✔ 3. 그 친구는 (**너무**) 바빠요.   She is too busy.

✔ 4. 그 친구는 너무 (**바빠요**).   She is too busy.

✔ 5. 그래서 (~~전~~ **저희**)는 보통 주말에 만나요.   So, we usually meet on the weekends.
    ↑ we, our
    (polite excluding the listener)

✔ 6. 그래서 저희는 (**보통**) 주말에 만나요.   So, we usually meet on the weekends.

✔ 7. 그래서 저희는 보통 (**주말**)에 만나요.   So, we usually meet on the weekends.

✔ 8. 그래서 저희는 보통 주말에 (**만나요**).   So, we usually meet on the weekends.

✘ 9. 만나면 (**영화**✘ ~~영화~~)를 보거나 카페에 가서 커피를 마셔요.   When we meet, we either watch a movie or go to a café and drink coffee.

✔ 10. 만나면 영화를 보거나 (**카페**)에 가서 커피를 마셔요.   When we meet, we either watch a movie or go to a café and drink coffee.

고 ~ connects verb → verb

도 ~ also, too

DAY 02

Check off the words
you already know.

○ 매일   ✓ every day

○ 일찍   ✓ early

○ 일어나다   ✓ to wake up/
                  to get up

✓ 물 ·   ✓ water

○ 마시다   ✓ to drink

○ 세수   ✓ to wash
                  ~~your~~ face
                  one's

○ 옷   ✓ clothes

○ 입다   ✓ to wear,
                  to put on

○ 화장   ✓ make-up

✓ 회사   ✓ company
                  (firm)
                  work

After you study these words, come back and
check off the ones you have memorized.

Day 02 *LET'S WARM UP!*

Imagine the situation in the story below to help you
remember the ten Korean words in context.

일어나다 일찍 매일
I <u>wake up</u>　　　<u>early</u>　<u>every</u> morning.

마시다 물　　세수
I <u>drink</u>　　　<u>water</u> and <u>wash my face.</u>

입다　　　　　화장
I <u>put on clothes</u> and put on <u>make-up.</u>

회사
Then I go to <u>work.</u>

I can do it again today!

LET'S KEEP THE BALL ROLLING!

Word	Meaning	Related Words	Meaning
매일 mae-il 매일	every day	매일 만나다 mae-il man-na-da	to meet every day 매일 만나 다
		매일 한 시간 mae-il han si-gan	one hour every day 매일 한 시 간
		매일매일 mae-il-mae-il	every day, every single day 매 일 매 일
일찍 il-jjik 일 찍	early	아침 일찍 a-chim il-jjik	early in the morning 아침 일 찍
		일찍 자다 il-jjik ja-da	to go to bed early 일찍 자다
		일찍 일어나다 il-jjik i-reo-na-da	to wake up early 일찍 일어나 다
		일찍 도착하다 il-jjik do-cha-ka-da	to arrive early 일 찍 도착하 다
일어나다 i-reo-na-da 일 어 나 다	to get up, to wake up	늦게 일어나다 neut-kke i-reo-na-da	to wake up late 늦게 일어 나 다
		먼저 일어나다 meon-jeo i-reo-na-da	to wake up first 머저 일어 나 다
		눕다 nup-tta	to lie down 눕 다
		앉다 an-tta	to sit down 앉 다

물	water	물을 마시다	to drink water
mul		mu-reul ma-si-da	물을 마시다
물		차가운 물	cold water
		cha-ga-un mul	차가운 물
		물을 끓이다	to boil water
		mu-reul kkeu-ri-da	물을 끓이다

마시다	to drink	차를 마시다	to drink tea
ma-si-da		cha-reul ma-si-da	차를 마시다
마시다		천천히 마시다	to drink slowly
		cheon-cheo-ni ma-si-da	천천히 마시다
		다 마시다	to drink up, to drink all
		da ma-si-da	다 마시다

세수	washing one's face	세수하다	to wash one's face
se-su		se-su-ha-da	세수하다
세수		세수를 하다	to wash one's face
		se-su-reul ha-da	세수를 하다

옷	clothes	옷을 사다	to buy clothes
ot		o-seul sa-da	옷을 사다
옷		옷 가게	clothing store
		ot ga-ge	옷 가게
		새 옷	new clothes
		sae ot	새 옷

입다
ip-tta

to wear, to put on

입 다

옷을 입다 *o-seul ip-tta*	to put on clothes 옷을을 입 다
벗다 *beot-tta*	to take off clothes 벗 다
갈아입다 *ga-ra-ip-tta*	to change clothes 갈아 입 다
입어 보다 *i-beo bo-da*	to try on clothes 입 어 보다

화장
hwa-jang

make-up

화 장

화장을 하다 *hwa-jang-eul ha-da*	to put on make-up 화 장을 하다
화장하다 *hwa-jang-ha-da*	to put on make-up 화 장 하 다
화장한 얼굴 *hwa-jang-han eol-gul*	a face with make-up on, a made-up face 화 장한 얼굴
화장품 *hwa-jang-pum*	make-up product, cosmetic product 화 장 품

회사
hoe-sa

company

회사

회사에 들어가다 *hoe-sa-e deu-reo-ga-da*	to join a company 회 사 에 들어 가 다
회사원 *hoe-sa-won*	company employee 회 사 원
회사에 다니다 *hoe-sa-e da-ni-da*	to work at a company 회 사 에 다 니 다

Read the story again, but this time in Korean!

저는 매일 아침 일찍 일어나요.

물을 마시고 세수를 해요.

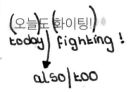
connects
verb → verb

옷을 입고 화장을 해요.

(그리고)회사에 가요.
and

(오늘도)(화이팅!)
today) fighting!

also/too

....

Translation

I wake up early every morning. I drink water and wash my face.
I put on clothes and put on make-up. Then I go to work. I can do it
again today!

Match each Korean word to its English translation.

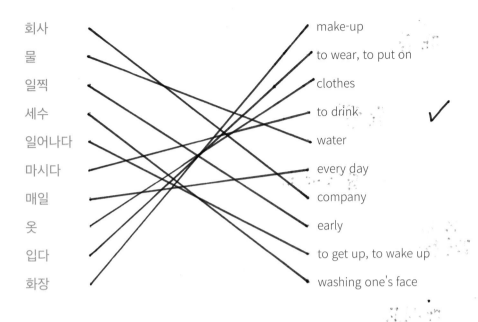

회사 — make-up
물 — to wear, to put on
일찍 — clothes
세수 — to drink ✓
일어나다 — water
마시다 — every day
매일 — company
옷 — early
입다 — to get up, to wake up
화장 — washing one's face

Crossword Puzzle

	01 물				02 입
		04,03→ 일	어	나	다
05 화	장	쩨 쩍			
				06 마	
	07 회	사		시	
				다	

01 water ✓
02 to wear, to put on ✓
03 to get up, to wake up ✓
04 early ✗ 일찍
05 make-up ✓
06 to drink ✓
07 company ✓

Fill in the blanks using one of the words that you learned in Day 02.
(Please refer to page 017 to review how to conjugate verbs/adjectives.)

✓ 1. 저는 (매 일) 아침 일찍 일어나요.   I wake up early every morning.

✓ 2. 저는 매일 아침 (일 찍) 일어나요.   I wake up early every morning.

✓ 3. 저는 매일 아침 일찍 (일어나요)   I wake up early every morning.

✗ 4. (저는)을 마시고 세수를 해요.   I drink water and wash my face.

✓ 5. 물을 (마시고) 세수를 해요.   I drink water and wash my face.

✓ 6. 물을 마시고 (세수)를 해요.   I drink water and wash my face.

✓ 7. (옷)을 입고 화장을 해요.   I put on clothes and put on make-up.

✗ 8. 옷을 (입타) 화장을 해요.   I put on clothes and put on make-up.
    입 다고 ← connects
          verb to verb

✓ 9. 옷을 입고 (화상)을 해요.   I put on clothes and put on make-up.

✓ 10. 그리고 (회사)에 가요.   Then I go to work.

내일 ~ tomorrow
매일 ~ every day
하루 ~ a day
오늘 ~ today
어제 ~ yesterday

DAY 03

Check off the words
you already know.

○ 시험   ✓ test / exam

✓ 의자   ✓ chair

○ 책상   ✓ desk

○ 더럽다   ✓ to be dirty

✓ 위   ✓ up / top

◉ 청소   ✓ cleaning

○ 깨끗하다   ✓ to be clean

✷ 공책   ✓ note book

✷ 필통   ✓ pencil case

✷ 시작하다   ✓ to start / to begin

After you study these words, come back and
check off the ones you have memorized.

LET'S WARM UP!

....

Imagine the situation in the story below to help you
remember the ten Korean words in context.

시험
I have an <u>exam</u> tomorrow.

의자
I sat down on the <u>chair.</u>

책상 더럽다
The <u>desk</u> is too <u>dirty.</u>

청소하다 위
I <u>clean</u> the   <u>top</u> of my desk.

깨끗하다
Now it's <u>clean.</u>

공책   필통
I take out my <u>notebook</u> and my <u>pencil case</u> from my bag.

시작하다
I <u>start</u> studying.

LET'S KEEP THE BALL ROLLING!

Word	Meaning	Related Words	Meaning
시험 *si-heom* 시험	test, exam	시험을 보다 *si-heo-meul bo-da*	to take an exam 시험을 보다
		시험 문제 *si-heom mun-je*	exam question 시험 문제
		시험 공부 *si-heom gong-bu*	study for an exam 시험 공부
		시험 기간 *si-heom gi-gan*	exam period 시험 기간
		성적 *seong-jeok*	exam score 성적
의자 *ui-ja* 의자	chair	의자에 앉다 *ui-ja-e an-tta*	to sit on a chair 의자에 앉다
		나무 의자 *na-mu ui-ja*	wooden chair 나무 의자
		편안한 의자 *pyeo-na-nan ui-ja*	comfortable chair 편안한 의자
책상 *chaek-ssang* 책상	desk	책상 위 *chaek-ssang wi*	on the desk 책상 위
		내 책상 *nae chaek-ssang*	my desk 내 책상
		책상을 정리하다 *chaek-ssang-eul jeong-li-ha-da*	to organize one's desk 책상을 정리하다

더럽다
deo-reop-tta

더럽다

to be dirty

옷이 더럽다 *o-si deo-reop-tta*	the clothes are dirty 옷이 더럽다
더러운 손 *deo-reo-un son*	dirty hand 더 러 운 손
더럽히다 *deo-reo-pi-da*	to make dirty, to dirty up 더 럽 히 다

위
wi

위

up, top

위를 보다 *wi-reul bo-da*	to look up 위를 보다
위로 *wi-ro*	up, upward 위 로
위에서 *wi-e-seo*	from up 위 에 서
아래 *a-rae*	down, below 아 래

청소
cheong-so

청 소

cleaning

화장실 청소 *hwa-jang-sil cheong-so*	cleaning the bathroom ㅋ화 장 실 청 소
청소하다 *cheong-so-ha-da*	to clean 청 소 하 다
교실을 청소하다 *gyo-si-reul cheong-so-ha-da*	to clean the classroom 교 실 을 청 소 하 다
청소기 *cheong-so-gi*	cleaner 청 소 기

깨끗하다
kkae-kkeu-ta-da
깨끗하다

to be clean

물이 깨끗하다
mu-ri kkae-kkeu-ta-da
the water is clean
물이 깨끗하다

깨끗한 손
kkae-kkeu-tan son
clean hand
깨끗한 손

깨끗하게
kkae-kkeu-ta-ge
cleanly
깨끗하게

깨끗해지다
kkae-kkeu-tae-ji-da
to become clean
깨끗해지다

공책
gong-chaek
공책

notebook

공책 열 권
gong-chaek yeol gwon
ten notebooks
공책 열 권

열 = 10
(native Korean
numeral)

권 = counter
(Volume)
for native
Korean numerals

공책에 쓰다
gong-chae-ge sseu-da
to write in a notebook
공책에 쓰다

노트
no-teu
note
노트

필통
pil-tong
필통

pencil case

필통에 담다
pil-tong-e dam-tta
to put into a pencil case
필통에 담다

필통 속
pil-tong sok
inside a pencil case
필통속

필통을 꺼내다
pil-tong-eul kkeo-nae-da
to take out one's pencil case
필통을 꺼내다

필통에서 꺼내다
pil-tong-e-seo kkeo-nae-da
to take out from one's pencil case
필통에서 꺼내다

시작하다
si-ja-ka-da
시작하다

to begin, to start

청소를 시작하다
cheong-so-reul si-ja-ka-da
to start cleaning
청소를 시작하다

시작되다
si-jak-ttoe-da
to be started
시작되다

시작
si-jak
start
시작

Read the story again, but this time in Korean!

내일 **시험**이 있어요. **의자**에 앉았어요.　~~changes to 'l'~~
　↑　　　↑　　　　　　↑　　　　　　~~sound~~
　tomorrow　I have　　on

책상 위가 너무 **더러워요.**

책상 **위**를 **청소**해요.
　　　↑
　object marking
　　particle

이제 **깨끗해요.**
　↑
　Now

가방에서 **공책**과 **필통**을 꺼내요 ↙ I take out
↑　　　　　　　　↑　　　↑
from ~~at~~　　　and　　object
　~~off~~　　　　　　　　marking
　　　　　　　　　　　particle

공부를 **시작해요.**

Translation

I have an exam tomorrow. I sat down on the chair. The desk is too dirty. I clean the top of my desk. Now it's clean. I take out my notebook and my pencil case from my bag. I start studying.

Match each Korean word to its English translation.

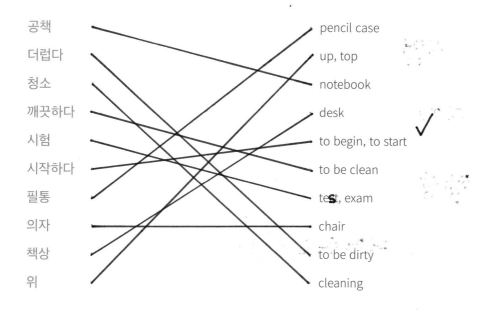

공책
더럽다
청소
깨끗하다
시험
시작하다
필통
의자
책상
위

pencil case
up, top
notebook
desk
to begin, to start ✓
to be clean
test, exam
chair
to be dirty
cleaning

Crossword Puzzle

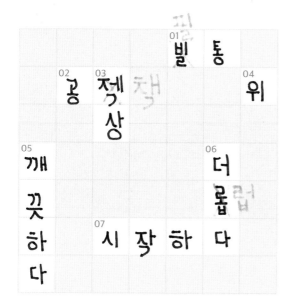

01 pencil case ✓ 필통
02 notebook ✗ 공책
03 desk ✗ 책상
04 up, top ✓
05 to be clean ✓
06 to be dirty 더럽다
07 to begin, to start ✓

Fill in the blanks using one of the words that you learned in Day 03.
(Please refer to page 017 to review how to conjugate verbs/adjectives.)

✓ 1. 내일 (시험)이 있어요. I have an exam tomorrow.

✓ 2. (의자)에 앉았어요. I sat down on the chair.

✓ 3. (책상) 위가 너무 더러워요. The desk is too dirty.

✓ 4. 책상 위가 너무 (더럽워요) see page 25 The desk is too dirty.

✓ 5. 책상 (위)를 청소해요. I clean the top of my desk.

✓ 6. 책상 위를 (청소)해요. I clean the top of my desk.

✗ 7. 이제 (깨끗 해)요 Now it's clean.
        깨

✓ 8. 가방에서 (공책)과 필통을 꺼내요. I take out my notebook and my pencil case from my bag.

✓ 9. 가방에서 공책과 (필통)을 꺼내요. I take out my notebook and my pencil case from my bag.

✓ 10. 공부를 (시작해)요 I start studying.

DAY 04

Check off the words
you already know.

○ 배고프다   ✓ to be hungry

○ 아까   ✓ earlier

✓ 빵   ✓ bread

✗ 음료수   ✓ beverage

○ 주다   ✓ to give

○ 지금   ✓ now

○ 배부르다   ✓ to be full (opposite of hungry)

✗ 졸다   ✓ to doze

○ 선생님   ✓ teacher

○ 무섭다   ✓ to be scary / to be scared

After you study these words, come back and
check off the ones you have memorized.

065

Day 04

Imagine the situation in the story below to help you remember the ten Korean words in context.

배고프다
I am so <u>hungry.</u>

아까　주다　빵
<u>Earlier,</u> my friend <u>gave</u> me some <u>bread</u> and a beverage.

지금
<u>Now</u> I am eating the bread and beverage.

배부르다
Now I'm <u>full.</u>

But I'm so sleepy.

졸다　　　선생님
If I <u>doze off</u> in my class, I get scolded by my <u>teacher.</u>

무섭다
My teacher is so <u>scary.</u>

LET'S KEEP THE BALL ROLLING!

Word	Meaning	Related Words	Meaning
배고프다 bae-go-peu-da 배 고프 다	to be hungry	배가 고프다 bae-ga go-peu-da 배고픈 사람 bae-go-peun sa-ram	to be hungry 배 가 고프다 hungry person 배고픈 사 람
아까 a-kka 아 까	earlier	아까부터 a-kka-bu-teo 방금 bang-geum 나중에 na-jung-e 이따가 i-tta-ga	from earlier, since earlier 아 까부터 just now 방금 later 나 중에 a short time later 이 따 가
빵 ppang 빵	bread	빵을 먹다 ppang-eul meok-tta 빵을 굽다 ppang-eul gup-tta 빵집 ppang-jjip	to eat bread 빵을 먹 다 to bake bread 빵을 굽다 bakery 빵 집
음료수 eum-nyo-su 음료수 (when ㅁ is followed by ㄹ ~ ㄹ becomes ㄴ)	beverage	음료수를 마시다 eum-nyo-su-reul ma-si-da 음료수 한 병 eum-nyo-su han byeong	to drink a beverage 음료수를 마시 다 one bottle of a beverage 음료수 한 병

주다	to give	선물을 주다	to give a present
ju-da		seon-mu-reul ju-da	선물을주다
주다		받다	to receive
		bat-tta	받 다
		주고받다	to give and receive
		ju-go-bat-tta	주고 받다

지금	now	지금 당장	right now
ji-geum		ji-geum dang-jang	지금당장
지금		지금부터	from now
		ji-geum-bu-teo	지금 부터
		지금까지	until now
		ji-geum-kka-ji	지금 까지
		지금 시작하다	to start now
		ji-geum si-ja-ka-da	지금 시작하다

배부르다	to be full (opposite of hungry)	배가 부르다	to be full
bae-bu-reu-da		bae-ga bu-reu-da	배가 부르다
배부르다		배부르게 먹다	to eat until one is full
		bae-bu-reu-ge meok-tta	배 부르게 먹다

졸다	to doze	잠깐 졸다	to doze for a short while
jol-da		jam-kkan jol-da	잠깐 졸다
졸다		깜박 졸다	to doze for a short while
		kkam-ppak jol-da	깜 박 졸다
		조는 사람	person who is dozing
		jo-neun sa-ram	조는 사 람
		졸리다	to feel sleepy
		jol-li-da	졸 리 다

선생님
seon-saeng-nim

선생님

teacher

수학 선생님	math teacher
su-hak seon-saeng-nim	수학 선생님
의사 선생님	doctor
ui-sa seon-saeng-nim	의사 선생님
학생	student
hak-ssaeng	학생

무섭다
mu-seop-tta

무섭다

to be scary,
to be scared

무서워하다	to dread
mu-seo-wo-ha-da	무서워하다
무서운 영화	scary movie
mu-seo-un yeong-hwa	무서운 영화
무서운 선생님	scary teacher
mu-seo-un seon-saeng-nim	무서운 선생님

LET'S REVIEW!

Read the story again, but this time in Korean!

너무 **배고파요.**

아까 친구가 **빵**(이랑)**음료수**를 **줬어요.**
↑
and
(connects noun
and noun)

지금 빵이랑 음료수를 (먹어요.)
↑
eating

(이제)**배불러요.** (그런데)너무 졸려요.
↑　　　　　↑
now　　　　"But"
　　　　　see pg 28

(수업)시간에 **졸면 선생님**(한테)(혼나요.) ← scolded
↑　　　　　　　　　　　　↑
class　　　　　　　　　by (my)

저희 선생님은(정말)**무서워요.**
　　　　　　　↑
　　　　　so/really

Translation

I am so hungry. Earlier, my friend gave me some bread and a beverage. Now I am eating the bread and beverage. Now I'm full. But I'm so sleepy. If I doze off in my class, I get scolded by my teacher. My teacher is so scary.

Match each Korean word to its English translation.

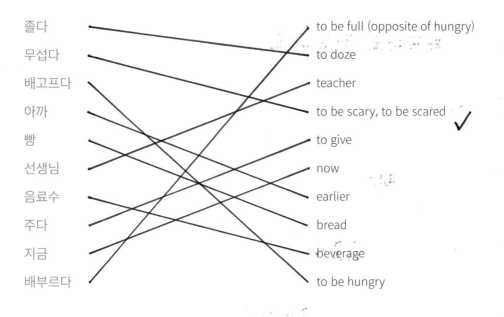

졸다 — to be full (opposite of hungry)

무섭다 — to doze

배고프다 — teacher

아까 — to be scary, to be scared ✓

빵 — to give

선생님 — now

음료수 — earlier

주다 — bread

지금 — beverage

배부르다 — to be hungry

Crossword Puzzle

01 bread ✓
02 to give ✓
03 to be full (opposite of hungry) ✗ 배부르다
04 beverage ✗ 음료수
05 to be hungry ✗ 배고프다
06 earlier ✓
07 now ✓

Fill in the blanks using one of the words that you learned in Day 04.
(Please refer to page 017 to review how to conjugate verbs/adjectives.)

✗ 1. 너무 (**배프나요**. 배고파요) I am so hungry.

✓ 2. (**아까**) 친구가 빵이랑 음료수를 줬어요. Earlier, my friend gave me some bread and a beverage.

✓ 3. 아까 친구가 (**빵**)이랑 음료수를 줬어요. Earlier, my friend gave me some bread and a beverage.

✓ 4. 아까 친구가 빵이랑 (**음료수**)를 줬어요. Earlier, my friend gave me some bread and a beverage.

✓ 5. 아까 친구가 빵이랑 음료수를 (**줬어요**). Earlier, my friend gave me some bread and a beverage.

✓ 6. (**지금**) 빵이랑 음료수를 먹어요. Now I am eating the bread and beverage.

✗ 7. 이제 (**빼불러**)요 Now I'm full.

✓ 8. 수업 시간에 (**졸면**) 선생님한테 혼나요. If I doze off in my class, I get scolded by my teacher.

✓ 9. 수업 시간에 졸면 (**쌀 선생님**)한테 혼나요. If I doze off in my class, I get scolded by my teacher.

~~졸어요~~ ~~졸면~~

✗ 10. 저희 선생님은 정말 (**무섶어요** 무서워요) My teacher is so scary.

DAY 05

Check off the words you already know.

○ 어린이 ○

✓ 학교 ○

○ 가족 ○

✓ 공원 ○

✓ 많다 ○

○ 어른 ○

○ 아기 ○

✗○ 적다 ○

✗○ 신기하다 ○

✓ 어떻게 ○

After you study these words, come back and check off the ones you have memorized.

Day 05

Imagine the situation in the story below to help you remember the ten Korean words in context.

어린이
Today is <u>Children</u>'s Day.

학교
On Children's Day, you don't go to <u>school.</u>

공원　　가족
I went to the <u>park</u> with my <u>family.</u>

많다
There were so <u>many</u> people.

어른　　　　아기
There were many <u>adults</u> and also many <u>babies.</u>

적다　　　　신기하다
There were <u>not many</u> children. It was <u>interesting.</u>

어떻게
<u>How</u> can there be more adults than children at a park?

LET'S KEEP THE BALL ROLLING!

Word	Meaning	Related Words	Meaning
어린이 *eo-ri-ni*	child	어린이날 *eo-ri-ni-nal*	Children's Day
		착한 어린이 *cha-kan eo-ri-ni*	good child
		어른 *eo-reun*	adult
		청소년 *cheong-so-nyeon*	youth, adolescent
학교 *hak-kkyo*	school	학교에 가다 *hak-kkyo-e ga-da*	to go to school
		초등학교 *cho-deung-hak-kkyo*	elementary school
		중학교 *jung-hak-kkyo*	middle school
		고등학교 *go-deung-hak-kkyo*	high school
가족 *ga-jok*	family	가족끼리 *ga-jok-kki-ri*	among family members, with family
		가족사진 *ga-jok-ssa-jin*	family photo
		가족 모임 *ga-jok mo-im*	family gathering
		친척 *chin-cheok*	relative

공원
gong-won

park

공원을 산책하다
gong-wo-neul san-chae-ka-da

to take a walk in the park

놀이공원
no-ri-gong-won

amusement park

공원에서 놀다
gong-wo-ne-seo nol-da

to hang out in the park

많다
man-ta

to be a lot,
to be numerous

사람이 많다
sa-ra-mi man-ta

to be many people

돈이 많다
do-ni man-ta

to have a lot of money

시간이 많다
si-ga-ni man-ta

to have a lot of time

어른
eo-reun

adult, grown-up

어른이 되다
eo-reu-ni doe-da

to become an adult

어른 같다
eo-reun gat-tta

to be like an adult

어른들
eo-reun-deul

adults

아이
a-i

child

ㄴ 어린이 = CHILD ? ?

아기
a-gi

baby

아기를 낳다
a-gi-reul na-ta

to give birth to a baby

아기가 태어나다
a-gi-ga tae-eo-na-da

a baby is born

우리 아기
u-ri a-gi

my baby, our baby

적다 *jeok-tta*	to be few, to be little	사람이 적다 *sa-ra-mi jeok-tta*	to not be many people
		양이 적다 *yang-i jeok-tta*	to not be much
		적은 월급 *jeo-geun wol-geup*	small salary
신기하다 *sin-gi-ha-da*	to be interesting, to be fascinating	신기한 물건 *sin-gi-han mul-geon*	interesting object
		신기하게 *sin-gi-ha-ge*	interestingly
어떻게 *eo-tteo-ke*	how	왜 *wae*	why
		언제 *eon-je*	when
		어디에서 *eo-di-e-seo*	where

어떻다 = TO BE HOW, TO BE LIKE WHAT

Read the story again, but this time in Korean!

오늘은 **어린이**날이에요. 어린이날은 **학교**에 안 가요.

저는 **가족**이랑 **공원**에 갔어요.

사람이 정말 **많았어요.**

어른도 많고 **아기**도 많았어요.

어린이는 **적었어요. 신기했어요.**

어떻게 공원에 어린이보다 어른이 더 많아요?

Translation

Today is Children's Day. On Children's Day, you don't go to school.
I went to the park with my family. There were so many people.
There were many adults and also many babies. There were not
many children. It was interesting. How can there be more adults
than children at a park?

Match each Korean word to its English translation.

어른 · · to be a lot, to be numerous

공원 · · adult, grown-up

아기 · · child

신기하다 · · to be few, to be little

어떻게 · · park

학교 · · family

적다 · · baby

어린이 · · school

가족 · · to be interesting, to be fascinating

많다 · · how

Crossword Puzzle

01 school
02 child
03 adult, grown-up
04 to be few, to be little
05 to be interesting,
    to be fascinating
06 how
07 family

Fill in the blanks using one of the words that you learned in Day 05.
(Please refer to page 017 to review how to conjugate verbs/adjectives.)

1. 오늘은 (어린이)날이에요.   Today is Children's Day.

2. 어린이날은 (학교)에 안 가요.   On Children's Day, you don't go to school.

3. 저는 (가족)이랑 공원에 갔어요.   I went to the park with my family.

4. 저는 가족이랑 (공원)에 갔어요.   I went to the park with my family.

5. 사람이 정말 (많았어요).   There were so many people.

6. (어른)도 많고 아기도 많았어요.   There were many adults and also many babies.

7. 어른도 많고 (아기)도 많았어요.   There were many adults and also many babies.

8. 어린이는 (적었어요).   There were not many children.

9. (신기해요).   It was interesting.

10. (어떻게) 공원에 어린이보다   How can there be more adults than children at a park?
    어른이 더 많아요?

DAY 06

Check off the words you already know.

- ○ 겨울 ○
- ○ 방학 ○
- ✓ 할머니 ○
- ✓ 가다 ○
- ✓ 버스 ○
- ✓ 지하철 ○
- ○ 타다 ○
- ✓ 고양이 ○
- ○ 동물 ○
- ○ 놀다 ○

After you study these words, come back and check off the ones you have memorized.

Day 06

LET'S WARM UP!

....

Imagine the situation in the story below to help you remember the ten Korean words in context.

겨울 방학

It is <u>winter</u> <u>vacation</u> time.

가다 할머니

I <u>go</u> to my <u>grandmother</u>'s house.

버스 타다 지하철

I take the <u>bus</u> and I <u>take</u> the <u>subway</u>, too.

고양이

My grandmother has a <u>cat</u>.

동물

I really like <u>animals</u>.

놀다

I want to <u>play</u> with her cat soon.

LET'S KEEP THE BALL ROLLING!

Word	Meaning	Related Words	Meaning
겨울 *gyeo-ul*	winter	**겨울옷** *gyeo-u-rot*	winter clothes
		겨울 날씨 *gyeo-ul nal-ssi*	winter weather
		춥다 *chup-tta*	to be cold
		눈 *nun*	snow
방학 *bang-hak*	school vacation	**여름 방학** *yeo-reum bang-hak*	summer vacation
		겨울 방학 *gyeo-ul bang-hak*	winter vacation
		방학 숙제 *bang-hak suk-jje*	vacation homework
		개학 *gae-hak*	beginning of a semester
할머니 *hal-meo-ni*	grandmother	**외할머니** *oe-hal-meo-ni*	♀ maternal grandmother
		친할머니 *chi-nal-meo-ni*	♀ paternal grandmother
		할아버지 *ha-ra-beo-ji*	grandfather
		할머니 집 *hal-meo-ni jip*	grandmother's house

가다	to go	만나러 가다 *man-na-reo ga-da*	to go meet (someone)
ga-da		집에 가다 *ji-be ga-da*	to go home
		오다 *o-da*	to come

버스	bus	버스를 타다 *beo-sseu-reul ta-da*	to take the bus
beo-sseu		버스 기사 *beo-sseu gi-sa*	bus driver
		버스 정류장 *beo-sseu jeong-lyu-jang*	bus stop

지하철	subway	지하철을 타다 *ji-ha-cheo-reul ta-da*	to take the subway
ji-ha-cheol		지하철역 *ji-ha-cheol-lyeok*	subway station
		지하철에서 내리다 *ji-ha-cheo-re-seo nae-ri-da*	to get off the subway

타다	to ride	차를 타다 *cha-reul ta-da*	to ride in a car
ta-da		자전거를 타다 *ja-jeon-geo-reul ta-da*	to ride a bicycle
		배를 타다 *bae-reul ta-da*	to ride a boat
		말을 타다 *ma-reul ta-da*	to ride a horse

고양이	cat	새끼 고양이	kitten
go-yang-i		*sae-kki go-yang-i*	
		길 고양이	stray cat
		gil go-yang-i	
		고양이를 키우다	to raise a cat
		go-yang-i-reul ki-u-da	

동물	animal	동물원	zoo
dong-mul		*dong-mu-rwon*	
		동물 병원	veterinary clinic
		dong-mul byeong-won	
		식물	plant
		sing-mul	

놀다	to hang out, to play	친구랑 놀다	to hang out with a friend
nol-da		*chin-gu-rang nol-da*	
		놀러 가다	to go out
		nol-leo ga-da	
		놀고 싶다	to want to play
		nol-go sip-tta	

LET'S REVIEW!

Read the story again, but this time in Korean!

겨울 방학이에요.

할머니 집에 **가요.**

버스도 타고 **지하철**도 **타요.**

할머니는 **고양이**를 키워요.

저는 **동물**이 정말 좋아요.

고양이랑 빨리 **놀고** 싶어요.

Translation

It is winter vacation time. I go to my grandmother's house. I take the bus and I take the subway, too. My grandmother has a cat. I really like animals. I want to play with her cat soon.

Match each Korean word to its English translation.

동물 ·   · bus

가다 ·   · subway

겨울 ·   · to ride

타다 ·   · school vacation

놀다 ·   · winter

할머니 ·   · cat

방학 ·   · animal

지하철 ·   · to hang out, to play

고양이 ·   · grandmother

버스 ·   · to go

Crossword Puzzle

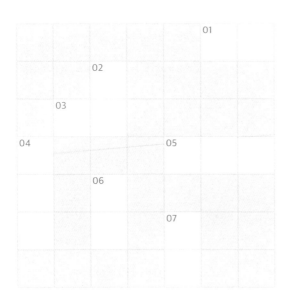

01   animal
02   to hang out, to play
03   to go
04   subway
05   grandmother
06   school vacation
07   winter

Fill in the blanks using one of the words that you learned in Day 06.
(Please refer to page 017 to review how to conjugate verbs/adjectives.)

1. (   ) 방학이에요.　　　　　It is winter vacation time.

2. 겨울 (   )이에요.　　　　　It is winter vacation time.

3. (   ) 집에 가요.　　　　　I go to my grandmother's house.

4. 할머니 집에 (   ).　　　　　I go to my grandmother's house.

5. (   )도 타고 지하철도 타요.　　　　　I take the bus and I take the subway, too.

6. 버스도 타고 (   )도 타요.　　　　　I take the bus and I take the subway, too.

7. 버스도 타고 지하철도 (   ).　　　　　I take the bus and I take the subway, too.

8. 할머니는 (   )를 키워요.　　　　　My grandmother has a cat.

9. 저는 (   )이 정말 좋아요.　　　　　I really like animals.

10. 고양이랑 빨리 (   ) 싶어요.　　　　　I want to play with her cat soon.

DAY 07

Check off the words
you already know.

○ 휴가 ○

○ 남자 ○

○ 여자 ○

○ 샴푸 ○

○ 린스 ○

○ 속옷 ○

○ 양말 ○

○ 드라이기 ○

○ 바지 ○

○ 티셔츠 ○

After you study these words, come back and
check off the ones you have memorized.

Day 07 *LET'S WARM UP!*

Imagine the situation in the story below to help you
remember the ten Korean words in context.

휴가
I went on <u>vacation</u> with my family.

남자
The <u>men</u> brought one bag each.

여자
The <u>women</u> brought two bags each.

샴푸   린스
In the women's bags, there were <u>shampoo</u>, <u>hair conditioner</u>,

속옷   양말
<u>underwear</u>, and <u>socks</u>.

드라이기
There was also a <u>hairdryer</u>.

바지 티셔츠
In the men's bags, there were only <u>pants</u> and <u>t-shirts</u>.

LET'S KEEP THE BALL ROLLING!

Word	Meaning	Related Words	Meaning
휴가 *hyu-ga*	vacation, leave	**휴가를 가다** *hyu-ga-reul ga-da*	to go on a vacation
		휴가를 받다 *hyu-ga-reul bat-tta*	to get a vacation, to get time off
		여름 휴가 *yeo-reum hyu-ga*	summer vacation
남자 *nam-ja*	man	**남자 화장실** *nam-ja hwa-jang-sil*	men's room
		남자 아이 *nam-ja a-i*	boy
		남학생 *na-mak-ssaeng*	male student
여자 *yeo-ja*	woman	**여자 화장실** *yeo-ja hwa-jang-sil*	women's room
		여자 아이 *yeo-ja a-i*	girl
		여학생 *yeo-hak-ssaeng*	female student
샴푸 *syam-pu*	shampoo	**샴푸 냄새** *syam-pu naem-sae*	shampoo smell
		머리를 감다 *meo-ri-reul gam-tta*	to wash one's hair
		비누 *bi-nu*	soap

린스
rin-seu

hair conditioner

린스를 바르다
rin-seu-reul ba-reu-da

to apply hair conditioner

머리를 헹구다
meo-ri-reul heng-gu-da

to rinse one's hair

속옷
so-got

underwear

속옷 몇 벌
so-got myeot beol

a few pieces of underwear

속치마
sok-chi-ma

slip, underskirt

팬티
paen-ti

underpants

브래지어
beu-rae-ji-eo

brassiere, bra

양말
yang-mal

socks

양말을 신다
yang-ma-reul sin-tta

to put on socks

양말을 빨다
yang-ma-reul ppal-da

to wash socks

양말 한 짝
yang-mal han jjak

a sock

드라이기
deu-ra-i-gi

hairdryer

헤어 드라이기
he-eo deu-ra-i-gi

hairdryer

머리를 말리다
meo-ri-reul mal-li-da

to dry one's hair

바지	pants	바지가 맞다	to be the right pants, the pants fit well
ba-ji		*ba-ji-ga mat-tta*	
		바지를 줄이다	to shorten one's pants
		ba-ji-reul ju-ri-da	
		청바지	jeans
		cheong-ba-ji	
		반바지	shorts
		ban-ba-ji	

티셔츠	t-shirt	하얀 티셔츠	white t-shirt
ti-syeo-cheu		*ha-yan ti-syeo-cheu*	
		티셔츠 두 장	two t-shirts
		ti-syeo-cheu du jang	
		티	t-shirt
		ti	

LET'S REVIEW!

....

Read the story again, but this time in Korean!

가족과 함께 **휴가**를 갔어요.

남자들은 가방을 한 개 가져왔어요.

여자들은 가방을 두 개 가져왔어요.

여자들 가방에는 **샴푸, 린스, 속옷,**

양말이 있었어요. **드라이기**도 있었어요.

남자들 가방에는 **바지**와 **티셔츠**만 있었어요.

....

Translation

I went on vacation with my family. The men brought one bag each.
The women brought two bags each. In the women's bags, there
were shampoo, hair conditioner, underwear, and socks. There
was also a hairdryer. In the men's bags, there were only pants and
t-shirts.

Match each Korean word to its English translation.

샴푸	·	· underwear
티셔츠	·	· socks
속옷	·	· hairdryer
휴가	·	· t-shirt
남자	·	· vacation, leave
양말	·	· pants
드라이기	·	· man
바지	·	· shampoo
린스	·	· woman
여자	·	· hair conditioner

Crossword Puzzle

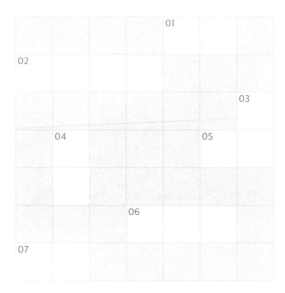

01 socks
02 hairdryer
03 woman
04 hair conditioner
05 man
06 t-shirt
07 shampoo

Fill in the blanks using one of the words that you learned in Day 07.
(Please refer to page 017 to review how to conjugate verbs/adjectives.)

1. 가족과 함께 (   )를 갔어요.   I went on vacation with my family.

2. (   )들은 가방을 한 개 가져왔어요.   The men brought one bag each.

3. (   )들은 가방을 두 개 가져왔어요.   The women brought two bags each.

4. 여자들 가방에는 (   ), 린스, 속옷,   In the women's bags, there were shampoo,
    양말이 있었어요.   hair conditioner, underwear, and socks.

5. 여자들 가방에는 샴푸, (   ), 속옷,   In the women's bags, there were shampoo,
    양말이 있었어요.   hair conditioner, underwear, and socks.

6. 여자들 가방에는 샴푸, 린스, (   ),   In the women's bags, there were shampoo,
    양말이 있었어요.   hair conditioner, underwear, and socks.

7. 여자들 가방에는 샴푸, 린스, 속옷,   In the women's bags, there were shampoo,
    (   )이 있었어요.   hair conditioner, underwear, and socks.

8. (   )도 있었어요.   There was also a hairdryer.

9. 남자들 가방에는 (   )와 티셔츠만   In the men's bags, there were only pants
    있었어요.   and t-shirts.

10. 남자들 가방에는 바지와 (   )만   In the men's bags, there were only pants
    있었어요.   and t-shirts.

DAY 08

Check off the words you already know.

- ○ 누나 ○
- ○ 텔레비전 ○
- ○ 드라마 ○
- ○ 뉴스 ○
- ○ 싸우다 ○
- ○ 지다 ○
- ○ 방 ○
- ○ 닫다 ○
- ○ 음악 ○
- ○ 듣다 ○

After you study these words, come back and check off the ones you have memorized.

Day 08

Imagine the situation in the story below to help you remember the ten Korean words in context.

텔레비전　　　누나

I watched <u>TV</u> in the living room with my <u>older sister</u>.

드라마

She likes <u>TV dramas</u>.

뉴스

I like the <u>news</u>.

싸우다

So, I <u>argued</u> with my sister.

지다

When I fight with my sister, I always <u>lose</u>.

방

I went into my <u>room</u>.

닫다　　　듣다 음악

I <u>closed</u> the door and <u>listened to</u> <u>music</u>.

LET'S KEEP THE BALL ROLLING!

Word	Meaning	Related Words	Meaning
누나 *nu-na*	older sister (for a boy)	친누나 *chin-nu-na*	real older sister, biological older sister
		사촌 누나 *sa-chon nu-na*	older female cousin (for a boy)
		아는 누나 *a-neun nu-na*	older woman a guy knows
텔레비전 *tel-le-bi-jeon*	television	텔레비전을 보다 *tel-le-bi-jeo-neul bo-da*	to watch television
		텔레비전을 켜다 *tel-le-bi-jeo-neul kyeo-da*	to turn on the television
		텔레비전을 끄다 *tel-le-bi-jeo-neul kkeu-da*	to turn off the television
드라마 *deu-ra-ma*	TV drama	드라마를 보다 *deu-ra-ma-reul bo-da*	to watch a TV drama
		인기 있는 드라마 *in-kki in-neun deu-ra-ma*	popular drama
		주인공 *ju-in-gong*	main character
뉴스 *nyu-sseu*	news	텔레비전 뉴스 *tel-le-bi-jeon nyu-sseu*	television news
		뉴스 기사 *nyu-sseu gi-sa*	news article
		소식 *so-sik*	news about a person

싸우다	to fight, to argue	크게 싸우다	to have a big fight,
ssa-u-da		*keu-ge ssa-u-da*	to have a big argument
		싸움	fight
		ssa-um	
		말싸움	argument, quarrel
		mal-ssa-um	
		화해하다	to make up (with),
		hwa-hae-ha-da	to reconcile (with)

지다	to lose	경기에서 지다	to lose a game/match
ji-da		*gyeong-gi-e-seo ji-da*	
		진 사람	someone who lost, loser
		jin sa-ram	
		이기다	to win
		i-gi-da	

방	room	방이 넓다	to be a spacious room
bang		*bang-i neol-tta*	
		방으로 들어가다	to go into a room
		bang-eu-ro deu-reo-ga-da	
		방에 있다	to be in a room
		bang-e it-tta	

닫다	to close	문을 닫다	to close a door
dat-tta		*mu-neul dat-tta*	
		닫히다	to be closed
		da-chi-da	
		열다	to open
		yeol-da	

음악
eu-mak

music

신나는 음악
sin-na-neun eu-mak

exciting music, uplifting music

음악을 틀다
eu-ma-geul teul-da

to turn on music

음악 소리
eu-mak so-ri

music sound

듣다
deut-tta

to listen, to hear

음악을 듣다
eu-ma-geul deut-tta

to listen to music

소리를 듣다
so-ri-reul deut-tta

to listen to a sound

들리다
deul-li-da

to be heard, can hear

들어 보다
deu-reo bo-da

to have a listen

Read the story again, but this time in Korean!

누나랑 거실에서 텔레비전을 봤어요.

누나는 드라마를 좋아해요. 저는 뉴스를 좋아해요.

그래서 누나랑 싸웠어요.

누나랑 싸우면 항상 제가 져요.

저는 방으로 들어갔어요.

문을 닫고 음악을 들었어요.

Translation

I watched TV in the living room with my older sister. She likes TV dramas. I like the news. So, I argued with my sister. When I fight with my sister, I always lose. I went into my room. I closed the door and listened to music.

Match each Korean word to its English translation.

닫다 ·   · TV drama

싸우다 ·   · news

음악 ·   · to lose

듣다 ·   · music

뉴스 ·   · to listen, to hear

방 ·   · older sister (for a boy)

누나 ·   · room

텔레비전 ·   · to fight, to argue

드라마 ·   · television

지다 ·   · to close

Crossword Puzzle

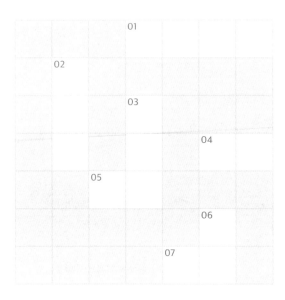

01 television
02 TV drama
03 to fight, to argue
04 older sister (for a boy)
05 to close
06 to listen, to hear
07 to lose

Fill in the blanks using one of the words that you learned in Day 08.
(Please refer to page 017 to review how to conjugate verbs/adjectives.)

1. (   )랑 거실에서 텔레비전을 봤어요.   I watched TV in the living room with my older sister.

2. 누나랑 거실에서 (   )을 봤어요.   I watched TV in the living room with my older sister.

3. 누나는 (   )를 좋아해요.   She likes TV dramas.

4. 저는 (   )를 좋아해요.   I like the news.

5. 그래서 누나랑 (   ).   So, I argued with my sister.

6. 누나랑 싸우면 항상 제가 (   ).   When I fight with my sister, I always lose.

7. 저는 (   )으로 들어갔어요.   I went into my room.

8. 문을 (   ) 음악을 들었어요.   I closed the door and listened to music.

9. 문을 닫고 (   )을 들었어요.   I closed the door and listened to music.

10. 문을 닫고 음악을 (   ).   I closed the door and listened to music.

DAY 09

Check off the words
you already know.

- ○ 개 ○
- ○ 있다 ○
- ○ 이름 ○
- ○ 시간 ○
- ○ 살다 ○
- ○ 죽다 ○
- ○ 슬프다 ○
- ○ 동생 ○
- ○ 울다 ○
- ○ 눈물 ○

After you study these words, come back and
check off the ones you have memorized.

LET'S WARM UP!

Imagine the situation in the story below to help you remember the ten Korean words in context.

있다 개
We <u>had</u> one <u>dog</u> at our house.

이름
Her <u>name</u> was Iseul.

살다   시간
She <u>lived</u> with us for a long <u>time</u>.

죽다
But yesterday, Iseul <u>died</u>.

슬프다
I am so <u>sad</u>.

동생   울다
My <u>younger brother</u> and I <u>cried</u> all day long.

눈물
I can't stop shedding <u>tears</u>.

LET'S KEEP THE BALL ROLLING!

Word	Meaning	Related Words	Meaning
개 *gae*	dog	개를 키우다 *gae-reul ki-u-da*	to raise a dog
		개 한 마리 *gae han ma-ri*	one dog
		강아지 *gang-a-ji*	puppy
있다 *it-tta*	to exist, to have, to be (at a place)	돈이 있다 *do-ni it-tta*	to have money
		약속이 있다 *yak-sso-gi it-tta*	to have plans, to have an appointment
		회사에 있다 *hoe-sa-e it-tta*	to be at work
		없다 *eop-tta*	to not have, to not exist, to not be
이름 *i-reum*	name	이름을 짓다 *i-reu-meul jit-tta*	to make up a name
		이름을 물어보다 *i-reu-meul mu-reo-bo-da*	to ask someone their name
		이름을 적다 *i-reu-meul jeok-tta*	to write down someone's name
		이름을 말하다 *i-reu-meul ma-ra-da*	to say someone's name

시간 *si-gan*	time	시간이 있다 *si-ga-ni it-tta*	to have time
		시간이 없다 *si-ga-ni eop-tta*	to not have time
		시 *si*	hour
		분 *bun*	minute
살다 *sal-da*	to live	혼자 살다 *hon-ja sal-da*	to live alone
		오래 살다 *o-rae sal-da*	to live for a long period of time
		살려 주다 *sal-lyeo ju-da*	to spare someone's life
		삶 *sam*	life
죽다 *juk-tta*	to die	일찍 죽다 *il-jjik juk-tta*	to die young
		죽이다 *ju-gi-da*	to kill
		죽음 *ju-geum*	death
		돌아가시다 *do-ra-ga-si-da*	to pass away

슬프다 *seul-peu-da*	to be sad	슬픈 *seul-peun*	sad
		슬프게 울다 *seul-peu-ge ul-da*	to cry sadly
		기쁘다 *gi-ppeu-da*	to be happy

동생 *dong-saeng*	younger sibling, younger brother, younger sister	동생이 있다 *dong-saeng-i it-tta*	to have a younger sibling
		여동생 *yeo-dong-saeng*	younger sister
		남동생 *nam-dong-saeng*	younger brother

울다 *ul-da*	to cry	펑펑 울다 *peong-peong ul-da*	to cry one's eyes out
		우는 *u-neun*	crying
		울음 *u-reum*	cry, weeping
		울음을 그치다 *u-reu-meul geu-chi-da*	to stop crying

눈물 *nun-mul*	tear	눈물이 나다 *nun-mu-ri na-da*	to shed tears, tears come out
		눈물을 닦다 *nun-mu-reul dak-tta*	to wipe one's tears
		눈물을 흘리다 *nun-mu-reul heul-li-da*	to shed tears

LET'S REVIEW!

Read the story again, but this time in Korean!

저희 집에는 **개**가 한 마리 **있었어요.**

이름은 이슬이었어요.

오랜 **시간** 동안 저희와 함께 **살았어요.**

그런데 어제 이슬이가 **죽었어요.** 너무 **슬퍼요.**

저와 제 **동생**은 하루 종일 **울었어요.**

눈물이 멈추지 않아요.

Translation

We had one dog at our house. Her name was Iseul. She lived with us for a long time. But yesterday, Iseul died. I am so sad. My younger brother and I cried all day long. I can't stop shedding tears.

Match each Korean word to its English translation.

죽다   ·   · name

슬프다   ·   · time

동생   ·   · to live

개   ·   · tear

시간   ·   · younger sibling

있다   ·   · dog

살다   ·   · to cry

이름   ·   · to exist, to have, to be (at a place)

눈물   ·   · to be sad

울다   ·   · to die

Crossword Puzzle

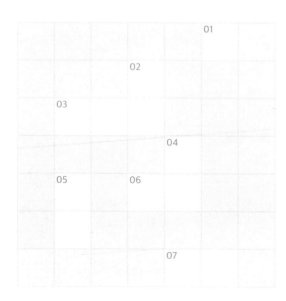

01 dog
02 to cry
03 to be sad
04 to exist, to have,
     to be (at a place)
05 name
06 to live
07 time

Fill in the blanks using one of the words that you learned in Day 09.
(Please refer to page 017 to review how to conjugate verbs/adjectives.)

1. 저희 집에는 (   )가 한 마리 있었어요.   We had one dog at our house.

2. 저희 집에는 개가 한 마리 (   ).   We had one dog at our house.

3. (   )은 이슬이었어요.   Her name was Iseul.

4. 오랜 (   ) 동안 저희와 함께 살았어요.   She lived with us for a long time.

5. 오랜 시간 동안 저희와 함께 (   ).   She lived with us for a long time.

6. 그런데 어제 이슬이가 (   ).   But yesterday, Iseul died.

7. 너무 (   ).   I am so sad.

8. 저와 제 (   )은 하루 종일 울었어요.   My younger brother and I cried all day long.

9. 저와 제 동생은 하루 종일 (   ).   My younger brother and I cried all day long.

10. (   )이 멈추지 않아요.   I can't stop shedding tears.

DAY 10

Check off the words you already know.

○ 수영 ○

○ 수건 ○

○ 가게 ○

○ 돈 ○

○ 빌리다 ○

○ 비누 ○

○ 차갑다 ○

○ 어깨 ○

○ 힘 ○

○ 가르치다 ○

After you study these words, come back and check off the ones you have memorized.

Day 10

....

Imagine the situation in the story below to help you
remember the ten Korean words in context.

수영
I wanted to <u>swim</u>. I went to the swimming pool.

수건   가게
But, I didn't have a <u>towel</u>. I went to a <u>store</u> nearby.

돈   빌리다
But, I didn't have <u>money</u>. I <u>borrowed</u> money from a friend.

비누
I bought a towel. I bought <u>soap</u>.

차갑다
The water in the swimming pool was <u>cold</u>.

어깨 힘   가르치다
My <u>shoulders</u> <u>tightened</u>. My swimming teacher <u>taught</u> me.

So, I was able to relax my shoulders.

LET'S KEEP THE BALL ROLLING!

Word	Meaning	Related Words	Meaning
수영 *su-yeong*	swimming	수영을 배우다 *su-yeong-eul bae-u-da*	to learn to swim
		수영하다 *su-yeong-ha-da*	to swim
		수영장 *su-yeong-jang*	swimming pool
		수영복 *su-yeong-bok*	swimwear
수건 *su-geon*	towel	수건으로 닦다 *su-geo-neu-ro dak-tta*	to wipe with a towel
		마른 수건 *ma-reun su-geon*	dry towel
		흰 수건 *huin su-geon*	white towel
		손수건 *son-su-geon*	handkerchief
가게 *ga-ge*	store	가게에 가다 *ga-ge-e ga-da*	to go to a store
		가게에서 사다 *ga-ge-e-seo sa-da*	to buy at a store
		가게가 열려 있다 *ga-ge-ga yeol-lyeo it-tta*	the store is open
		가게 주인 *ga-ge ju-in*	store owner

돈	money	돈을 벌다	to earn money
don		do-neul beol-da	
		돈을 쓰다	to spend money
		do-neul sseu-da	
		돈이 없다	to have no money
		do-ni eop-tta	
		돈을 모으다	to save money
		do-neul mo-eu-da	

빌리다	to borrow, to rent	돈을 빌리다	to borrow money
bil-li-da		do-neul bil-li-da	
		책을 빌리다	to borrow a book
		chae-geul bil-li-da	
		빌린 차	rented car
		bil-lin cha	

비누	soap	비누로 씻다	to wash with soap
bi-nu		bi-nu-ro ssit-tta	
		비누 거품	soap foam
		bi-nu geo-pum	
		비누칠	lathering
		bi-nu-chil	

차갑다	to be cold	물이 차갑다	the water is cold
cha-gap-tta		mu-ri cha-gap-tta	
		차가운 바람	cold wind
		cha-ga-un ba-ram	
		뜨겁다	to be hot
		tteu-geop-tta	

어깨 *eo-kkae*	shoulder	어깨가 넓다 *eo-kkae-ga neol-tta*	one's shoulders are broad
		어깨를 펴다 *eo-kkae-reul pyeo-da*	to straighten one's shoulders
		어깨에 메다 *eo-kkae-e me-da*	to carry over one's shoulders
힘 *him*	strength, power	힘이 세다 *hi-mi se-da*	to be strong
		힘이 들어가다 *hi-mi deu-reo-ga-da*	to clench, to tighten
		힘주다 *him-ju-da*	to tense your muscles, to emphasize
		힘을 빼다 *hi-meul ppae-da*	to relax one's body, to relax a certain body part
가르치다 *ga-reu-chi-da*	to teach	운전을 가르치다 *un-jeo-neul ga-reu-chi-da*	to teach driving
		잘 가르치다 *jal ga-reu-chi-da*	to teach well
		가르쳐 주다 *ga-reu-chyeo ju-da*	to teach
		선생님 *seon-saeng-nim*	teacher

LET'S REVIEW!

Read the story again, but this time in Korean!

수영을 하고 싶었어요. 수영장에 갔어요.

그런데 **수건**이 없었어요. 근처 **가게**에 갔어요.

그런데 **돈**이 없었어요. 친구한테 돈을 **빌렸어요.**

수건을 샀어요. **비누**도 샀어요. 수영장 물이 **차가웠어요.**

어깨에 **힘**이 들어갔어요. 수영 선생님이 **가르쳐** 줬어요.

그래서 어깨에 힘을 뺄 수 있었어요.

Translation

I wanted to swim. I went to the swimming pool. But, I didn't have a
towel. I went to a store nearby. But, I didn't have money.
I borrowed money from a friend. I bought a towel. I bought soap.
The water in the swimming pool was cold. My shoulders tightened.
My swimming teacher taught me. So, I was able to relax my
shoulders.

Match each Korean word to its English translation.

수영	·	·	store
수건	·	·	soap
차갑다	·	·	to teach
돈	·	·	strength, power
어깨	·	·	swimming
빌리다	·	·	to be cold
비누	·	·	towel
가게	·	·	money
가르치다	·	·	shoulder
힘	·	·	to borrow, to rent

Crossword Puzzle

01 store
02 to teach
03 strength, power
04 to borrow, to rent
05 towel
06 swimming
07 to be cold

02,01→
↓
03
04
06,05→
↓
07

Fill in the blanks using one of the words that you learned in Day 10.
(Please refer to page 017 to review how to conjugate verbs/adjectives.)

1. (   )을 하고 싶었어요.   I wanted to swim.

2. 그런데 (   )이 없었어요.   But, I didn't have a towel.

3. 근처 (   )에 갔어요.   I went to a store nearby.

4. 그런데 (   )이 없었어요.   But, I didn't have money.

5. 친구한테 돈을 (   ).   I borrowed money from a friend.

6. (   )도 샀어요.   I bought soap, too.

7. 수영장 물이 (   ).   The water in the swimming pool was cold.

8. (   )에 힘이 들어갔어요.   My shoulders tightened.

9. 어깨에 (   )이 들어갔어요.   My shoulders tightened.

10. 수영 선생님이 (   ) 줬어요.   My swimming teacher taught me.

01 In Korean, 나 means "I, me". How do you say **"we, us"**?

    a. 우리   b. 여자   c. 아기   d. 어른

02 Choose the term that is an edible item.

    a. 린스   b. 싸우다   c. 음료수   d. 어떻게

03 Which one syllable word means **"bread"**?

    a. 뻥   b. 빵   c. 뽕   d. 팡

04 How do you say **"name"** in Korean?

    a. 의자   b. 뉴스   c. 이름   d. 휴가

05 In Korean, what is the name of the animal pictured?

    a. 고임이

    b. 고은이

    c. 고엉이

    d. 고양이

06 Which of the following is **NOT** a place?

    a. 학교   b. 주말   c. 카페   d. 공원

07 Choose the item that is **NOT** a toiletry.

    a. 동물   b. 수건   c. 비누   d. 샴푸

08 Which of the following words is **NOT** related to school?

    a. 시험   b. 회사원   c. 선생님   d. 방학

09 Which of the following words is **NOT** related to time?

    a. 일찍   b. 아까   c. 가게   d. 지금

10 Choose the term that is **NOT** a loanword from English.

    a. 매일   b. 텔레비전   c. 드라마   d. 버스

11 What does 책상 위 mean?

    a. beside the desk   b. in front of the desk

    c. on the desk   d. under the desk

12 Which season is 겨울?

    a. spring   b. summer   c. fall/autumn   d. winter

13 Which word is not related to the others?

    a. 바지   b. 티셔츠   c. 양말   d. 눈물

14 What is the Korean word for the item in the picture?

    a. 드라이

    b. 드라이기

    c. 드로이기

    d. 드러이기

15 Choose the pair of antonyms that are matched incorrectly.

    a. 울다 - 슬프다   b. 살다 - 죽다

    c. 배고프다 - 배부르다   d. 깨끗하다 - 더럽다

16 Choose which term also includes the others.

    a. 할머니   b. 누나   c. 동생   d. 가족

17 Puppy is 강아지 in Korean. What is **"dog"** in Korean?

    a. 힘   b. 개   c. 방   d. 물

18 Which of the following does **NOT** make sense if it comes after 너무?

    a. 바쁘다   b. 시작하다   c. 무섭다   d. 차갑다

19 Choose the noun-verb pair that is matched incorrectly.

    a. 지하철 - 타다   b. 옷 - 입다

    c. 음악 - 듣다   d. 세수 - 만나다

20 Which of the following does **NOT** become a verb if you attach -하다?

    a. 수영   b. 청소   c. 어깨   d. 화장

QUIZ
DAY 01-10

Answers : a c b c d / b a b c a / c d d b a / d b b d c

DAY 11

Check off the words you already know. ↗

- ○ 내일 ○
- ○ 친하다 ○
- ○ 쓰다 01 ○
- ○ 받다 ○
- ○ 기쁘다 ○
- ○ 선물 ○
- ○ 무엇 ○
- ○ 좋다 ○
- ○ 귀고리 ○
- ○ 목걸이 ○

↖ After you study these words, come back and check off the ones you have memorized.

125

LET'S WARM UP!

Imagine the situation in the story below to help you
remember the ten Korean words in context.

내일 　 친하다
Tomorrow is my close friend's birthday.

쓰다 01
Therefore, I am going to write a congratulatory letter.

기쁘다 　 받다
Will they be happy when they receive the letter?

무엇 　 좋다 선물
What will be a good 　 present?

귀고리
Will earrings be good?

목걸이
Will a necklace be good?

LET'S KEEP THE BALL ROLLING!

Word	Meaning	Related Words	Meaning
내일 *nae-il*	tomorrow	**내일 날씨** *nae-il nal-ssi*	tomorrow's weather
		다음날 *da-eum-nal*	the next day
		모레 *mo-re*	the day after tomorrow
친하다 *chi-na-da*	to be close (with someone)	**동생이랑 친하다** *dong-saeng-i-rang chi-na-da*	to be close to one's younger sibling
		친한 형 *chi-nan hyeong*	a close older male friend (for a boy)
		친하게 지내다 *chi-na-ge ji-nae-da*	to be close to someone
쓰다 01 *sseu-da*	to write	**이름을 쓰다** *i-reu-meul sseu-da*	to write a name
		글씨를 쓰다 *geul-ssi-reul sseu-da*	to write (by hand)
		일기를 쓰다 *il-gi-reul sseu-da*	to write in one's journal
		쓰이다 *sseu-i-da*	to be written

받다
bat-tta

to receive

선물을 받다
seon-mu-reul bat-tta

to receive a present

공을 받다
gong-eul bat-tta

to receive a ball,
to catch a ball

전화를 받다
jeo-nwa-reul bat-tta

to receive a phone call,
to answer a phone call

기쁘다
gi-ppeu-da

to be glad,
to be happy

정말 기쁘다
jeong-mal gi-ppeu-da

to be really glad,
to be really happy

기쁜 마음
gi-ppeun ma-eum

joyful heart, glad heart

기뻐하다
gi-ppeo-ha-da

to be glad, to be joyful

슬프다
seul-peu-da

to be sad

선물
seon-mul

present, gift

선물하다
seon-mu-ra-da

to give as a present

축하 선물
chu-ka seon-mul

congratulatory present

선물을 주다
seon-mu-reul ju-da

to give a present

무엇
mu-eot

what

뭐
mwo

what, something

무슨
mu-seun

what kind of

좋다	to be good	성격이 좋다	to have a good personality
jo-ta		*seong-kkyeo-gi jo-ta*	
		좋은 사람	good person, nice person
		jo-eun sa-ram	
		좋아하다	to like
		jo-a-ha-da	

귀고리	earrings	귀고리를 끼다	to put on earrings
gwi-go-ri		*gwi-go-ri-reul kki-da*	
		귀고리를 하다	to wear earrings
		gwi-go-ri-reul ha-da	
		은 귀고리	silver earrings
		eun gwi-go-ri	
		귀걸이	earrings (different spelling, same meaning)
		gwi-geo-ri	

목걸이	necklace	진주 목걸이	pearl necklace
mok-kkeo-ri		*jin-ju mok-kkeo-ri*	
		금 목걸이	gold necklace
		geum mok-kkeo-ri	
		목걸이를 하다	to wear a necklace
		mok-kkeo-ri-reul ha-da	

LET'S REVIEW!

Read the story again, but this time in Korean!

내일은 친한 친구 생일이에요.

그래서 축하 편지를 쓸 거예요.

편지를 받으면 기뻐할까요?

선물은 뭐가 좋을까요?

귀고리가 좋을까요?

목걸이가 좋을까요?

Translation

Tomorrow is my close friend's birthday. Therefore, I am going to write a congratulatory letter. Will they be happy when they receive the letter? What will be a good present? Will earrings be good? Will a necklace be good?

Match each Korean word to its English translation.

쓰다 01 ·   · to receive

기쁘다 ·   · to be good

받다 ·   · earrings

무엇 ·   · necklace

목걸이 ·   · to write

좋다 ·   · tomorrow

선물 ·   · to be close (with someone)

친하다 ·   · present, gift

귀고리 ·   · to be glad, to be happy

내일 ·   · what

Crossword Puzzle

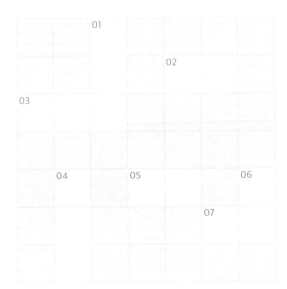

01   to be glad, to be happy
02   tomorrow
03   to be close (with someone)
04   earrings
05   present, gift
06   to be good
07   to receive

Fill in the blanks using one of the words that you learned in Day 11.
(Please refer to page 017 to review how to conjugate verbs/adjectives.)

1. (   )은 친한 친구 생일이에요.   Tomorrow is my close friend's birthday.

2. 내일은 (   ) 친구 생일이에요.   Tomorrow is my close friend's birthday.

3. 그래서 축하 편지를 (   ) 거예요.   Therefore, I am going to write a
                                                    congratulatory letter.

4. 편지를 (   ) 기뻐할까요?   Will they be happy when they receive the
                                                    letter?

5. 편지를 받으면 (   )?   Will they be happy when they receive the
                                                    letter?

6. (   )은 뭐가 좋을까요?   What will be a good present?

7. 선물은 (   )가 좋을까요?   What will be a good present?

8. 선물은 뭐가 (   )?   What will be a good present?

9. (   )가 좋을까요?   Will earrings be good?

10. (   )가 좋을까요?   Will a necklace be good?

DAY 12

Check off the words you already know.

- ○ 오늘 ○
- ○ 생일 ○
- ○ 교실 ○
- ○ 먹다 ○
- ○ 친구 ○
- ○ 노래 ○
- ○ 춤 ○
- ○ 축하하다 ○
- ○ 재미있다 ○
- ○ 하루 ○

After you study these words, come back and check off the ones you have memorized.

LET'S WARM UP!

Imagine the situation in the story below to help you remember the ten Korean words in context.

오늘   생일

Today is my birthday.

교실

We had a birthday party in the classroom.

먹다

We ate cake and also ate snacks.

친구   노래

My friends sang a song for me.

춤

We also sang and danced.

축하하다

I was happy because my friends celebrated my birthday.

재미있다 하루

It was a really fun   day.

LET'S KEEP THE BALL ROLLING!

Word	Meaning	Related Words	Meaning
오늘 *o-neul*	today	**어제** *eo-je*	yesterday
		내일 *nae-il*	tomorrow
생일 *saeng-il*	birthday	**친구 생일** *chin-gu saeng-il*	friend's birthday
		생일 파티 *saeng-il pa-ti*	birthday party
		생일 선물 *saeng-il seon-mul*	birthday present
		생신 *saeng-sin*	birthday (honorific)
교실 *gyo-sil*	classroom	**학교** *hak-kkyo*	school
		칠판 *chil-pan*	blackboard
		책상 *chaek-ssang*	desk
		의자 *ui-ja*	chair

먹다 *meok-tta*	to eat	밥을 먹다 *ba-beul meok-tta*	to have a meal
		많이 먹다 *ma-ni meok-tta*	to eat a lot
		마시다 *ma-si-da*	to drink
친구 *chin-gu*	friend	친구를 사귀다 *chin-gu-reul sa-gwi-da*	to make a friend
		친한 친구 *chi-nan chin-gu*	close friend
		친구들 *chin-gu-deul*	friends
노래 *no-rae*	song	노래하다 *no-rae-ha-da*	to sing
		노래를 듣다 *no-rae-reul deut-tta*	to listen to a song
		노래를 부르다 *no-rae-reul bu-reu-da*	to sing a song
춤 *chum*	dance	춤추다 *chum-chu-da*	to dance
		춤을 추다 *chu-meul chu-da*	to dance
		춤을 잘 추다 *chu-meul jal chu-da*	to dance well
		음악 *eu-mak*	music

축하하다	to congratulate,	생일을 축하하다	to celebrate someone's
chu-ka-ha-da	to celebrate	saeng-i-reul chu-ka-ha-da	birthday
		졸업을 축하하다	to celebrate someone's
		jo-reo-beul chu-ka-ha-da	graduation
		축하해 주다	to congratulate,
		chu-ka-hae ju-da	to celebrate
		축하 파티	celebration,
		chu-ka pa-ti	congratulatory party

재미있다	to be fun	재미있는	fun
jae-mi-it-tta		jae-mi-in-neun	
		정말 재미있다	to be a lot of fun
		jeong-mal jae-mi-it-tta	
		재미없다	to be boring,
		jae-mi-eop-tta	to not be fun

하루	day, one day	하루 종일	all day long
ha-ru		ha-ru jong-il	
		하루를 시작하다	to start one's day
		ha-ru-reul si-ja-ka-da	
		하루 동안	for a day
		ha-ru dong-an	

Read the story again, but this time in Korean!

오늘은 제 **생일**이에요. **교실**에서 생일 파티를 했어요.

케이크도 먹고 과자도 **먹었어요**.

친구들이 **노래**를 불러 줬어요.

노래도 부르고 **춤**도 췄어요.

친구들이 **축하해** 줘서 기분이 좋았어요.

정말 **재미있는 하루**였어요.

Translation

Today is my birthday. We had a birthday party in the classroom. We ate cake and also ate snacks. My friends sang a song for me. We also sang and danced. I was happy because my friends celebrated my birthday. It was a really fun day.

Match each Korean word to its English translation.

친구 ·   · to congratulate, to celebrate

축하하다 ·   · birthday

춤 ·   · friend

오늘 ·   · day, one day

먹다 ·   · song

생일 ·   · today

하루 ·   · classroom

재미있다 ·   · to eat

교실 ·   · dance

노래 ·   · to be fun

Crossword Puzzle

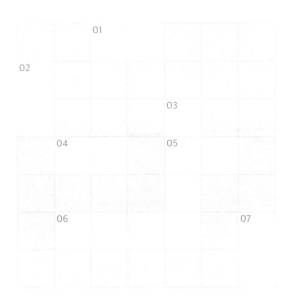

01 today
02 to eat
03 to congratulate, to celebrate
04 song
05 day, one day
06 to be fun
07 friend

Fill in the blanks using one of the words that you learned in Day 12.
(Please refer to page 017 to review how to conjugate verbs/adjectives.)

1. (　　　　　　)은 제 생일이에요.　　　Today is my birthday.

2. 오늘은 제 (　　　　　　)이에요.　　　Today is my birthday.

3. (　　　　　　)에서 생일 파티를 했어요.　　　We had a birthday party in the classroom.

4. 케이크도 먹고 과자도 (　　　　　　).　　　We ate cake and also ate snacks.

5. (　　　　　　)들이 노래를 불러 줬어요.　　　My friends sang a song for me.

6. 친구들이 (　　　　　　)를 불러 줬어요.　　　My friends sang a song for me.

7. 노래도 부르고 (　　　　　　)도 췄어요.　　　We also sang and danced.

8. 친구들이 (　　　　　　) 줘서 기분이 좋았어요.　　　I was happy because my friends celebrated my birthday.

9. 정말 (　　　　　　) 하루였어요.　　　It was a really fun day.

10. 정말 재미있는 (　　　　　　)였어요.　　　It was a really fun day.

DAY 13

Check off the words you already know.

○ 아빠 ○

○ 바다 ○

○ 걷다 ○

○ 식당 ○

○ 맛있다 ○

○ 음식 ○

○ 커피 ○

○ 별 ○

○ 보다 ○

○ 행복하다 ○

After you study these words, come back and check off the ones you have memorized.

Day 13

LET'S WARM UP!

Imagine the situation in the story below to help you remember the ten Korean words in context.

바다   아빠
I went to the <u>ocean</u> with my <u>dad</u>.

걷다
We <u>walked</u> along the beach.

식당   맛있다 음식
We went to a <u>restaurant</u> and had <u>delicious</u>   <u>food</u>.

커피
We went to a café and drank <u>coffee</u>.

보다 별
Night fell. We also <u>saw</u> the   <u>stars</u>.

행복하다
I was very <u>happy</u>.

LET'S KEEP THE BALL ROLLING!

Word	Meaning	Related Words	Meaning
아빠 *a-ppa*	dad	우리 아빠 *u-ri a-ppa*	my dad
		새아빠 *sae-a-ppa*	stepfather
		아빠가 되다 *a-ppa-ga doe-da*	to become a dad
		엄마 *eom-ma*	mom
바다 *ba-da*	sea, ocean	바다에 가다 *ba-da-e ga-da*	to go to the ocean
		바다낚시 *ba-da-nak-ssi*	sea fishing
		바닷가 *ba-dat-kka*	beach
		바닷물 *ba-dan-mul*	sea water
걷다 *geot-tta*	to walk	길을 걷다 *gi-reul geot-tta*	to walk in the street
		빨리 걷다 *ppal-li geot-tta*	to walk quickly
		천천히 걷다 *cheon-cheo-ni geot-tta*	to walk slowly
		걸어가다 *geo-reo-ga-da*	to walk (somewhere)

식당
sik-ttang

restaurant

식당에 가다
sik-ttang-e ga-da

to go to a restaurant

맛있는 식당
ma-sin-neun sik-ttang

delicious place, restaurant with delicious food

유명한 식당
yu-myeong-han sik-ttang

famous restaurant

새로운 식당
sae-ro-un sik-ttang

new restaurant

맛있다
ma-sit-tta

to be delicious

밥이 맛있다
ba-bi ma-sit-tta

the food is delicious, the meal is delicious

맛있는 음식
ma-sin-neun eum-sik

delicious food

맛없다
ma-deop-tta

to not be tasty, to be a bad taste

음식
eum-sik

food

음식을 먹다
eum-si-geul meok-tta

to eat food

음식을 만들다
eum-si-geul man-deul-da

to make food

밀가루 음식
mil-kka-ru eum-sik

flour-based food

커피
keo-pi

coffee

커피 한 잔
keo-pi han jan

a cup of coffee

따뜻한 커피
tta-tteu-tan keo-pi

hot coffee

커피를 마시다
keo-pi-reul ma-si-da

to drink coffee

별	star	반짝반짝	twinkling
byeol		ban-jjak-ban-jjak	
		빛나다	to shine
		bin-na-da	
		달	moon
		dal	
		해	sun
		hae	
		하늘	sky
		ha-neul	

보다	to see, to watch, to meet, to read	영화를 보다	to watch a movie
bo-da		yeong-haw-reul bo-da	
		신문을 보다	to read the newspaper
		sin-mu-neul bo-da	
		보이다	to be visible, to be seen, can see
		bo-i-da	
		보여 주다	to show
		bo-yeo ju-da	

행복하다	to be happy	너무 행복하다	to be very happy
haeng-bo-ka-da		neo-mu haeng-bo-ka-da	
		행복하게 살다	to live happily
		haeng-bo-ka-ge sal-da	
		행복한 사람	happy person
		haeng-bo-kan sa-ram	
		행복	happiness
		haeng-bok	

Read the story again, but this time in Korean!

아빠랑 같이 바다에 갔어요.

바닷가를 걸었어요.

식당에 가서 맛있는 음식을 먹었어요.

카페에 가서 커피를 마셨어요.

밤이 됐어요. 별도 봤어요.

너무 행복했어요.

Translation

I went to the ocean with my dad. We walked along the beach. We went to a restaurant and had delicious food. We went to a café and drank coffee. Night fell. We also saw the stars. I was very happy.

Match each Korean word to its English translation.

보다 ·   · restaurant

커피 ·   · to walk

음식 ·   · to see, to watch, to meet, to read

식당 ·   · dad

아빠 ·   · to be happy

행복하다 ·   · sea, ocean

바다 ·   · coffee

별 ·   · to be delicious

맛있다 ·   · star

걷다 ·   · food

Crossword Puzzle

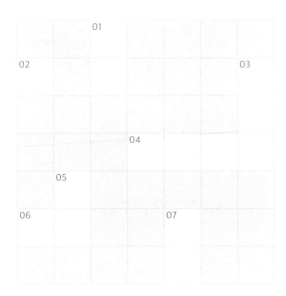

01 coffee
02 star
03 to be delicious
04 to be happy
05 to see, to watch
06 sea, ocean
07 food

Fill in the blanks using one of the words that you learned in Day 13.
(Please refer to page 017 to review how to conjugate verbs/adjectives.)

1. ( )랑 같이 바다에 갔어요.   I went to the ocean with my dad.

2. 아빠랑 같이 ( )에 갔어요.   I went to the ocean with my dad.

3. 바닷가를 ( ).   We walked along the beach.

4. ( )에 가서 맛있는 음식을 먹었어요.   We went to a restaurant and had delicious food.

5. 식당에 가서 ( ) 음식을 먹었어요.   We went to a restaurant and had delicious food.

6. 식당에 가서 맛있는 ( )을 먹었어요.   We went to a restaurant and had delicious food.

7. 카페에 가서 ( )를 마셨어요.   We went to a café and drank coffee.

8. ( )도 봤어요.   We also saw the stars.

9. 별도 ( ).   We also saw the stars.

10. 너무 ( ).   I was very happy.

DAY 14

Check off the words
you already know.

- 여름
- 싫어하다
- 덥다
- 밖
- 나가다
- 집
- 에어컨
- 켜다
- 시원하다
- 얼음

After you study these words, come back and
check off the ones you have memorized.

Day 14

Imagine the situation in the story below to help you
remember the ten Korean words in context.

싫어하다 여름
I <u>hate</u>   <u>summer</u>.

덥다
In the summer it is too <u>hot</u>. So, I hate summer.

나가다 밖
During the summer, I don't <u>go</u>   <u>outside</u> that often.

켜다 에어컨 집
I <u>turn on</u> the <u>air conditioner</u> at <u>home</u>.

시원하다 얼음
I drink <u>cold</u>   <u>ice</u> water.

In the summer, I like staying at home the most.

LET'S KEEP THE BALL ROLLING!

Word	Meaning	Related Words	Meaning
여름 *yeo-reum*	summer	**여름 방학** *yeo-reum bang-hak*	summer vacation
		여름옷 *yeo-reu-mot*	summer clothes
		덥다 *deop-tta*	to be hot
싫어하다 *si-reo-ha-da*	to dislike, to hate	**싫어하는** *si-reo-ha-neun*	that one hates
		싫어하는 사람 *si-reo-ha-neun sa-ram*	a person who one dislikes
		하기 싫어하다 *ha-gi si-reo-ha-da*	to hate doing something
덥다 *deop-tta*	to be hot	**더운** *deo-un*	hot
		더운 날씨 *deo-un nal-ssi*	hot weather
		여름 *yeo-reum*	summer
밖 *bak*	outside	**밖에 나가다** *ba-kke na-ga-da*	to go outside
		밖으로 *ba-kkeu-ro*	to the outside
		안 *an*	inside

나가다	to go out	방에서 나가다	to leave the room
na-ga-da		*bang-e-seo na-ga-da*	
		들어오다	to come in
		deu-reo-o-da	
		들어가다	to go in
		deu-reo-ga-da	
		나오다	to come out
		na-o-da	

집	house, home	집에 오다	to come home
jip		*ji-be o-da*	
		집에 가다	to go home
		ji-be ga-da	
		집에 있다	to stay at home
		ji-be it-tta	
		가족	family
		ga-jok	

에어컨	air conditioner	에어컨을 켜다	to turn on the air conditioner
e-eo-keon		*e-eo-keo-neul kyeo-da*	
		에어컨을 끄다	to turn off the air conditioner
		e-eo-keo-neul kkeu-da	
		에어컨 바람	wind from the air conditioner
		e-eo-keon ba-ram	

켜다	to turn on	불을 켜다	to turn on the light
kyeo-da		*bu-reul kyeo-da*	
		텔레비전을 켜다	to turn on the television
		tel-le-bi-jeo-neul kyeo-da	
		끄다	to turn off
		kkeu-da	

시원하다	to be cool	시원한	cool, cold
si-wo-na-da	(temperature)	*si-wo-nan*	
		시원한 물	cold water
		si-wo-nan mul	
		바람이 시원하다	the wind is cool
		ba-ra-mi si-wo-na-da	

얼음	ice	얼음이 얼다	ice forms
eo-reum		*eo-reu-mi eol-da*	
		얼음이 녹다	ice melts
		eo-reu-mi nok-tta	
		얼음물	ice water
		eo-reum-mul	

LET'S REVIEW!

Read the story again, but this time in Korean!

저는 **여름**을 **싫어해요.**

여름에는 너무 **더워요.** 그래서 여름을 싫어해요.

여름에는 **밖**에 잘 안 **나가요.**

집에서 **에어컨**을 **켜요.**

시원한 얼음물을 마셔요.

여름에는 집에 있는 것이 제일 좋아요.

Translation

I hate summer. In the summer it is too hot. So, I hate summer.
During the summer, I don't go outside that often. I turn on the air
conditioner at home. I drink cold ice water. In the summer, I like
staying at home the most.

Match each Korean word to its English translation.

집 · · to be hot

나가다 · · summer

얼음 · · to be cool (temperature)

에어컨 · · to turn on

여름 · · to dislike, to hate

시원하다 · · outside

덥다 · · to go out

싫어하다 · · ice

켜다 · · house, home

밖 · · air conditioner

Crossword Puzzle

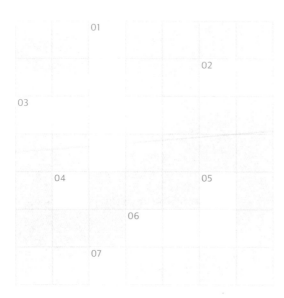

01 to dislike, to hate
02 summer
03 to be cool (temperature)
04 outside
05 to turn on
06 to go out
07 house, home

Fill in the blanks using one of the words that you learned in Day 14.
(Please refer to page 017 to review how to conjugate verbs/adjectives.)

1. 저는 (   )을 싫어해요.　　　　I hate summer.

2. 저는 여름을 (   ).　　　　I hate summer.

3. 여름에는 너무 (   ).　　　　In the summer it is too hot.

4. 여름에는 (   )에 잘 안 나가요.　　　During the summer, I don't go outside that often.

5. 여름에는 밖에 잘 안 (   ).　　　During the summer, I don't go outside that often.

6. (   )에서 에어컨을 켜요.　　　I turn on the air conditioner at home.

7. 집에서 (   )을 켜요.　　　I turn on the air conditioner at home.

8. 집에서 에어컨을 (   ).　　　I turn on the air conditioner at home.

9. (   ) 얼음물을 마셔요.　　　I drink cold ice water.

10. 시원한 (   )물을 마셔요.　　　I drink cold ice water.

DAY 15

Check off the words you already know.

○ 벌써   ○

○ 밤   ○

○ 침대   ○

○ 눕다   ○

○ 잠   ○

○ 화장실   ○

○ 책   ○

○ 읽다   ○

○ 냉장고   ○

○ 우유   ○

After you study these words, come back and check off the ones you have memorized.

Day 15

LET'S WARM UP!

Imagine the situation in the story below to help you remember the ten Korean words in context.

벌써   밤

It is <u>already</u> 12 o'clock at <u>night</u>.

눕다   침대   잠

I <u>lie down</u> in my <u>bed</u>. But I can't <u>sleep</u>.

화장실

I go to the <u>bathroom</u> and come back.

읽다 책

I <u>read</u> a   <u>book</u>. But I still can't sleep.

냉장고

I take out some milk from the <u>refrigerator</u>.

우유

I drink <u>milk</u>. Now I can sleep. I sleep well.

LET'S KEEP THE BALL ROLLING!

Word	Meaning	Related Words	Meaning
벌써 *beol-sseo*	already	벌써 10년 *beol-sseo sim-nyeon*	already 10 years
		벌써 끝나다 *beol-sseo kkeun-na-da*	to already be over
		이미 *i-mi*	already
밤 *bam*	night	오늘 밤 *o-neul bam*	tonight
		밤 10시 *bam yeol-ssi*	10 o'clock at night
		낮 *nat*	day, daytime
		캄캄하다 *kam-ka-ma-da*	to be dark
침대 *chim-dae*	bed	침대에 눕다 *chim-dae-e nup-tta*	to lie in the bed
		싱글 침대 *ssing-geul chim-dae*	single bed
		더블 침대 *deo-beul chim-dae*	double bed
		이층 침대 *i-cheung chim-dae*	bunk bed

눕다	to lie down	침대에 눕다	to lie in the bed
nup-tta		*chim-dae-e nup-tta*	
		똑바로 눕다	to lie flat on one's back
		ttok-ppa-ro nup-tta	
		누워 있다	to be lying (down)
		nu-wo it-tta	
		일어나다	to get up
		i-reo-na-da	

잠	sleep	늦잠	oversleep, sleeping in
jam		*neut-jjam*	
		자다	to sleep
		ja-da	
		잠을 자다	to sleep
		ja-meul ja-da	
		낮잠	nap
		nat-jjam	

화장실	bathroom	화장실에 가다	to go to the bathroom
hwa-jang-sil		*hwa-jang-si-re ga-da*	
		화장지	toilet paper
		hwa-jang-ji	

책	book	책을 읽다	to read a book
chaek		*chae-geul ik-tta*	
		책을 펴다	to open a book
		chae-geul pyeo-da	
		책을 덮다	to close a book
		chae-geul deop-tta	

읽다
ik-tta

to read

잡지를 읽다 jap-jji-reul ik-tta	to read a magazine
읽기 il-kki	reading
빨리 읽다 ppal-li ik-tta	to read quickly
다 읽다 da ik-tta	to finish reading, to read all

냉장고
naeng-jang-go

refrigerator

냉장고 문 naeng-jang-go mun	refrigerator door
큰 냉장고 keun naeng-jang-go	big refrigerator
냉장고에 넣다 naeng-jang-go-e neo-ta	to put in the refrigerator
냉장고를 열다 naeng-jang-go-reul yeol-da	to open the refrigerator

우유
u-yu

milk

우유 한 잔 u-yu han jan	a glass of milk
우유를 마시다 u-yu-reul ma-si-da	to drink milk

LET'S REVIEW!

Read the story again, but this time in Korean!

벌써 밤 12시예요.

침대에 **누워요.** 그런데 **잠**이 안 와요.

화장실에 갔다 와요.

책을 **읽어요.** 그래도 잠이 안 와요.

냉장고에서 우유를 꺼내요.

우유를 마셔요. 이제 잠이 와요. 잘 자요.

Translation

It is already 12 o'clock at night. I lie down in my bed. But I can't sleep. I go to the bathroom and come back. I read a book. But I still can't sleep. I take out some milk from the refrigerator. I drink milk. Now I can sleep. I sleep well.

Match each Korean word to its English translation.

눕다 ·   · bed

벌써 ·   · book

읽다 ·   · milk

냉장고 ·   · already

침대 ·   · bathroom

잠 ·   · to read

화장실 ·   · night

우유 ·   · to lie down

밤 ·   · sleep

책 ·   · refrigerator

Crossword Puzzle

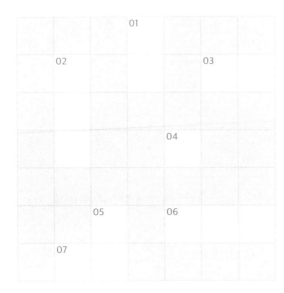

01 bed
02 refrigerator
03 milk
04 night
05 to lie down
06 bathroom
07 to read

Fill in the blanks using one of the words that you learned in Day 15.
(Please refer to page 017 to review how to conjugate verbs/adjectives.)

1.   (   ) 밤 12시예요.   It is already 12 o'clock at night.

2.   벌써 (   ) 12시예요.   It is already 12 o'clock at night.

3.   (   )에 누워요.   I lie down in my bed.

4.   침대에 (   ).   I lie down in my bed.

5.   그런데 (   )이 안 와요.   But I can't sleep.

6.   (   )에 갔다 와요.   I go to the bathroom and come back.

7.   (   )을 읽어요.   I read a book.

8.   책을 (   ).   I read a book.

9.   (   )에서 우유를 꺼내요.   I take out some milk from the refrigerator.

10. (   )를 마셔요.   I drink milk.

DAY 16

Check off the words you already know.

○ 컵 ○

○ 뜨겁다 ○

○ 컴퓨터 ○

○ 이메일 ○

○ 노트북 ○

○ 충전하다 ○

○ 중요하다 ○

○ 거울 ○

○ 화장품 ○

○ 바르다 ○

After you study these words, come back and check off the ones you have memorized.

Day 16

Imagine the situation in the story below to help you
remember the ten Korean words in context.

뜨겁다   컵

I pour <u>hot</u> coffee into a <u>cup</u>.

컴퓨터

I turn on my <u>computer</u>.

이메일

I read my <u>e-mails</u>.

충전하다   노트북

I <u>charge</u> my phone with my <u>laptop computer</u>.

중요하다

I have an <u>important</u> appointment in the afternoon.

거울

I look in the <u>mirror</u>.

바르다 화장품

I <u>put on</u>   <u>make-up</u>.

LET'S KEEP THE BALL ROLLING!

Word	Meaning	Related Words	Meaning
컵 *keop*	cup	컵에 따르다 *keo-be tta-reu-da*	to pour into a cup
		컵을 씻다 *keo-beul ssit-tta*	to wash a cup
		빈 컵 *bin keop*	empty cup
		한 컵 *han keop*	one cup
뜨겁다 *tteu-geop-tta*	to be hot	냄비가 뜨겁다 *naem-bi-ga tteu-geop-tta*	the pot is hot
		온몸이 뜨겁다 *on-mo-mi tteu-geop-tta*	one's whole body is hot
		뜨거운 커피 *tteu-geo-un keo-pi*	hot coffee
		차갑다 *cha-gap-tta*	to be cold
컴퓨터 *keom-pyu-teo*	computer	컴퓨터를 켜다 *keom-pyu-teo-reul kyeo-da*	to turn on a computer
		컴퓨터가 오래되다 *keom-pyu-teo-ga o-rae-doe-da*	the computer is old
		컴퓨터 한 대 *keom-pyu-teo han dae*	one computer
		컴퓨터하다 *keom-pyu-teo-ha-da*	to use a computer, to work on a computer

이메일	e-mail	이메일이 오다	an e-mail comes,
		i-me-i-ri o-da	to receive an e-mail
i-me-il			
		이메일을 읽다	to read an e-mail
		i-me-i-reul ik-tta	
		이메일을 쓰다	to write an e-mail
		i-me-i-reul sseu-da	
		이메일을 보내다	to send an e-mail
		i-me-i-reul bo-nae-da	

노트북	laptop computer	노트북 컴퓨터	laptop computer
		no-teu-buk keom-pyu-teo	
no-teu-buk		노트북으로 일하다	to work on a laptop
		no-teu-bu-geu-ro i-ra-da	computer

충전하다	to charge	노트북을 충전하다	to charge a laptop
		no-teu-bu-geul chung-jeo-na-da	computer
chung-jeo-na-da		휴대폰을 충전하다	to charge a cell phone
		hyu-dae-po-neul chung-jeo-na-da	
		충전기	charger
		chung-jeon-gi	
		배터리가 없다	to have no battery
		bae-teo-ri-ga eop-tta	

중요하다	to be important	중요한 약속	important appointment
		jung-yo-han yak-ssok	
jung-yo-ha-da		중요한 시험	important test
		jung-yo-han si-heom	

거울
geo-ul

mirror

거울을 보다
geo-u-reul bo-da

to look in the mirror

거울이 깨지다
geo-u-ri kkae-ji-da

the mirror breaks

큰 거울
keun geo-ul

big mirror

손거울
son-kkeo-ul

hand mirror

화장품
hwa-jang-pum

make-up product

화장품을 바르다
hwa-jang-pu-meul ba-reu-da

to apply make-up

화장품을 다 쓰다
hwa-jang-pu-meul da sseu-da

to run out of a make-up product

새 화장품
sae hwa-jang-pum

a new make-up product

화장품 정리
hwa-jang-pum jeong-li

organizing make-up products

바르다
ba-reu-da

to apply, to put on

로션을 바르다
lo-syeo-neul ba-reu-da

to apply lotion

연고를 바르다
yeon-go-reul ba-reu-da

to apply ointment

잼을 바르다
jae-meul ba-reu-da

to spread jam
(on bread, cracker, etc.)

LET'S REVIEW!

Read the story again, but this time in Korean!

컵에 뜨거운 커피를 따라요.

컴퓨터를 켜요. 이메일을 읽어요.

노트북으로 휴대폰을 충전해요.

오후에 중요한 약속이 있어요.

거울을 봐요.

화장품을 발라요.

Translation

I pour hot coffee into a cup. I turn on my computer. I read my
e-mails. I charge my phone with my laptop computer. I have an
important appointment in the afternoon. I look in the mirror.
I put on make-up.

Match each Korean word to its English translation.

뜨겁다 ·   · computer

이메일 ·   · to charge

중요하다 ·   · to be hot

컵 ·   · e-mail

바르다 ·   · make-up product

컴퓨터 ·   · cup

충전하다 ·   · to be important

화장품 ·   · to apply, to put on

거울 ·   · laptop computer

노트북 ·   · mirror

Crossword Puzzle

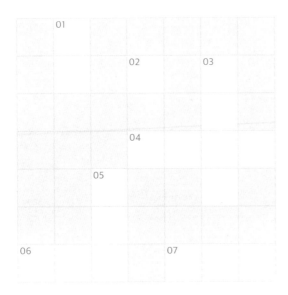

01 mirror
02 cup
03 to charge
04 to be important
05 to apply, to put on
06 to be hot
07 laptop computer

Fill in the blanks using one of the words that you learned in Day 16.
(Please refer to page 017 to review how to conjugate verbs/adjectives.)

1. (   )에 뜨거운 커피를 따라요.   I pour hot coffee into a cup.

2. 컵에 (   ) 커피를 따라요.   I pour hot coffee into a cup.

3. (   )를 켜요.   I turn on my computer.

4. (   )을 읽어요.   I read my e-mails.

5. (   )으로 휴대폰을 충전해요.   I charge my phone with my laptop computer.

6. 노트북으로 휴대폰을 (   ).   I charge my phone with my laptop computer.

7. 오후에 (   ) 약속이 있어요.   I have an important appointment in the afternoon.

8. (   )을 봐요.   I look in the mirror.

9. (   )을 발라요.   I put on make-up.

10. 화장품을 (   ).   I put on make-up.

DAY 17

Check off the words you already know.

- ○ 옆
- ○ 부부
- ○ 초대
- ○ 오후
- ○ 도착
- ○ 딸
- ○ 나이
- ○ 같다
- ○ 유치원
- ○ 사이

After you study these words, come back and check off the ones you have memorized.

Day 17

Imagine the situation in the story below to help you remember the ten Korean words in context.

초대하다　옆　　부부

Today I <u>invited</u> the　　<u>next</u> door <u>couple</u> over.

도착　　　　오후

They will <u>arrive</u> at my house at 6 <u>p.m.</u>

딸

The <u>daughter</u> of the next door couple

같다 나이

and my daughter are the <u>same</u>　　<u>age</u>.

유치원

They both go to the same <u>kindergarten</u>.

사이

So they have a good <u>relationship</u>.

LET'S KEEP THE BALL ROLLING!

Word	Meaning	Related Words	Meaning
옆 *yeop*	side, next to	옆집 *yeop-jjip*	next door, next house
		옆자리 *yeop-jja-ri*	next seat
		옆 사람 *yeop sa-ram*	next person
		옆에 *yeo-pe*	next to
부부 *bu-bu*	married couple	부부 사이 *bu-bu sa-i*	between a married couple, married couple
		부부 싸움 *bu-bu ssa-um*	married couple's fight, fight between husband and wife
		남편 *nam-pyeon*	husband
		아내 *a-nae*	wife
초대 *cho-dae*	invitation	초대하다 *cho-dae-ha-da*	to invite
		초대를 받다 *cho-dae-reul bat-tta*	to be invited, to receive an invitation
		저녁 초대 *jeo-nyeok cho-dae*	invitation to dinner
		초대장 *cho-dae-jjang*	invitation, invitation card

오후
o-hu

afternoon

오늘 오후	this afternoon
o-neul o-hu	
오전	morning
o-jeon	
오후에	in the afternoon
o-hu-e	

도착
do-chak

arrival

도착하다	to arrive
do-cha-ka-da	
도착 시간	arrival time
do-chak si-gan	
늦게 도착하다	to arrive late
neut-kke do-cha-ka-da	
일찍 도착하다	to arrive early
il-jjik do-cha-ka-da	

딸
ttal

daughter

첫째 딸	first daughter
cheot-jjae ttal	
막내 딸	youngest daughter, last daughter
mang-nae ttal	
딸을 낳다	to give birth to a daughter
tta-reul na-ta	
아들	son
a-deul	

나이	age	나이가 어리다	to be young
na-i		na-i-ga eo-ri-da	
		나이가 많다	to be old
		na-i-ga man-ta	
		나이가 들다	to get older
		na-i-ga deul-da	
		나이를 먹다	to get older
		na-i-reul meok-tta	
		살	counting unit for age
		sal	

같다	to be the same, to be like	나이가 같다	to be the same age
gat-tta		na-i-ga gat-tta	
		같은	the same
		ga-teun	
		같은 유치원	the same kindergarten
		ga-teun yu-chi-won	
		똑같다	to be exactly the same
		ttok-kkat-tta	

유치원	kindergarten	유치원에 다니다	to attend kindergarten
yu-chi-won		yu-chi-wo-ne da-ni-da	
		유치원 놀이터	playground at the kindergarten
		yu-chi-won no-ri-teo	

사이	relationship, relation	사이가 좋다	to be on good terms
sa-i		sa-i-ga jo-ta	
		친구 사이	(to be) friends, friendly relationship
		chin-gu sa-i	
		친한 사이	(to be) close friends, close relationship
		chi-nan sa-i	

Read the story again, but this time in Korean!

오늘 옆집 부부를 초대했어요.

오후 6시에 집에 도착할 거예요.

옆집 부부의 딸과 제 딸은 나이가 같아요.

둘 다 같은 유치원에 다녀요.

그래서 사이가 좋아요.

Translation

Today I invited the next door couple over. They will arrive at my house at 6 p.m. The daughter of the next door couple and my daughter are the same age. They both go to the same kindergarten. So they have a good relationship.

Match each Korean word to its English translation.

부부 ·   · invitation

오후 ·   · arrival

딸 ·   · side, next to

같다 ·   · age

사이 ·   · kindergarten

옆 ·   · married couple

유치원 ·   · relationship, relation

초대 ·   · afternoon

나이 ·   · daughter

도착 ·   · to be the same, to be like

Crossword Puzzle

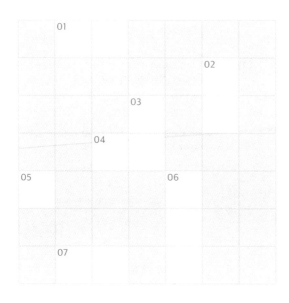

01 afternoon
02 married couple
03 age
04 relationship, relation
05 daughter
06 kindergarten
07 invitation

....

Fill in the blanks using one of the words that you learned in Day 17.
(Please refer to page 017 to review how to conjugate verbs/adjectives.)

1. 오늘 (   )집 부부를 초대했어요.　　Today I invited the next door couple over.

2. 오늘 옆집 (   )를 초대했어요.　　Today I invited the next door couple over.

3. 오늘 옆집 부부를 (   )했어요.　　Today I invited the next door couple over.

4. (   ) 6시에 집에 도착할 거예요.　　They will arrive at my house at 6 p.m.

5. 오후 6시에 집에 (   )할 거예요.　　They will arrive at my house at 6 p.m.

6. 옆집 부부의 (   )과 제 딸은 나이가
    같아요.　　The daughter of the next door couple and my daughter are the same age.

7. 옆집 부부의 딸과 제 딸은 (   )가
    같아요.　　The daughter of the next door couple and my daughter are the same age.

8. 옆집 부부의 딸과 제 딸은 나이가 (   ).　　The daughter of the next door couple and my daughter are the same age.

9. 둘 다 같은 (   )에 다녀요.　　They both go to the same kindergarten.

10. 그래서 (   )가 좋아요.　　So they have a good relationship.

DAY 18

Check off the words
you already know. ↗

- ○ 아들 ○
- ○ 게임 ○
- ○ 요일 ○
- ○ 아침 ○
- ○ 점심 ○
- ○ 밥 ○
- ○ 화나다 ○
- ○ 걱정 ○
- ○ 왜 ○
- ○ 공부 ○

After you study these words, come back and
check off the ones you have memorized. ↖

Day 18

....

Imagine the situation in the story below to help you remember the ten Korean words in context.

아들   게임

My <u>son</u> plays video <u>games</u> all day long.

토요일

Today is a <u>Saturday</u>.

아침   점심

My son played video games in the <u>morning</u> and also at <u>lunch</u>.

밥

He even skipped <u>meals</u> and played games.

화나다   걱정

I was really <u>angry</u>. And I was <u>worried</u>.

왜

<u>Why</u> does my son only play video games?

공부

Why doesn't he <u>study</u>?

LET'S KEEP THE BALL ROLLING!

Word	Meaning	Related Words	Meaning
아들 *a-deul*	son	첫째 아들 *cheot-jjae a-deul*	first son
		막내 아들 *mang-nae a-deul*	last son, youngest son
		아들을 낳다 *a-deu-reul na-ta*	to give birth to a son
		딸 *ttal*	daughter
게임 *kke-im*	game	게임을 하다 *kke-i-meul ha-da*	to play a game
		컴퓨터 게임 *keom-pyu-teo kke-im*	computer game
		보드게임 *bo-deu-kke-im*	board game
요일 *yo-il*	day of the week	월요일 *wo-ryo-il*	Monday
		화요일 *hwa-yo-il*	Tuesday
		수요일 *su-yo-il*	Wednesday
		목요일 *mo-gyo-il*	Thursday
		금요일 *geu-myo-il*	Friday
		토요일 *to-yo-il*	Saturday
		일요일 *i-ryo-il*	Sunday

아침 a-chim	morning	아침에 a-chi-me	in the morning
		아침 인사 a-chim in-sa	morning greeting
		아침 일찍 a-chim il-jjik	early in the morning
		아침밥 a-chim-ppap	breakfast

점심 jeom-sim	lunch	점심시간 jeom-sim-ssi-gan	lunch time
		늦은 점심 neu-jeun jeom-sim	late lunch
		점심을 먹다 jeom-si-meul meok-tta	to have lunch

밥 bap	rice, food, meal	밥을 먹다 ba-beul meok-tta	to eat (a meal)
		밥을 차리다 ba-beul cha-ri-da	to prepare a meal
		저녁밥 jeo-nyeok-ppap	dinner, supper
		비빔밥 bi-bim-ppap	mixed rice, rice mixed with various ingredients

화나다 hwa-na-da	to feel angry, to get angry	화난 hwa-nan	angry
		화가 나다 hwa-ga na-da	to feel angry
		화내다 hwa-nae-da	to get angry at someone, to show one's anger

걱정	worry, concern	걱정하다	to worry
geok-jjeong		geok-jjeong-ha-da	
		걱정되다	to be worried
		geok-jjeong-doe-da	
		걱정이 없다	to have no worries
		geok-jjeong-i eop-tta	

왜	why	왜 그렇게	why so
wae		wae geu-reo-ke	
		때문에	because, because of
		ttae-mu-ne	

공부	study	공부하다	to study
gong-bu		gong-bu-ha-da	
		공부를 안 하다	to not study
		gong-bu-reul an ha-da	
		열심히 공부하다	to study hard
		yeol-ssi-mi gong-bu-ha-da	

LET'S REVIEW!

Read the story again, but this time in Korean!

제 **아들**은 하루 종일 **게임**을 해요.

오늘은 **토요일**이에요.

아들은 **아침**에도 **점심**에도 게임을 했어요.

밥도 안 먹고 게임을 했어요.

저는 정말 **화났어요.** 그리고 **걱정**되었어요.

제 아들은 **왜** 게임만 할까요? 왜 **공부**를 안 할까요?

Translation

My son plays video games all day long. Today is a Saturday. My son played video games in the morning and also at lunch. He even skipped meals and played games. I was really angry. And I was worried. Why does my son only play video games? Why doesn't he study?

Match each Korean word to its English translation.

아침　·　　　　　　　　　　　　· game

점심　·　　　　　　　　　　　　· rice, food, meal

아들　·　　　　　　　　　　　　· to feel angry, to get angry

화나다　·　　　　　　　　　　　· morning

걱정　·　　　　　　　　　　　　· son

공부　·　　　　　　　　　　　　· why

밥　·　　　　　　　　　　　　　· lunch

게임　·　　　　　　　　　　　　· study

왜　·　　　　　　　　　　　　　· day of the week

요일　·　　　　　　　　　　　　· worry, concern

Crossword Puzzle

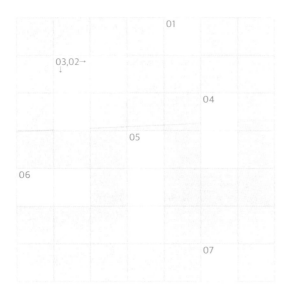

01　rice, food, meal
02　morning
03　son
04　day of the week
05　to feel angry, to get angry
06　worry, concern
07　why

Fill in the blanks using one of the words that you learned in Day 18.
(Please refer to page 017 to review how to conjugate verbs/adjectives.)

1. 제 (   )은 하루 종일 게임을 해요.   My son plays video games all day long.

2. 제 아들은 하루 종일 (   )을 해요.   My son plays video games all day long.

3. 오늘은 (   )이에요.   Today is a Saturday.

4. 아들은 (   )에도 점심에도 게임을   My son played video games in the morning
   했어요.   and also at lunch.

5. 아들은 아침에도 (   )에도 게임을   My son played video games in the morning
   했어요.   and also at lunch.

6. (   )도 안 먹고 게임을 했어요.   He even skipped meals and played games.

7. 저는 정말 (   ).   I was really angry.

8. 그리고 (   )되었어요.   And I was worried.

9. 제 아들은 (   ) 게임만 할까요?   Why does my son only play video games?

10. 왜 (   )를 안 할까요?   Why doesn't he study?

DAY 19

Check off the words you already know. ↱

○ 느낌 ○

○ 달력 ○

○ 날짜 ○

○ 모양 ○

○ 아래 ○

○ 전화번호 ○

○ 잊어버리다 ○

○ 빨리 ○

○ 예약 ○

○ 출발하다 ○

After you study these words, come back and check off the ones you have memorized. ↖

Day 19

Imagine the situation in the story below to help you remember the ten Korean words in context.

I worked until late again today.

느낌 　 달력

I had a weird <u>feeling</u>, so I checked the <u>calendar</u>.

날짜 　 모양

On today's <u>date</u>, there is a circle <u>shape</u>.

아래 　 전화번호

<u>Below</u> the date, there is also a <u>phone number</u>.

잊어버리다

Oh, it's my dad's birthday today! I <u>forgot</u>.

빨리 　 예약

I <u>quickly</u> <u>reserved</u> a restaurant.

출발하다

I am <u>leaving</u> for the restaurant now.

LET'S KEEP THE BALL ROLLING!

Word	Meaning	Related Words	Meaning
느낌 neu-kkim	feeling	느낌이 들다 neu-kki-mi deul-da	to feel, to have a certain feeling
		느낌이 이상하다 neu-kki-mi i-sang-ha-da	to have a weird feeling
		좋은 느낌 jo-eun neu-kkim	good feeling
		그런 느낌 geu-reon neu-kkim	such a feeling, feeling like that
달력 dal-lyeok	calendar	달력을 보다 dal-lyeo-geul bo-da	to check the calendar
		달력에 표시하다 dal-lyeo-ge pyo-si-ha-da	to mark the calendar
		년 nyeon	year
		월 wol	month
		일 il	day
날짜 nal-jja	date	오늘 날짜 o-neul nal-jja	today's date
		약속 날짜 yak-ssok nal-jja	date of appointment
		결혼 날짜 gyeo-ron nal-jja	wedding date
		날짜를 잡다 nal-jja-reul jap-tta	to set a date

모양
mo-yang

shape

같은 모양	same shape
ga-teun mo-yang	
다른 모양	different shape
da-reun mo-yang	
비슷한 모양	similar shape
bi-seu-tan mo-yang	
동그라미	circle
dong-geu-ra-mi	
세모	triangle
se-mo	
네모	rectangle
ne-mo	

아래
a-rae

down, below

책상 아래	below the desk
chaek-ssang a-rae	
나무 아래에서	below a tree
na-mu a-rae-e-seo	
위	up, top
wi	
옆	side
yeop	

전화번호
jeo-nwa-beon-ho

phone number

집 전화번호	home phone number
jip jeo-nwa-beo-no	
전화번호를 외우다	to memorize a number
jeo-nwa-beo-no-reul oe-u-da	
전화번호를 물어보다	to ask someone's number
jeo-nwa-beo-no-reul mu-reo-bo-da	
전화번호를 알려 주다	to give one's number
jeo-nwa-beo-no-reul al-lyeo ju-da	

잊어버리다	to forget	깜빡 잊어버리다	to forget, something slips one's mind
i-jeo-beo-ri-da		kkam-ppak i-jeo-beo-ri-da	
		약속을 잊어버리다	to forget about a plan/ appointment
		yak-sso-geul i-jeo-beo-ri-da	
		기억하다	to remember
		gi-eo-ka-da	

빨리	fast, quickly	빨리 가다	to go quickly
ppal-li		ppal-li ga-da	
		빠르다	to be quick
		ppa-reu-da	
		빠르게	quickly
		ppa-reu-ge	

예약	reservation	예약하다	to reserve
ye-yak		ye-ya-ka-da	
		전화로 예약하다	to reserve on the phone
		jeo-nwa-ro ye-ya-ka-da	
		예약 취소	reservation cancellation
		ye-yak chwi-so	

출발하다	to depart	일찍 출발하다	to depart early
chul-bal-ha-da		il-jjik chul-ba-ra-da	
		서울로 출발하다	to depart for Seoul
		seo-ul-lo chul-ba-ra-da	
		출발	departure
		chul-bal	
		도착하다	to arrive
		do-cha-ka-da	

LET'S REVIEW!

Read the story again, but this time in Korean!

오늘도 늦게까지 일을 했어요.

느낌이 이상해서 **달력**을 봤어요.

오늘 **날짜**에 동그라미 **모양**이 있어요.

날짜 **아래 전화번호**도 있어요.

아, 오늘 아빠 생신이에요! 깜빡 **잊어버렸어요.**

빨리 식당을 **예약**했어요. 지금 식당으로 **출발해요.**

Translation

I worked until late again today. I had a weird feeling, so I checked the calendar. On today's date, there is a circle shape. Below the date, there is also a phone number. Oh, it's my dad's birthday today! I forgot. I quickly reserved a restaurant. I am leaving for the restaurant now.

Match each Korean word to its English translation.

날짜 ·   · feeling

전화번호 ·   · calendar

빨리 ·   · to forget

느낌 ·   · shape

아래 ·   · date

출발하다 ·   · phone number

잊어버리다 ·   · reservation

달력 ·   · to depart

예약 ·   · fast, quickly

모양 ·   · down, below

Crossword Puzzle

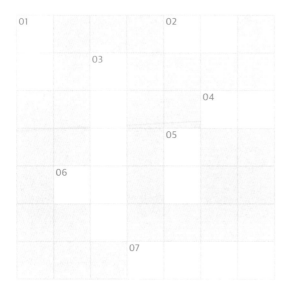

01 down, below
02 shape
03 to forget
04 calendar
05 feeling
06 fast, quickly
07 phone number

Fill in the blanks using one of the words that you learned in Day 19.
(Please refer to page 017 to review how to conjugate verbs/adjectives.)

1. (   )이 이상해서 달력을 봤어요.   I had a weird feeling, so I checked the calendar.

2. 느낌이 이상해서 (   )을 봤어요.   I had a weird feeling, so I checked the calendar.

3. 오늘 (   )에 동그라미 모양이 있어요.   On today's date, there is a circle shape.

4. 오늘 날짜에 동그라미 (   )이 있어요.   On today's date, there is a circle shape.

5. 날짜 (   ) 전화번호도 있어요.   Below the date, there is also a phone number.

6. 날짜 아래 (   )도 있어요.   Below the date, there is also a phone number.

7. 깜빡 (   ).   I forgot.

8. (   ) 식당을 예약했어요.   I quickly reserved a restaurant.

9. 빨리 식당을 (   )했어요.   I quickly reserved a restaurant.

10. 지금 식당으로 (   ).   I am leaving for the restaurant now.

DAY 20

Check off the words you already know.

- ○ 시골 ○
- ○ 도시 ○
- ○ 시끄럽다 ○
- ○ 조용하다 ○
- ○ 등산 ○
- ○ 높다 ○
- ○ 낮다 ○
- ○ 해 ○
- ○ 어둡다 ○
- ○ 내려가다 ○

After you study these words, come back and check off the ones you have memorized.

Day 20

Imagine the situation in the story below to help you
remember the ten Korean words in context.

시골

I was born in the countryside.

도시　　　시끄럽다

Now I live in the city. The city is too noisy.

조용하다

But if I go to the mountain, it's really quiet.

등산

So, I like hiking up the mountain.

높다　　　낮다

I like both high mountains and low mountains.

I usually go to the mountain in the morning.

어둡다 해　　내려가다

It is dark when the sun sets. So, I go down before the sun sets.

LET'S KEEP THE BALL ROLLING!

Word	Meaning	Related Words	Meaning
시골 *si-gol*	countryside	**시골 사람** *si-gol sa-ram*	country person
		시골 풍경 *si-gol pung-gyeong*	rural scene
		시골에서 태어나다 *si-go-re-seo tae-eo-na-da*	to be born in the countryside
도시 *do-si*	city	**도시 생활** *do-si saeng-hwal*	city life
		대도시 *dae-do-si*	big city
		도시에 살다 *do-si-e sal-da*	to live in a city
시끄럽다 *si-kkeu-reop-tta*	to be noisy	**교실이 시끄럽다** *gyo-si-ri si-kkeu-reop-tta*	to be noisy in the classroom
		시끄러운 소리 *si-kkeu-reo-un so-ri*	noisy sound, loud sound
		시끄럽게 *si-kkeu-reop-kke*	noisily, loudly
		시끄럽게 하다 *si-kkeu-reop-kke ha-da*	to make a loud noise

조용하다
jo-yong-ha-da

to be quiet

집이 조용하다
ji-bi jo-yong-ha-da

the house is quiet

조용한 동네
jo-yong-han dong-ne

quiet neighborhood

조용하게
jo-yong-ha-ge

quietly

조용하게 말하다
jo-yong-ha-ge ma-ra-da

to talk quietly

등산
deung-san

hiking

등산을 가다
deung-sa-neul ga-da

to go hiking in the mountain

등산을 하다
deung-sa-neul ha-da

to hike in the mountain

등산하다
deung-sa-na-da

to hike in the mountain

높다
nop-tta

to be high

하늘이 높다
ha-neu-ri nop-tta

the sky is high

천장이 높다
cheon-jang-i nop-tta

the ceiling is high

높은 건물
no-peun geon-mul

tall building

낮다
nat-tta

to be low

책상이 낮다
chaek-ssang-i nat-tta

the desk is low

낮은 산
na-jeun san

low mountain

낮은 계단
na-jeun gye-dan

low steps

해 *hae*	the sun	해가 뜨다 *hae-ga tteu-da*	the sun rises
		해가 지다 *hae-ga ji-da*	the sun sets
		햇빛 *haet-ppit*	sunlight

어둡다 *eo-dup-tta*	to be dark	색깔이 어둡다 *saek-kka-ri eo-dup-tta*	the color is dark
		어두운 골목 *eo-du-un gol-mok*	dark alley
		어두워지다 *eo-du-wo-ji-da*	to get dark
		밝다 *bak-tta*	to be bright

내려가다 *nae-ryeo-ga-da*	to go down	산을 내려가다 *sa-neul nae-ryeo-ga-da*	to go down the mountain
		지하실로 내려가다 *ji-ha-sil-lo nae-ryeo-ga-da*	to go down to the basement
		내려가는 엘리베이터 *nae-ryeo-ga-neun el-li-be-i-teo*	descending elevator
		올라가다 *ol-la-ga-da*	to go up

LET'S REVIEW!

Read the story again, but this time in Korean!

저는 **시골**에서 태어났어요.

지금은 **도시**에 살아요. 도시는 너무 **시끄러워요.**

그런데 산에 가면 정말 **조용해요.**

그래서 **등산**을 좋아해요. **높은** 산도 **낮은** 산도 다 좋아요.

보통 아침에 산에 가요. **해**가 지면 **어두워요.**

그래서 해가 지기 전에 산을 **내려가요.**

Translation

I was born in the countryside. Now I live in the city. The city is too noisy. But if I go to the mountain, it's really quiet. So, I like hiking up the mountain. I like both high mountains and low mountains. I usually go to the mountain in the morning. It is dark when the sun sets. So, I go down before the sun sets.

Match each Korean word to its English translation.

도시 ·	· to be quiet
등산 ·	· the sun
낮다 ·	· to be noisy
내려가다 ·	· to be high
어둡다 ·	· to go down
시골 ·	· hiking
시끄럽다 ·	· city
해 ·	· to be dark
높다 ·	· to be low
조용하다 ·	· countryside

Crossword Puzzle

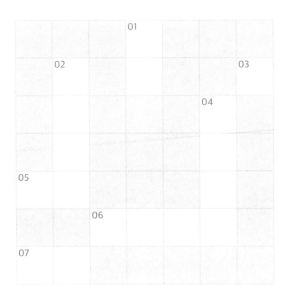

01 city
02 to go down
03 the sun
04 to be noisy
05 to be low
06 to be quiet
07 hiking

Fill in the blanks using one of the words that you learned in Day 20.
(Please refer to page 017 to review how to conjugate verbs/adjectives.)

1. 저는 (   )에서 태어났어요. I was born in the countryside.

2. 지금은 (   )에 살아요. Now I live in the city.

3. 도시는 너무 (   ). The city is too noisy.

4. 그런데 산에 가면 정말 (   ). But if I go to the mountain, it's really quiet.

5. 그래서 (   )을 좋아해요. So, I like hiking up the mountain.

6. (   ) 산도 낮은 산도 다 좋아요. I like both high mountains and low mountains.

7. 높은 산도 (   ) 산도 다 좋아요. I like both high mountains and low mountains.

8. (   )가 지면 어두워요. It is dark when the sun sets.

9. 해가 지면 (   ). It is dark when the sun sets.

10. 그래서 해가 지기 전에 (   ). So, I go down before the sun sets.

01 How do you say **"calendar"** in Korean?

    a. 사이   b. 달력   c. 예약   d. 아들

02 Which word is related to 여름?

    a. 쓰다   b. 노트북   c. 덥다   d. 맛있다

03 Choose the word that is a non-edible item.

    a. 우유   b. 커피   c. 시골   d. 밥

04 Choose the term that is **NOT** a loanword from English.

    a. 컴퓨터   b. 내일   c. 이메일   d. 게임

05 How do you say **"to be glad"** or **"to be happy"** in Korean?

    a. 기쁘다   b. 기쁘다   c. 기쁘다   d. 기뻐다

06 Choose the word pair that is matched incorrectly.

    a. 낮다 - to be high   b. 어둡다 - to be dark

    c. 재미있다 - to be fun   d. 행복하다 - to be happy

07 Which of the following Korean words means **"one day"**?

    a. 하루   b. 아빠   c. 오늘   d. 교실

08 Which word do Korean people commonly refer to as **"air conditioner"**?

    a. 에어컨디셔너   b. 에어린스   c. 에어컨디   d. 에어컨

09 Choose the word that best replaces ○○.

    월○○   **화**○○   **수**○○   **목**○○   **금**○○   **토**○○   **일**○○

    a. 선물   b. 요일   c. 아침   d. 얼음

10 What is the antonym of 시끄럽다?

    a. 출발하다   b. 충전하다   c. 중요하다   d. 조용하다

11   Which of the following does **NOT** become a verb if you attach -하다?

a. 거울   b. 등산   c. 걱정   d. 노래

12   Which one syllable word means **"sleep"**?

a. 잠   b. 밤   c. 집   d. 밖

13   How do you say **"married couple"** in Korean?

a. 도도   b. 두두   c. 부부   d. 보보

14   Choose the noun-verb pair that is matched incorrectly.

a. 생일 - 축하하다   b. 전화번호 - 잊어버리다

c. 화장품 - 바르다   d. 귀고리 - 목걸이

15   Choose the word that best replaces ○○.

○○에 눕다   싱글○○   더블○○   이층○○

a. 초대   b. 점심   c. 침대   d. 친구

16   Which of the following does **NOT** refer to an action?

a. 내려가다   b. 나가다   c. 걷다   d. 높다

17 Which of the following is the equivalent of **"why"** in Korean?

    a. 딸   b. 왜   c. 춤   d. 옆

18 What does 나이가 같다 mean?

    a. to be old   b. to be young

    c. to be the same age   d. to be different ages

19 What kind of 모양 is the item in the picture?

    a. 해 모양

    b. 컵 모양

    c. 책 모양

    d. 별 모양

20 What is the Korean word for the place in the picture?

    a. 바다

    b. 식당

    c. 도시

    d. 화장실

QUIZ

DAY 11-20

DAY 21

Check off the words
you already know.

○ 연예인 ○

○ 누구 ○

○ 키 ○

○ 크다 ○

○ 웃다 ○

○ 얼굴 ○

○ 귀엽다 ○

○ 눈 [01] ○

○ 다리 ○

○ 길다 ○

After you study these words, come back and
check off the ones you have memorized.

209

Day 21

LET'S WARM UP!

Imagine the situation in the story below to help you remember the ten Korean words in context.

누구　　　　　　연예인

<u>Who</u> do you think is my favorite <u>celebrity</u>?

키가 크다

He <u>is tall</u>.

웃다 얼굴　귀엽다

His <u>smiling</u>　<u>face</u> is really <u>cute</u>.

눈 ⁰¹ 길다 다리

He has big <u>eyes</u> and <u>long</u>　　<u>legs</u>.

Word	Meaning	Related Words	Meaning
연예인 *yeo-nye-in*	entertainer, celebrity	유명한 연예인 *yu-myeong-han yeo-nye-in*	famous celebrity
		연예인이 되다 *yeo-nye-i-ni doe-da*	to become a celebrity
		연예인을 만나다 *yeo-nye-i-neul man-na-da*	to meet a celebrity
누구 *nu-gu*	who	누가 *nu-ga*	who (subject)
		누구든지 *nu-gu-deun-ji*	whoever, anyone
		누구나 *nu-gu-na*	anyone
키 *ki*	one's height	키가 크다 *ki-ga keu-da*	to be tall
		키가 작다 *ki-ga jak-tta*	to be short
		키를 재다 *ki-reul jae-da*	to measure someone's height
크다 *keu-da*	to be big	옷이 크다 *o-si keu-da*	the clothes are big
		큰 눈 *keun nun*	big eyes
		작다 *jak-tta*	to be small

웃다 ut-tta	to laugh, to smile	크게 웃다 keu-ge ut-tta	to laugh loudly
		웃음 u-seum	laughter
		웃음소리 u-seum-sso-ri	laughter sound
		미소 mi-so	smile
얼굴 eol-gul	face	웃는 얼굴 un-neun eol-gul	laughing face, smiling face
		얼굴이 예쁘다 eol-gu-ri ye-ppeu-da	one's face is pretty
		표정 pyo-jeong	facial expression, look
귀엽다 gwi-yeop-tta	to be cute	강아지가 귀엽다 gang-a-ji-ga gwi-yeop-tta	the puppy is cute
		귀여운 얼굴 gwi-yeo-un eol-gul	cute face
		귀엽게 생기다 gwi-yeop-kke saeng-gi-da	to look cute, to have a cute face
눈 01 nun	eye	눈을 뜨다 nu-neul tteu-da	to open one's eyes
		눈을 감다 nu-neul gam-tta	to close one's eyes
		눈동자 nun-ttong-ja	pupil

다리
da-ri

leg

다리를 다치다
da-ri-reul da-chi-da

to hurt one's leg(s)

다리가 아프다
da-ri-ga a-peu-da

one's leg hurts

팔
pal

arm

팔다리
pal-da-ri

arms and legs, limbs

길다
gil-da

to be long

줄이 길다
ju-ri gil-da

the line is long

머리가 길다
meo-ri-ga gil-da

one's hair is long

긴 다리
gin da-ri

long legs

Read the story again, but this time in Korean!

제가 좋아하는 **연예인**은 **누구**일까요?

키가 **커요.**

웃는 얼굴이 정말 **귀여워요.**

눈이 크고 **다리**가 **길어요.**

Translation

Who do you think is my favorite celebrity? He is tall.
His smiling face is really cute. He has big eyes and long legs.

Match each Korean word to its English translation.

키　　　　·　　　　　　　　　· eye

얼굴　　　·　　　　　　　　　· to be big

웃다　　　·　　　　　　　　　· entertainer, celebrity

귀엽다　　·　　　　　　　　　· who

연예인　　·　　　　　　　　　· one's height

눈 01　　·　　　　　　　　　· to be long

길다　　　·　　　　　　　　　· face

다리　　　·　　　　　　　　　· to laugh, to smile

크다　　　·　　　　　　　　　· to be cute

누구　　　·　　　　　　　　　· leg

Crossword Puzzle

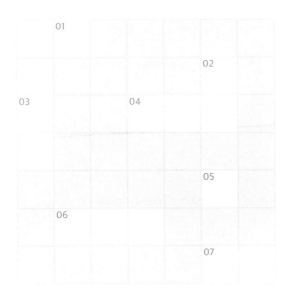

01　one's height
02　to be long
03　who
04　to be cute
05　eye
06　entertainer, celebrity
07　leg

Fill in the blanks using one of the words that you learned in Day 21.
(Please refer to page 017 to review how to conjugate verbs/adjectives.)

1. 제가 좋아하는 (   )은 누구일까요?   Who do you think is my favorite celebrity?

2. 제가 좋아하는 연예인은 (   )일까요?   Who do you think is my favorite celebrity?

3. (   )가 커요.   He is tall.

4. 키가 (   ).   He is tall.

5. (   ) 얼굴이 정말 귀여워요.   His smiling face is really cute.

6. 웃는 (   )이 정말 귀여워요.   His smiling face is really cute.

7. 웃는 얼굴이 정말 (   ).   His smiling face is really cute.

8. (   )이 크고 다리가 길어요.   He has big eyes and long legs.

9. 눈이 크고 (   )가 길어요.   He has big eyes and long legs.

10. 눈이 크고 다리가 (   ).   He has big eyes and long legs.

DAY 22

Check off the words you already know.

- ○ 언니 ○
- ○ 같이 ○
- ○ 여행 ○
- ○ 비행기 ○
- ○ 처음 ○
- ○ 창문 ○
- ○ 앉다 ○
- ○ 이따가 ○
- ○ 하늘 ○
- ○ 구름 ○

After you study these words, come back and check off the ones you have memorized.

Day 22

Imagine the situation in the story below to help you
remember the ten Korean words in context.

여행 같이   언니

I am going on a <u>trip</u> <u>together</u> with my <u>older sister</u>.

비행기

We will go there by <u>airplane</u>.

처음

I will ride in an airplane <u>for the first time</u>.

창문

I <u>sat</u> in the seat next to the <u>window</u>.

하늘 이따가

I will be able to see the <u>sky</u>   <u>later</u>.

구름

Will I be able to see the <u>clouds</u>, too?

LET'S KEEP THE BALL ROLLING!

Word	Meaning	Related Words	Meaning
언니 *eon-ni*	older sister (for a girl)	친언니 *chi-neon-ni*	biological older sister (for a girl)
		사촌 언니 *sa-chon eon-ni*	older female cousin (for a girl)
		친한 언니 *chi-nan eon-ni*	close older female friend (for a girl)
같이 *ga-chi*	together	친구랑 같이 *chin-gu-rang ga-chi*	together with a friend
		다 같이 *da ga-chi*	all together
		같이 하다 *ga-chi ha-da*	to do something together
여행 *yeo-haeng*	travel	여행하다 *yeo-haeng-ha-da*	to travel
		여행 가다 *yeo-haeng ga-da*	to go on a trip
		기차 여행 *gi-cha yeo-haeng*	train trip
비행기 *bi-haeng-gi*	airplane	비행기를 타다 *bi-haeng-gi-reul ta-da*	to ride in an airplane
		공항 *gong-hang*	airport
		비행기 표 *bi-haeng-gi pyo*	airplane ticket

처음
cheo-eum

beginning,
for the first time

처음 보다
cheo-eum bo-da

to see for the first time

맨 처음
maen cheo-eum

in the very beginning

처음에
cheo-eu-me

at first

처음으로
cheo-eu-meu-ro

for the first time

창문
chang-mun

window

창문을 열다
chang-mu-neul yeol-da

to open the window

창문을 닫다
chang-mu-neul dat-tta

to close the window

유리창
yu-ri-chang

glass window

창가
chang-kka

by the window

앉다
an-tta

to sit

의자에 앉다
ui-ja-e an-tta

to sit on a chair

바닥에 앉다
ba-da-ge an-tta

to sit on the floor

서다
seo-da

to stand

이따가
i-tta-ga

later

이따가 전화하다
i-tta-ga jeo-nwa-ha-da

to call later

이따가 만나다
i-tta-ga man-na-da

to meet later

아까
a-kka

earlier

하늘	sky	파란 하늘	blue sky
ha-neul		pa-ran ha-neul	
		하늘이 맑다	the sky is clear
		ha-neu-ri mak-tta	
		땅	ground
		ttang	

구름	cloud	구름이 끼다	to be cloudy
gu-reum		gu-reu-mi kki-da	
		구름이 많다	to be very cloudy
		gu-reu-mi man-ta	
		흐리다	to be overcast
		heu-ri-da	
		흰 구름	white cloud
		huin gu-reum	

Read the story again, but this time in Korean!

언니랑 같이 여행을 가요.

비행기를 타고 가요.

저는 비행기를 처음 타요.

창문 옆자리에 앉았어요.

이따가 하늘을 볼 수 있을 거예요.

구름도 볼 수 있을까요?

Translation

I am going on a trip together with my older sister. We will go there by airplane. I will ride in an airplane for the first time. I sat in the seat next to the window. I will be able to see the sky later.
Will I be able to see the clouds, too?

Match each Korean word to its English translation.

비행기 ·   · beginning, for the first time

창문 ·   · together

이따가 ·   · to sit

구름 ·   · later

앉다 ·   · older sister (for a girl)

여행 ·   · sky

언니 ·   · travel

하늘 ·   · cloud

처음 ·   · window

같이 ·   · airplane

Crossword Puzzle

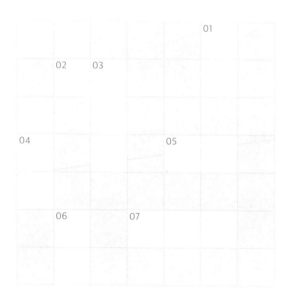

01 older sister (for a girl)
02 together
03 later
04 beginning, for the first time
05 cloud
06 sky
07 airplane

Fill in the blanks using one of the words that you learned in Day 22.
(Please refer to page 017 to review how to conjugate verbs/adjectives.)

1. (   )랑 같이 여행을 가요.　　　I am going on a trip together with my older sister.

2. 언니랑 (   ) 여행을 가요.　　　I am going on a trip together with my older sister.

3. 언니랑 같이 (   )을 가요.　　　I am going on a trip together with my older sister.

4. (   )를 타고 가요.　　　We will go there by airplane.

5. 저는 비행기를 (   ) 타요.　　　I will ride in an airplane for the first time.

6. (   ) 옆자리에 앉았어요.　　　I sat in the seat next to the window.

7. 창문 옆자리에 (   ).　　　I sat in the seat next to the window.

8. (   ) 하늘을 볼 수 있을 거예요.　　　I will be able to see the sky later.

9. 이따가 (   )을 볼 수 있을 거예요.　　　I will be able to see the sky later.

10. (   )도 볼 수 있을까요?　　　Will I be able to see the clouds, too?

DAY 23

Check off the words
you already know.

○ 연락 ○

○ 도와주다 ○

○ 층 ○

○ 엘리베이터 ○

○ 무겁다 ○

○ 상자 ○

○ 들다 ○

○ 넣다 ○

○ 좁다 ○

○ 빼다 ○

After you study these words, come back and
check off the ones you have memorized.

Day 23

....

Imagine the situation in the story below to help you remember the ten Korean words in context.

연락

I am moving today. I <u>contacted</u> my friend.

도와주다

My friend will <u>help</u> me move.

층   엘리베이터

My place is on the fifth <u>floor</u>. We don't have an <u>elevator</u>.

들다 무겁다 상자

I go up the stairs <u>carrying</u> a <u>heavy</u>   <u>box</u>.

넣다   좁다

I <u>put</u> my bed in the room. But, the room is too <u>small</u>.

빼다

I <u>take</u> the bed out again.

LET'S KEEP THE BALL ROLLING!

Word	Meaning	Related Words	Meaning
연락 *yeol-lak*	contact, contacting	연락이 되다 *yeol-la-gi doe-da*	to be able to reach, to be able to contact, to be within reach
		전화 연락 *jeo-nwa yeol-lak*	contact by phone
		연락하다 *yeol-la-ka-da*	to contact
		연락처 *yeol-lak-cheo*	contact information
도와주다 *do-wa-ju-da*	to help	남을 도와주다 *na-meul do-wa-ju-da*	to help someone else
		일을 도와주다 *i-reul do-wa-ju-da*	to help with work
		도와준 사람 *do-wa-jun sa-ram*	person who helped
		돕다 *dop-tta*	to help
층 *cheung*	floor	5층 *o-cheung*	5th floor
		다른 층 *da-reun cheung*	different floor
		높은 층 *no-peun cheung*	high floor
		몇 층 *myeot cheung*	what floor

엘리베이터 *el-li-be-i-teo*	elevator	엘리베이터를 타다 *el-li-be-i-teo-reul ta-da*	to take an elevator
		엘리베이터에서 내리다 *el-li-be-i-teo-e-seo nae-ri-da*	to get out of an elevator
		엘리베이터가 멈추다 *el-li-be-i-teo-ga meom-chu-da*	the elevator stops

무겁다 *mu-geop-tta*	to be heavy	들기 무겁다 *deul-gi mu-geop-tta*	to be heavy to carry
		무거운 짐 *mu-geo-un jim*	heavy luggage
		무게 *mu-ge*	weight
		가볍다 *ga-byeop-tta*	to be light

상자 *sang-ja*	box	상자를 열다 *sang-ja-reul yeol-da*	to open a box
		상자에 담다 *sang-ja-e dam-tta*	to put in a box
		종이 상자 *jong-i sang-ja*	paper box
		박스 *bak-sseu*	box

들다	to lift, to carry	상자를 들다	to lift a box,
deul-da		*sang-ja-reul deul-da*	to carry a box
		가방을 들다	to carry a bag
		ga-bang-eul deul-da	
		들고 다니다	to carry around
		deul-go da-ni-da	
		들어 주다	to carry for someone
		deu-reo ju-da	

넣다	to put in	봉투에 넣다	to put into an envelope
neo-ta		*bong-tu-e neo-ta*	
		바람을 넣다	to put air in
		ba-ra-meul neo-ta	
		설탕을 넣다	to put sugar in
		seol-tang-eul neo-ta	
		넣는 곳	a place to put something
		neon-neun got	

좁다	to be narrow	방이 좁다	the room is small
jop-tta		*bang-i jop-tta*	
		좁은 길	narrow road,
		jo-beun gil	narrow path
		넓다	to be spacious,
		neol-tta	to be wide

빼다	to take out,	차를 빼다	to pull out a car
ppae-da	to pull out	*cha-reul ppae-da*	
		돈을 빼다	to withdraw money
		do-neul ppae-da	
		3을 빼다	to subtract three
		sa-meul ppae-da	

Read the story again, but this time in Korean!

저는 오늘 이사를 가요. 친구에게 **연락**을 했어요.

친구가 이사를 **도와줄** 거예요.

저희 집은 5**층**이에요. **엘리베이터**가 없어요.

무거운 상자를 **들고** 계단을 올라가요.

방에 침대를 **넣어요.** 그런데 방이 너무 **좁아요.**

침대를 다시 **빼요.**

Translation

I am moving today. I contacted my friend. My friend will help me
move. My place is on the fifth floor. We don't have an elevator.
I go up the stairs carrying a heavy box. I put my bed in the room.
But, the room is too small. I take the bed out again.

Match each Korean word to its English translation.

넣다 ·　　　　　　　　　　· to be heavy

엘리베이터 ·　　　　　　　· to lift, to carry

무겁다 ·　　　　　　　　　· to be narrow

빼다 ·　　　　　　　　　　· floor

들다 ·　　　　　　　　　　· contact, contacting

좁다 ·　　　　　　　　　　· to help

상자 ·　　　　　　　　　　· elevator

도와주다 ·　　　　　　　　· to put in

연락 ·　　　　　　　　　　· to take out, to pull out

층 ·　　　　　　　　　　　· box

Crossword Puzzle

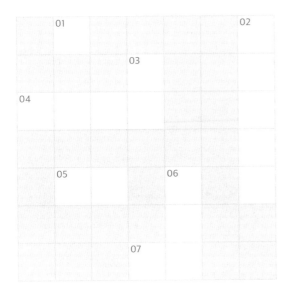

01 floor
02 elevator
03 to lift, to carry
04 to help
05 box
06 to be heavy
07 to put in

Fill in the blanks using one of the words that you learned in Day 23.
(Please refer to page 017 to review how to conjugate verbs/adjectives.)

1. 친구에게 (   )을 했어요.   I contacted my friend.

2. 친구가 이사를 (   ) 거예요.   My friend will help me move.

3. 저희 집은 5(   )이에요.   My place is on the fifth floor.

4. (   )가 없어요.   We don't have an elevator.

5. (   ) 상자를 들고 계단을 올라가요.   I go up the stairs carrying a heavy box.

6. 무거운 (   )를 들고 계단을 올라가요.   I go up the stairs carrying a heavy box.

7. 무거운 상자를 (   ) 계단을 올라가요.   I go up the stairs carrying a heavy box.

8. 방에 침대를 (   ).   I put my bed in the room.

9. 그런데 방이 너무 (   ).   But, the room is too small.

10. 침대를 다시 (   ).   I take the bed out again.

DAY 24

Check off the words
you already know.

○ 이사 ○

○ 혼자 ○

○ 멋있다 ○

○ 거실 ○

○ 벽 ○

○ 그림 ○

○ 시계 ○

○ 부엌 ○

○ 만들다 ○

○ 쓰다 02 ○

After you study these words, come back and
check off the ones you have memorized.

Day 24

....

Imagine the situation in the story below to help you
remember the ten Korean words in context.

이사   혼자

I <u>moved</u> yesterday. I am finally living <u>by myself</u>.

멋있다

I want to decorate my house in a <u>cool</u> way.

그림   거실   벽

I want to hang a <u>picture</u> on the <u>living room</u> <u>wall</u>.

시계

I also bought a pretty wall <u>clock</u>.

만들다   부엌

I will also <u>make</u> food by myself in the <u>kitchen</u>.

쓰다 ⁰²

I will <u>use</u> new plates.

LET'S KEEP THE BALL ROLLING!

Word	Meaning	Related Words	Meaning
이사 *i-sa*	moving	이사하다 *i-sa-ha-da*	to move (to another place)
		이사 가다 *i-sa ga-da*	to move (to another place)
		이사 오다 *i-sa o-da*	to move in, to move here
		이삿짐 *i-sat-jjim*	things to move
		이삿짐 센터 *i-sat-jjim ssen-teo*	moving company, movers
혼자 *hon-ja*	alone	나 혼자 *na hon-ja*	alone, by myself
		혼자 살다 *hon-ja sal-da*	to live by oneself
		혼잣말 *hon-jan-mal*	talking to oneself
멋있다 *meo-sit-tta*	to be cool, to be awesome	멋있는 사람 *meo-sin-neun sa-ram*	cool person, awesome person
		멋있는 옷 *meo-sin-neun ot*	cool-looking clothes
		멋있게 *meo-sit-kke*	in a cool manner

거실 *geo-sil*	living room	거실에 앉다 *geo-si-re an-tta*	to sit in the living room
		거실에 모이다 *geo-si-re mo-i-da*	to gather in the living room
		소파 *so-pa*	couch, sofa
벽 *byeok*	wall	벽이 무너지다 *byeo-gi mu-neo-ji-da*	the wall collapses
		벽에 걸다 *byeo-ge geol-da*	to hang on the wall
		벽을 칠하다 *byeo-geul chi-ra-da*	to paint the wall
그림 *geu-rim*	painting, drawing, picture	그림을 그리다 *geu-ri-meul geu-ri-da*	to paint a picture
		그림을 걸다 *geu-ri-meul geol-da*	to hang a picture
		액자 *aek-jja*	frame
		사진 *sa-jin*	photo
시계 *si-gye*	clock	벽시계 *byeok-ssi-gye*	wall clock
		손목시계 *son-mok-ssi-gye*	wrist watch
		시계가 느리다 *si-gye-ga neu-ri-da*	the watch is slow
		시계가 빠르다 *si-gye-ga ppa-reu-da*	the watch is fast

부엌
bu-eok

kitchen

부엌에서 요리하다
bu-eo-ke-seo yo-ri-ha-da

to cook in the kitchen

부엌이 좁다
bu-eo-ki jop-tta

the kitchen is small

만들다
man-deul-da

to make

음식을 만들다
eum-si-geul man-deul-da

to make food,
to cook food

직접 만들다
jik-jjeop man-deul-da

to make for oneself

손으로 만들다
so-neu-ro man-deul-da

to make with one's
hands

쓰다 02
sseu-da

to use

집에서 쓰다
ji-be-seo sseu-da

to use at home

쓰는 물건
sseu-neun mul-geon

things that are being
used

써 보다
sseo bo-da

to try using

쓰이다
sseu-i-da

to be used

LET'S REVIEW!

Read the story again, but this time in Korean!

어제 **이사**했어요. 드디어 **혼자** 살아요.

집을 **멋있게** 꾸미고 싶어요.

거실 벽에 **그림**을 걸고 싶어요.

예쁜 벽**시계**도 샀어요.

부엌에서 음식도 직접 **만들** 거예요.

새 접시를 **쓸** 거예요.

Translation

I moved yesterday. I am finally living by myself. I want to decorate my house in a cool way. I want to hang a picture on the living room wall. I also bought a pretty wall clock. I will also make food by myself in the kitchen. I will use new plates.

Match each Korean word to its English translation.

거실 ·   · clock

그림 ·   · to be cool, to be awesome

혼자 ·   · wall

시계 ·   · alone

부엌 ·   · to make

쓰다 02 ·   · moving

이사 ·   · living room

벽 ·   · painting, drawing, picture

만들다 ·   · to use

멋있다 ·   · kitchen

Crossword Puzzle

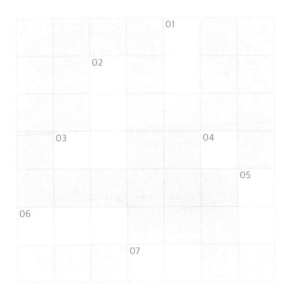

01 alone
02 to make
03 to use
04 wall
05 living room
06 to be cool, to be awesome
07 moving

Fill in the blanks using one of the words that you learned in Day 24.
(Please refer to page 017 to review how to conjugate verbs/adjectives.)

1. 어제 (   )했어요.   I moved yesterday.

2. 드디어 (   ) 살아요.   I am finally living by myself.

3. 집을 (   ) 꾸미고 싶어요.   I want to decorate my house in a cool way.

4. (   ) 벽에 그림을 걸고 싶어요.   I want to hang a picture on the living room wall.

5. 거실 (   )에 그림을 걸고 싶어요.   I want to hang a picture on the living room wall.

6. 거실 벽에 (   )을 걸고 싶어요.   I want to hang a picture on the living room wall.

7. 예쁜 벽(   )도 샀어요.   I also bought a pretty wall clock.

8. (   )에서 음식도 직접 만들 거예요.   I will also make food by myself in the kitchen.

9. 부엌에서 음식도 직접 (   ) 거예요.   I will also make food by myself in the kitchen.

10. 새 접시를 (   ) 거예요.   I will use new plates.

DAY 25

Check off the words
you already know.

○ 지우다 ○

○ 씻다 ○

○ 버섯 ○

○ 당근 ○

○ 부르다 ○

○ 다 ○

○ 산책 ○

○ 밝다 ○

○ 편하다 ○

○ 감사 ○

After you study these words, come back and
check off the ones you have memorized.

LET'S WARM UP!

Imagine the situation in the story below to help you remember the ten Korean words in context.

지우다   씻다

I come home. I <u>wash off</u> my make-up. I <u>wash</u> my hands.

Today's dinner is soybean paste stew.

버섯   당근

I put in <u>mushrooms</u> and <u>carrots</u>.

부르다

I <u>call</u> my kids. We have dinner all together.

산책 다   밝다

We go for a <u>walk</u>   <u>all</u> together. The streets are still <u>bright</u>.

편하다

When I walk with my kids, I feel <u>at ease</u>.

감사

I am <u>thankful</u> for another happy day.

LET'S KEEP THE BALL ROLLING!

Word	Meaning	Related Words	Meaning
지우다 *ji-u-da*	to erase, to wash off	화장을 지우다 *hwa-jang-eul ji-u-da*	to wash off make-up
		낙서를 지우다 *nak-sseo-reul ji-u-da*	to erase scribbles
		지우개로 지우다 *ji-u-gae-ro ji-u-da*	to erase with an eraser
씻다 *ssit-tta*	to wash	손을 씻다 *so-neul ssit-tta*	to wash one's hands
		얼굴을 씻다 *eol-gu-reul ssit-tta*	to wash one's face
		깨끗하게 씻다 *kkae-kkeu-ta-ge ssit-tta*	to wash cleanly
버섯 *beo-seot*	mushroom	버섯을 따다 *beo-seo-seul tta-da*	to pick a mushroom
		버섯을 넣다 *beo-seo-seul neo-ta*	to put a mushroom in
		버섯 요리 *beo-seot yo-ri*	mushroom dish
당근 *dang-geun*	carrot	당근을 볶다 *dang-geu-neul bok-tta*	to stir fry a carrot
		당근을 썰다 *dang-geu-neul sseol-da*	to chop a carrot
		생당근 *saeng-dang-geun*	raw carrot

부르다 *bu-reu-da*	to call	큰 소리로 부르다 *keun so-ri-ro bu-reu-da*	to call out loud
		이름을 부르다 *i-reu-meul bu-reu-da*	to call someone's name
		아이들을 부르다 *a-i-deu-reul bu-reu-da*	to call the children
		부르는 소리 *bu-reu-neun so-ri*	sound of calling someone

다 *da*	all, every	모두 *mo-du*	all, everyone
		전부 *jeon-bu*	all
		다 함께 *da ham-kke*	all together

산책 *san-chaek*	walk	산책을 나가다 *san-chae-geul na-ga-da*	to go out for a walk
		공원을 산책하다 *gong-wo-neul san-chae-ka-da*	to take a walk in the park
		강아지를 산책시키다 *gang-a-ji-reul san-chaek-si-ki-da*	to walk a dog

밝다 bak-tta	to be bright	거리가 밝다 geo-ri-ga bak-tta	the street is bright
		표정이 밝다 pyo-jeong-i bak-tta	one's facial expression is bright
		밝은 빛 bal-geun bit	bright light
		어둡다 eo-dup-tta	to be dark
편하다 pyeo-na-da	to be comfortable	마음이 편하다 ma-eu-mi pyeo-na-da	to feel comfortable, to feel at ease
		몸이 편하다 mo-mi pyeo-na-da	one's body is comfortable
		편한 신발 pyeo-nan sin-bal	comfortable shoes
감사 gam-sa	gratitude	감사 편지 gam-sa pyeon-ji	thank you letter
		감사 기도 gam-sa gi-do	prayer of gratitude
		감사하다 gam-sa-ha-da	to thank

LET'S REVIEW!

Read the story again, but this time in Korean!

집에 왔어요. 화장을 **지워요**. 손을 **씻어요**.

오늘 저녁은 된장찌개예요. **버섯**과 **당근**을 넣어요.

아이들을 **불러요**. 저녁을 같이 먹어요.

다 함께 산책을 가요. 거리가 아직 **밝아요**.

아이들이랑 산책하면 마음이 **편해요**.

오늘도 행복한 하루에 **감사**해요.

Translation

I come home. I wash off my make-up. I wash my hands. Today's dinner is soybean paste stew. I put in mushrooms and carrots. I call my kids. We have dinner all together. We go for a walk all together. The streets are still bright. When I walk with my kids, I feel at ease. I am thankful for another happy day.

Match each Korean word to its English translation.

부르다 ·   · to wash

편하다 ·   · all, every

버섯 ·   · to call

산책 ·   · mushroom

감사 ·   · gratitude

지우다 ·   · to be comfortable

씻다 ·   · to erase, to wash off

당근 ·   · walk

밝다 ·   · carrot

다 ·   · to be bright

Crossword Puzzle

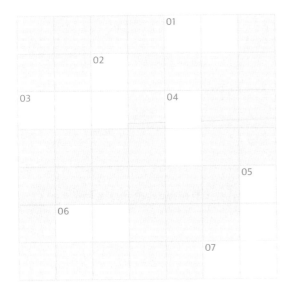

01 mushroom
02 to wash
03 to call
04 gratitude
05 to be comfortable
06 carrot
07 to be bright

Fill in the blanks using one of the words that you learned in Day 25.
(Please refer to page 017 to review how to conjugate verbs/adjectives.)

1. 화장을 (   ).   I wash off my make-up.

2. 손을 (   ).   I wash my hands.

3. (   )과 당근을 넣어요.   I put in mushrooms and carrots.

4. 버섯과 (   )을 넣어요.   I put in mushrooms and carrots.

5. 아이들을 (   ).   I call my kids.

6. (   ) 함께 산책을 가요.   We go for a walk all together.

7. 다 함께 (   )을 가요.   We go for a walk all together.

8. 거리가 아직 (   ).   The streets are still bright.

9. 아이들이랑 산책하면 마음이 (   ).   When I walk with my kids, I feel at ease.

10. 오늘도 행복한 하루에 (   )해요.   I am thankful for another happy day.

DAY 26

Check off the words you already know.

- ○ 꿈 ○
- ○ 사진 ○
- ○ 배우다 ○
- ○ 카메라 ○
- ○ 가격 ○
- ○ 비싸다 ○
- ○ 휴대폰 ○
- ○ 찍다 ○
- ○ 연습하다 ○
- ○ 유명하다 ○

After you study these words, come back and check off the ones you have memorized.

Day 26

LET'S WARM UP!

Imagine the situation in the story below to help you
remember the ten Korean words in context.

꿈
My <u>dream</u> is to be a photographer.

배우다 사진
I am <u>learning</u>   <u>photography</u> in school.

카메라
But my <u>camera</u> broke.

가격   비싸다
I want to buy a new camera. But the <u>price</u> is too <u>high</u>.

찍다   휴대폰
So I <u>take</u> photos with my <u>cell phone</u>.

연습하다
I will <u>practice</u> hard.

유명하다
I want to become a <u>famous</u> photographer.

LET'S KEEP THE BALL ROLLING!

Word	Meaning	Related Words	Meaning
꿈 *kkum*	dream	꿈을 꾸다 *kku-meul kku-da*	to dream
		슬픈 꿈 *seul-peun kkum*	sad dream
		꿈을 이루다 *kku-meul i-ru-da*	to realize one's dream
사진 *sa-jin*	photo	사진을 찍다 *sa-ji-neul jjik-tta*	to take a photo
		사진 작가 *sa-jin jak-kka*	photographer
		사진 한 장 *sa-jin han jang*	one photo
		사진이 잘 나오다 *sa-ji-ni jal na-o-da*	the photo turns out well
배우다 *bae-u-da*	to learn	한국어를 배우다 *han-gu-geo-reul bae-u-da*	to learn Korean
		아빠한테 배우다 *a-ppa-han-te bae-u-da*	to learn from one's dad
		가르치다 *ga-reu-chi-da*	to teach

카메라
ka-me-ra

camera

비디오카메라
bi-di-o-ka-me-ra

video camera

카메라를 사다
ka-me-ra-reul sa-da

to buy a camera

수동 카메라
su-dong ka-me-ra

manual camera

렌즈
ren-jeu

lens

가격
ga-gyeok

price

가격이 내리다
ga-gyeo-gi nae-ri-da

the price goes down

가격이 오르다
ga-gyeo-gi o-reu-da

the price goes up

가격을 물어보다
ga-gyeo-geul mu-reo-bo-da

to ask the price

비싸다
bi-ssa-da

to be expensive

비싼 가방
bi-ssan ga-bang

expensive bag

비싼 가격
bi-ssan ga-gyeok

expensive price

옷이 비싸다
o-si bi-ssa-da

the clothes are expensive

싸다
ssa-da

to be cheap

휴대폰	mobile phone,	휴대폰을 사다	to buy a mobile phone
hyu-dae-pon	cell phone	*hyu-dae-po-neul sa-da*	
		휴대폰으로 통화하다	to talk on the mobile phone
		hyu-dae-po-neu-ro tong-hwa-ha-da	
		핸드폰	mobile phone, cell phone
		haen-deu-pon	
		스마트폰	smart phone
		seu-ma-teu-pon	

찍다	to take, to film	사진을 찍다	to take a photo
jjik-tta		*sa-ji-neul jjik-tta*	
		동영상을 찍다	to take a video
		dong-yeong-sang-eul jjik-tta	
		셀카를 찍다	to take a selfie
		ssel-ka-reul jjik-tta	

연습하다	to practice	기타를 연습하다	to practice the guitar
yeon-seu-pa-da		*gi-ta-reul yeon-seu-pa-da*	
		열심히 연습하다	to practice hard
		yeol-ssi-mi yeon-seu-pa-da	
		연습	practice
		yeon-seup	

유명하다	to be famous	유명한 사람	famous person
yu-myeong-ha-da		*yu-myeong-han sa-ram*	
		아주 유명하다	to be very famous
		a-ju yu-myeong-ha-da	
		유명해지다	to become famous
		yu-myeong-hae-ji-da	

LET'S REVIEW!

Read the story again, but this time in Korean!

제 **꿈**은 사진 작가예요.

학교에서 **사진**을 배우고 있어요.

그런데 **카메라**가 고장이 났어요.

새 카메라를 사고 싶어요. 그런데 **가격**이 너무 **비싸요.**

그래서 **휴대폰**으로 사진을 **찍어요.**

열심히 **연습할** 거예요. **유명한** 사진 작가가 되고 싶어요.

Translation

My dream is to be a photographer. I am learning photography in school. But my camera broke. I want to buy a new camera. But the price is too high. So I take photos with my cell phone. I will practice hard. I want to become a famous photographer.

Match each Korean word to its English translation.

사진 ·   · camera

비싸다 ·   · price

휴대폰 ·   · to be famous

연습하다 ·   · dream

유명하다 ·   · to learn

찍다 ·   · to be expensive

꿈 ·   · photo

가격 ·   · to practice

카메라 ·   · to take, to film

배우다 ·   · mobile phone, cell phone

Crossword Puzzle

01 to be famous
02 price
03 dream
04 to practice
05 camera
06 to take, to film
07 to learn

Fill in the blanks using one of the words that you learned in Day 26.
(Please refer to page 017 to review how to conjugate verbs/adjectives.)

1. 제 (   )은 사진 작가예요.   My dream is to be a photographer.

2. 학교에서 (   )을 배우고 있어요.   I am learning photography in school.

3. 학교에서 사진을 (   ) 있어요.   I am learning photography in school.

4. 그런데 (   )가 고장이 났어요.   But my camera broke.

5. 그런데 (   )이 너무 비싸요.   But the price is too high.

6. 그런데 가격이 너무 (   ).   But the price is too high.

7. 그래서 (   )으로 사진을 찍어요.   So I take photos with my cell phone.

8. 그래서 휴대폰으로 사진을 (   ).   So I take photos with my cell phone.

9. 열심히 (   ) 거예요.   I will practice hard.

10. (   ) 사진 작가가 되고 싶어요.   I want to become a famous photographer.

DAY 27

Check off the words you already know.

○ 봄 ○

○ 오다 ○

○ 날씨 ○

○ 따뜻하다 ○

○ 예쁘다 ○

○ 꽃 ○

○ 딸기 ○

○ 빨간색 ○

○ 좋아하다 ○

○ 과일 ○

After you study these words, come back and check off the ones you have memorized.

Day 27

Imagine the situation in the story below to help you remember the ten Korean words in context.

봄　오다
Spring has come.

날씨　따뜻하다
The weather is warm.

예쁘다 꽃
Pretty flowers have blossomed.

딸기
In the spring, a lot of strawberries come out.

빨간색
Strawberries are red.

좋아하다 과일
Strawberries are my favorite fruit.

Therefore, I like spring the best.

LET'S KEEP THE BALL ROLLING!

Word	Meaning	Related Words	Meaning
봄 *bom*	spring (season)	3월 *sa-mwol*	March
		따뜻하다 *tta-tteu-ta-da*	to be warm
		계절 *gye-jeol*	season
		가을 *ga-eul*	fall, autumn
오다 *o-da*	to come	빨리 오다 *ppal-li o-da*	to come quickly
		갔다 오다 *gat-tta o-da*	to go and come back
		가다 *ga-da*	to go
날씨 *nal-ssi*	weather	날씨가 좋다 *nal-ssi-ga jo-ta*	the weather is good
		오늘 날씨 *o-neul nal-ssi*	today's weather
		날씨가 흐리다 *nal-ssi-ga heu-ri-da*	the weather is cloudy

따뜻하다	to be warm	방이 따뜻하다	the room is warm
tta-tteu-ta-da		bang-i tta-tteu-ta-da	
		날씨가 따뜻하다	the weather is warm
		nal-ssi-ga tta-tteu-ta-da	
		따뜻한	warm
		tta-tteu-tan	

예쁘다	to be pretty	너무 예쁘다	to be very pretty
ye-ppeu-da		neo-mu ye-ppeu-da	
		예쁜	pretty
		ye-ppeun	
		예쁘게	prettily, beautifully
		ye-ppeu-ge	

꽃	flower	꽃 한 송이	one flower
kkot		kkot han song-i	
		꽃이 피다	a flower blossoms
		kko-chi pi-da	
		꽃이 지다	a flower falls
		kko-chi ji-da	
		꽃다발	a bunch of flowers
		kkot-tta-bal	

딸기	strawberry	맛있는 딸기	delicious strawberries
ttal-gi		ma-sin-neun ttal-gi	
		딸기잼	strawberry jam
		ttal-gi-jjaem	
		딸기를 따다	to pick strawberries
		ttal-gi-reul tta-da	

빨간색 *ppal-gan-saek*	red (color)	**빨간** *ppal-gan*	red
		빨간색 옷 *ppal-gan-saek ot*	red clothes

좋아하다 *jo-a-ha-da*	to like	**제일 좋아하다** *je-il jo-a-ha-da*	to like the most
		좋아하는 *jo-a-ha-neun*	that one likes
		좋아하는 영화 *jo-a-ha-neun yeong-hwa*	a movie that one likes

과일 *gwa-il*	fruit	**과일을 먹다** *gwa-i-reul meok-tta*	to eat fruit
		과일 주스 *gwa-il ju-sseu*	fruit juice
		사과 *sa-gwa*	apple
		채소 *chae-so*	vegetable

Read the story again, but this time in Korean!

봄이 왔어요.

날씨가 따뜻해요.

예쁜 꽃이 피었어요.

봄에는 **딸기**가 많이 나와요. 딸기는 **빨간색**이에요.

딸기는 제가 제일 **좋아하는 과일**이에요.

그래서 저는 봄이 제일 좋아요.

Translation

Spring has come. The weather is warm. Pretty flowers have blossomed. In the spring, a lot of strawberries come out. Strawberries are red. Strawberries are my favorite fruit. Therefore, I like spring the best.

Match each Korean word to its English translation.

오다 ·   · weather

예쁘다 ·   · to be warm

딸기 ·   · flower

빨간색 ·   · to come

과일 ·   · strawberry

봄 ·   · to be pretty

날씨 ·   · red (color)

좋아하다 ·   · fruit

꽃 ·   · spring (season)

따뜻하다 ·   · to like

Crossword Puzzle

01 to come
02 to be warm
03 flower
04 strawberry
05 to like
06 spring (season)
07 to be pretty

Fill in the blanks using one of the words that you learned in Day 27.
(Please refer to page 017 to review how to conjugate verbs/adjectives.)

1. (   )이 왔어요.   Spring has come.

2. 봄이 (   ).   Spring has come.

3. (   )가 따뜻해요.   The weather is warm.

4. 날씨가 (   ).   The weather is warm.

5. (   ) 꽃이 피었어요.   Pretty flowers have blossomed.

6. 예쁜 (   )이 피었어요.   Pretty flowers have blossomed.

7. 봄에는 (   )가 많이 나와요.   In the spring, a lot of strawberries come out.

8. 딸기는 (   )이에요.   Strawberries are red.

9. 딸기는 제가 제일 (   )   Strawberry is my favorite fruit.
   과일이에요.

10. 딸기는 제가 제일 좋아하는 (   )   Strawberry is my favorite fruit.
    이에요.

DAY 28

Check off the words
you already know.

○ 기다리다 ○

○ 눈 02 ○

○ 바람 ○

○ 춥다 ○

○ 자주 ○

○ 안 ○

○ 전화하다 ○

○ 알다 ○

○ 장갑 ○

○ 목도리 ○

After you study these words, come back and
check off the ones you have memorized.

Day 28 *LET'S WARM UP!*

Imagine the situation in the story below to help you
remember the ten Korean words in context.

기다리다   눈 ⁰²

I am <u>waiting</u> for a friend. But it suddenly <u>snows</u>.

바람   춥다

The <u>wind</u> blows, too. It is so <u>cold</u>.

자주

I went into a café that I go to <u>often</u>.

안   전화하다

I will wait <u>inside</u>. I <u>called</u> my friend.

알다

My friend also <u>knows</u> this café.

I will meet my friend and go shopping.

장갑   목도리

I am going to buy <u>gloves</u> and a <u>scarf</u>.

LET'S KEEP THE BALL ROLLING!

Word	Meaning	Related Words	Meaning
기다리다 *gi-da-ri-da*	to wait	밖에서 기다리다 *ba-kke-seo gi-da-ri-da*	to wait outside
		방학을 기다리다 *bang-ha-geul gi-da-ri-da*	to wait for school vacation
		잠깐 기다리다 *jam-kkan gi-da-ri-da*	to wait for a little bit
		오래 기다리다 *o-rae gi-da-ri-da*	to wait for a long time
눈 02 *nun*	snow	눈이 오다 *nu-ni o-da*	to snow
		눈이 내리다 *nu-ni nae-ri-da*	to snow
		눈이 쌓이다 *nu-ni ssa-i-da*	the snow piles up
바람 *ba-ram*	wind	바람이 불다 *ba-ra-mi bul-da*	the wind blows
		바람이 세다 *ba-ra-mi se-da*	the wind is strong
		시원한 바람 *si-wo-nan ba-ram*	cool wind

춥다 *chup-tta*	to be cold	너무 춥다 *neo-mu chup-tta*	to be too cold
		날씨가 춥다 *nal-ssi-ga chup-tta*	the weather is cold
		추운 겨울 *chu-un gyeo-ul*	cold winter
자주 *ja-ju*	often	자주 가다 *ja-ju ga-da*	to go often
		자주 하다 *ja-ju ha-da*	to do often
안 *an*	inside	건물 안 *geon-mul an*	inside a building
		안에서 *a-ne-seo*	inside, indoors
		안으로 *a-neu-ro*	into
		밖 *bak*	outside
전화하다 *jeo-nwa-ha-da*	to call, to telephone	친구한테 전화하다 *chin-gu-han-te jeo-nwa-ha-da*	to call a friend
		집으로 전화하다 *ji-beu-ro jeo-nwa-ha-da*	to call home
		휴대폰으로 전화하다 *hyu-dae-po-neu-ro jeo-nwa-ha-da*	to call on one's cell phone
		전화번호 *jeo-nwa-beo-no*	phone number

알다 *al-da*	to know	잘 알다 *jal al-da*	to know well
		알리다 *al-li-da*	to let someone know, to announce
		알려 주다 *al-lyeo ju-da*	to let someone know
		모르다 *mo-reu-da*	to not know

장갑 *jang-gap*	glove	털장갑 *teol-jang-gap*	fur gloves, woolen gloves
		고무장갑 *go-mu-jang-gap*	rubber gloves
		가죽 장갑 *ga-juk jang-gap*	leather gloves

목도리 *mok-tto-ri*	scarf	목도리를 하다 *mok-tto-ri-reul ha-da*	to put on a scarf
		목도리를 두르다 *mok-tto-ri-reul du-reu-da*	to wrap a scarf around one's neck
		털목도리 *teol-mok-tto-ri*	woolen scarf

Read the story again, but this time in Korean!

친구를 **기다리고** 있어요. 그런데 갑자기 **눈**이 와요.

바람도 불어요. 너무 **추워요**.

자주 가는 카페에 들어갔어요.

안에서 기다릴 거예요. 친구한테 **전화했어요.**

친구도 이 카페를 **알아요**. 친구를 만나서 쇼핑을 할 거예요.

장갑이랑 **목도리**를 살 거예요.

Translation

I am waiting for a friend. But it suddenly snows. The wind blows, too. It is so cold. I went into a café that I go to often. I will wait inside. I called my friend. My friend also knows this café. I will meet my friend and go shopping. I am going to buy gloves and a scarf.

Match each Korean word to its English translation.

눈 02   ·   · to be cold

자주   ·   · inside

전화하다   ·   · wind

목도리   ·   · to wait

장갑   ·   · scarf

기다리다   ·   · snow

알다   ·   · glove

바람   ·   · often

안   ·   · to know

춥다   ·   · to call, to telephone

Crossword Puzzle

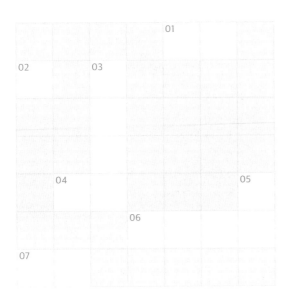

01   often
02   snow
03   to wait
04   to know
05   to be cold
06   to call, to telephone
07   wind

Fill in the blanks using one of the words that you learned in Day 28.
(Please refer to page 017 to review how to conjugate verbs/adjectives.)

1. 친구를 (   ) 있어요.   I am waiting for a friend.

2. 그런데 갑자기 (   )이 와요.   But it suddenly snows.

3. (   )도 불어요.   The wind blows, too.

4. 너무 (   ).   It is so cold.

5. (   ) 가는 카페에 들어갔어요.   I went into a café that I go to often.

6. (   )에서 기다릴 거예요.   I will wait inside.

7. 친구한테 (   ).   I called my friend.

8. 친구도 이 카페를 (   ).   My friend also knows this café.

9. (   )이랑 목도리를 살 거예요.   I am going to buy gloves and a scarf.

10. 장갑이랑 (   )를 살 거예요.   I am going to buy gloves and a scarf.

DAY 29

Check off the words
you already know.

○ 잘하다 ○

○ 맛 ○

○ 못하다 ○

○ 사랑 ○

○ 양파 ○

○ 감자 ○

○ 칼 ○

○ 썰다 ○

○ 손가락 ○

○ 배달 ○

After you study these words, come back and
check off the ones you have memorized.

Day 29

LET'S WARM UP!

Imagine the situation in the story below to help you
remember the ten Korean words in context.

잘하다
My mom cooks <u>well</u>.

맛   못하다
All the food my mom makes is <u>delicious</u>. I <u>can't</u> cook.

사랑
But today, for my <u>dear</u> mom, I am going to cook.

양파
I peeled an <u>onion</u>.

썰다 감자   칼
I <u>chopped</u> a <u>potato</u> with a <u>knife</u>.

손가락   배달
I hurt my <u>finger</u>. In the end, I ordered <u>delivery</u> food.

LET'S KEEP THE BALL ROLLING!

Word	Meaning	Related Words	Meaning
잘하다 *ja-ra-da*	to do well, to be good at something, to be skillful	요리를 잘하다 *yo-ri-reul ja-ra-da*	to cook well
		공부를 잘하다 *gong-bu-reul ja-ra-da*	to be good in school
		잘하는 운동 *ja-ra-neun un-dong*	a sport that one is good at
		못하다 *mo-ta-da*	to be bad at
맛 *mat*	taste	무슨 맛 *mu-seun mat*	what flavor
		맛있다 *ma-sit-tta*	to be delicious
		맛없다 *ma-deop-tta*	to not be tasty
		맛보다 *mat-ppo-da*	to taste
못하다 *mo-ta-da*	to not do well, to be bad at something, to be unskillful	노래를 못하다 *no-rae-reul mo-ta-da*	to sing terribly, to not sing well
		운전을 못하다 *un-jeo-neul mo-ta-da*	to be terrible at driving
		못하는 것 *mo-ta-neun geot*	something that one is not good at
		잘하다 *ja-ra-da*	to do well

사랑 *sa-rang*	love	짝사랑 *jjak-ssa-rang*	unrequited love, crush
		사랑하다 *sa-rang-ha-da*	to love
		사랑하는 엄마 *sa-rang-ha-neun eom-ma*	one's dear mom
		사랑스럽다 *sa-rang-seu-reop-tta*	to be lovely
양파 *yang-pa*	onion	양파를 까다 *yang-pa-reul kka-da*	to peel an onion
		양파 껍질 *yang-pa kkeop-jjil*	skin of an onion
		양파 냄새 *yang-pa naem-sae*	smell of an onion
감자 *gam-ja*	potato	감자가 익다 *gam-ja-ga ik-tta*	the potato is cooked
		찐 감자 *jjin gam-ja*	steamed potato
		고구마 *go-gu-ma*	sweet potato
칼 *kal*	knife	칼로 자르다 *kal-lo ja-reu-da*	to cut with a knife
		칼에 베이다 *ka-re be-i-da*	to get a cut from a knife
		칼 한 자루 *kal han ja-ru*	one knife
		부엌칼 *bu-eok-kal*	kitchen knife

썰다 *sseol-da*	to chop, to cut	양파를 썰다 *yang-pa-reul sseol-da*	to chop an onion
		칼로 썰다 *kal-lo sseol-da*	to chop with a knife
		자르다 *ja-reu-da*	to cut
손가락 *son-kka-rak*	finger	손가락이 길다 *son-kka-ra-gi gil-da*	one's finger is long
		손가락이 두껍다 *son-kka-ra-gi du-kkeop-tta*	one's finger is thick
		엄지손가락 *eom-ji-son-kka-rak*	thumb
		새끼손가락 *sae-kki-son-kka-rak*	pinky finger
배달 *bae-dal*	delivery	배달 음식 *bae-dal eum-sik*	delivery food
		우유 배달 *u-yu bae-dal*	milk delivery
		신문 배달 *sin-mun bae-dal*	newspaper delivery
		배달하다 *bae-da-ra-da*	to deliver

Read the story again, but this time in Korean!

엄마는 요리를 **잘**해요.

엄마가 만든 음식은 다 **맛**있어요. 저는 요리를 **못**해요.

하지만 오늘은 **사랑**하는 엄마를 위해서 요리를 할 거예요.

양파를 깎았어요.

감자를 칼로 **썰었어요.**

손가락을 다쳤어요. 결국 **배달** 음식을 시켰어요.

Translation

My mom cooks well. All the food my mom makes is delicious.
I can't cook. But today, for my dear mom, I am going to cook.
I peeled an onion. I chopped a potato with a knife. I hurt my finger.
In the end, I ordered delivery food.

Match each Korean word to its English translation.

못하다 ·   · potato

양파 ·   · knife

칼 ·   · to do well, to be skillful

썰다 ·   · taste

맛 ·   · love

배달 ·   · onion

잘하다 ·   · to not do well, to be unskillful

손가락 ·   · delivery

감자 ·   · finger

사랑 ·   · to chop, to cut

Crossword Puzzle

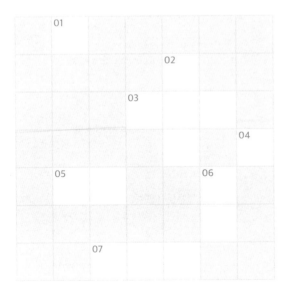

01 knife
02 to do well
03 to not do well
04 taste
05 potato
06 delivery
07 finger

Fill in the blanks using one of the words that you learned in Day 29.
(Please refer to page 017 to review how to conjugate verbs/adjectives.)

1. 엄마는 요리를 (   ).　　　　My mom cooks well.

2. 엄마가 만든 음식은 다 (   )있어요.　　All the food my mom makes is delicious.

3. 저는 요리를 (   ).　　　　I can't cook.

4. 하지만 오늘은 (   )하는 엄마를　　But today, for my dear mom, I am going to
   위해서 요리를 할 거예요.　　　　　　　　　cook.

5. (   )를 깠어요.　　　　I peeled an onion.

6. (   )를 칼로 썰었어요.　　I chopped a potato with a knife.

7. 감자를 (   )로 썰었어요.　　I chopped a potato with a knife.

8. 감자를 칼로 (   ).　　　I chopped a potato with a knife.

9. (   )을 다쳤어요.　　　I hurt my finger.

10. 결국 (   ) 음식을 시켰어요.　　In the end, I ordered delivery food.

DAY 30

Check off the words you already know.

- ○ 손님 ○
- ○ 빨래 ○
- ○ 설거지 ○
- ○ 이불 ○
- ○ 베개 ○
- ○ 쓰레기 ○
- ○ 버리다 ○
- ○ 시장 ○
- ○ 과자 ○
- ○ 준비하다 ○

After you study these words, come back and check off the ones you have memorized.

LET'S WARM UP!

Imagine the situation in the story below to help you
remember the ten Korean words in context.

손님

Tonight, guests will come to my house.

빨래   설거지

I washed my clothes and did the dishes.

이불   베개

I tidied up the blankets and pillows.

버리다   쓰레기

I threw away the trash.

시장

I went to the market and did some grocery shopping.

과자

I bought some snacks for the kids.

준비하다

Now I am going to prepare food.

LET'S KEEP THE BALL ROLLING!

Word	Meaning	Related Words	Meaning
손님 *son-nim*	guest	손님이 오다 *son-ni-mi o-da*	a guest comes
		손님이 많다 *son-ni-mi man-ta*	there are many guests
		손님들 *son-nim-deul*	guests
빨래 *ppal-lae*	laundry	빨래를 널다 *ppal-lae-reul neol-da*	to hang up the laundry
		빨래를 개다 *ppal-lae-reul gae-da*	to fold the laundry
		빨래하다 *ppal-lae-ha-da*	to wash clothes
		세탁기 *se-tak-kki*	washing machine
설거지 *seol-geo-ji*	doing the dishes	설거지하다 *seol-geo-ji-ha-da*	to do the dishes
		부엌 *bu-eok*	kitchen
		싱크대 *sing-keu-dae*	sink
		그릇 *geu-reut*	dish, plate, bowl

이불 *i-bul*	blanket	이불을 개다 *i-bu-reul gae-da*	to fold a blanket
		이불을 덮다 *i-bu-reul deop-tta*	to cover oneself with a blanket
		이불 빨래 *i-bul ppal-lae*	washing blankets
베개 *be-gae*	pillow	베개를 베다 *be-gae-reul be-da*	to rest one's head on the pillow
		베개가 높다 *be-gae-ga nop-tta*	the pillow is big
		무릎베개 *mu-reup-ppe-gae*	resting one's head on someone's lap
쓰레기 *sseu-re-gi*	trash	쓰레기를 버리다 *sseu-re-gi-reul beo-ri-da*	to throw away trash
		쓰레기를 치우다 *sseu-re-gi-reul chi-u-da*	to get rid of trash
		쓰레기봉투 *sseu-re-gi-bong-tu*	trash bag
		쓰레기통 *sseu-re-gi-tong*	trash bin
버리다 *beo-ri-da*	to throw away	휴지를 버리다 *hyu-ji-reul beo-ri-da*	to throw away trash
		쓰레기통에 버리다 *sseu-re-gi-tong-e beo-ri-da*	to throw away in a trash bin
		아무 데나 버리다 *a-mu de-na beo-ri-da*	to litter
		버린 물건 *beo-rin mul-geon*	an object that has been thrown away

시장
si-jang

market

시장에 가다
si-jang-e ga-da

to go to the market

시장에서 사다
si-jang-e-seo sa-da

to buy at the market

전통 시장
jeon-tong si-jang

traditional market

장을 보다
jang-eul bo-da

to do grocery shopping

과자
gwa-ja

snack

과자 한 봉지
gwa-ja han bong-ji

a bag of snacks

맛있는 과자
ma-sin-neun gwa-ja

delicious snacks

준비하다
jun-bi-ha-da

to prepare

선물을 준비하다
seon-mu-reul jun-bi-ha-da

to prepare a present

식사를 준비하다
sik-ssa-reul jun-bi-ha-da

to prepare a meal

준비
jun-bi

preparation

LET'S REVIEW!

Read the story again, but this time in Korean!

오늘 밤 저희 집에 **손님**들이 올 거예요.

빨래도 하고 **설거지**도 했어요.

이불과 **베개**를 정리했어요.

쓰레기를 버렸어요.

시장에 가서 장을 봤어요. 아이들을 위해 **과자**도 샀어요.

이제 음식을 **준비할 거예요.**

Translation

Tonight, guests will come to my house. I washed my clothes and did the dishes. I tidied up the blankets and pillows. I threw away the trash. I went to the market and did some grocery shopping. I bought some snacks for the kids. Now I am going to prepare food.

Match each Korean word to its English translation.

베개 ·   · laundry

쓰레기 ·   · doing the dishes

준비하다 ·   · blanket

손님 ·   · pillow

빨래 ·   · guest

버리다 ·   · trash

과자 ·   · market

설거지 ·   · snack

이불 ·   · to prepare

시장 ·   · to throw away

Crossword Puzzle

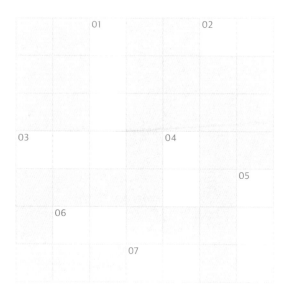

01 to prepare
02 laundry
03 to throw away
04 pillow
05 doing the dishes
06 market
07 snack

Fill in the blanks using one of the words that you learned in Day 30.
(Please refer to page 017 to review how to conjugate verbs/adjectives.)

1. 오늘 밤 저희 집에 (   )들이
    올 거예요.   Tonight, guests will come to my house.

2. (   )도 하고 설거지도 했어요.   I washed my clothes and did the dishes.

3. 빨래도 하고 (   )도 했어요.   I washed my clothes and did the dishes.

4. (   )과 베개를 정리했어요.   I tidied up the blankets and pillows.

5. 이불과 (   )를 정리했어요.   I tidied up the blankets and pillows.

6. (   )를 버렸어요.   I threw away the trash.

7. 쓰레기를 (   ).   I threw away the trash.

8. (   )에 가서 장을 봤어요.   I went to the market and did some grocery
                                                    shopping.

9. 아이들을 위해 (   )도 샀어요.   I bought some snacks for the kids.

10. 이제 음식을 (   ).   Now I am going to prepare food.

01 What is the Korean word for the item in the picture?

a. 캐메라

b. 캐머러

c. 캠러

d. 카메라

02 Besides **"eye"**, what does 눈 mean?

a. carrot   b. mushroom   c. snow   d. rain

03 How can you say in Korean, the item that your head rests upon when you sleep?

a. 봄   b. 베개   c. 그림   d. 상자

04 Which item is 과일?

a. 버섯   b. 당근   c. 양파   d. 딸기

05 What color is 빨간색?

    a. black   b. yellow   c. green   d. red

06 What is the antonym of 잘하다?

    a. 못하다   b. 멋있다   c. 비싸다   d. 배우다

07 Choose the noun-verb pair that is matched incorrectly.

    a. 쓰레기 - 버리다   b. 감자 - 썰다

    c. 사진 - 찍다   d. 빨래 - 좁다

08 Choose the word that is **NOT** a body part.

    a. 다리   b. 창문   c. 손가락   d. 얼굴

09 Which of the following can you see when you look at the 하늘?

    a. 장갑   b. 과일   c. 구름   d. 거실

10 What is the area in the house where you cook?

    a. 부엌   b. 산책   c. 층   d. 손님

11 Choose the word pair that is matched incorrectly.

   a. 자주 - often   b. 혼자 - alone
   c. 누구 - where   d. 다 - all

12 What do you call the item you wrap around your neck to feel warm in the winter?

   a. 시계   b. 이사   c. 목도리   d. 벽

13 Choose the term that has a kinship meaning.

   a. 처음   b. 언니   c. 연예인   d. 시장

14 Choose the term that is the opposite of 넣다.

   a. 빼다   b. 들다   c. 오다   d. 쓰다

15 Which of the following does **NOT** become a verb if you attach –하다?

   a. 여행   b. 사랑   c. 꽃   d. 연락

16 Which of the following is **NOT** related to 날씨?

   a. 바람   b. 춥다   c. 따뜻하다   d. 전화하다

17 With which item can you chop vegetables?

    a. 꿈   b. 칼   c. 맛   d. 설거지

18 Which of the following refers to an action?

    a. 앉다   b. 무겁다   c. 귀엽다   d. 좋아하다

19 How do you say **"to be tall"** in Korean?

    a. 키가 길다   b. 키가 크다   c. 키가 웃다   d. 키가 씻다

20 What is the Korean word for the item in the picture?

    a. 비행기

    b. 이불

    c. 엘리베이터

    d. 과자

Answers : d c b d d / a d b c a / c c b a c / d b a b a

QUIZ

DAY 21-30

DAY 31

Check off the words you already know.

- ○ 인터넷 ○
- ○ 치마 ○
- ○ 주문하다 ○
- ○ 실패 ○
- ○ 작다 ○
- ○ 쇼핑 ○
- ○ 어렵다 ○
- ○ 성공 ○
- ○ 다음 ○
- ○ 모자 ○

After you study these words, come back and check off the ones you have memorized.

Day 31

LET'S WARM UP!

Imagine the situation in the story below to help you
remember the ten Korean words in context.

주문하다 치마   인터넷
I ordered a   skirt on the Internet.

실패
This time was also a failure.

작다
The skirt is too small.

쇼핑   어렵다
Shopping online is too difficult.

성공
When will I succeed?

다음   모자
Next time, I will order a hat.

LET'S KEEP THE BALL ROLLING!

Word	Meaning	Related Words	Meaning
인터넷 *in-teo-net*	the Internet	인터넷 쇼핑 *in-teo-net syo-ping*	Internet shopping, online shopping
		인터넷에 연결하다 *in-teo-ne-se yeon-gyeo-ra-da*	to connect to the Internet
		인터넷으로 *in-teo-ne-seu-ro*	via the Internet
치마 *chi-ma*	skirt	치마를 입다 *chi-ma-reul ip-tta*	to put on a skirt, to wear a skirt
		치마를 벗다 *chi-ma-reul beot-tta*	to take off a skirt
		긴 치마 *gin chi-ma*	long skirt
		짧은 치마 *jjal-beun chi-ma*	short skirt
주문하다 *ju-mu-na-da*	to order	옷을 주문하다 *o-seul ju-mu-na-da*	to order clothes
		음식을 주문하다 *eum-si-geul ju-mu-na-da*	to order food
		주문한 책 *ju-mu-nan chaek*	a book that was ordered

실패	failure	실패하다	to fail
sil-pae		*sil-pae-ha-da*	
		실패 원인	reason for failure, cause for failure
		sil-pae wo-nin	
		성공	success
		seong-gong	
작다	to be small	치마가 작다	the skirt is small
jak-tta		*chi-ma-ga jak-tta*	
		키가 작다	to be short (height)
		ki-ga jak-tta	
		작은 집	small house
		ja-geun jip	
쇼핑	shopping	쇼핑을 좋아하다	to like shopping
syo-ping		*syo-ping-eul jo-a-ha-da*	
		쇼핑하다	to shop
		syo-ping-ha-da	
		쇼핑몰	shopping mall
		syo-ping-mol	
		백화점	department store
		bae-kwa-jeom	
어렵다	to be difficult, to be hard	문제가 어렵다	the question is difficult
eo-ryeop-tta		*mun-je-ga eo-ryeop-tta*	
		어려운 시험	difficult test
		eo-ryeo-un si-heom	
		어려운 일	difficult thing to do, difficult task, difficult work
		eo-ryeo-un il	

| 성공
seong-gong | success | 성공하다
seong-gong-ha-da | to succeed |
| | | 실패
sil-pae | fail, failure |

다음 da-eum	next	다음 날 da-eum nal	next day
		다음 역 da-eum yeok	next stop, next station
		다음 페이지 da-eum pe-i-ji	next page
		다음에 da-eu-me	next time

모자 mo-ja	hat, cap	모자를 쓰다 mo-ja-reul sseu-da	to put on a hat, to wear a hat
		모자를 벗다 mo-ja-reul beot-tta	to take off a hat
		야구 모자 ya-gu mo-ja	baseball cap

Read the story again, but this time in Korean!

인터넷으로 치마를 주문했어요.

이번에도 실패예요.

치마가 너무 작아요.

인터넷 쇼핑은 너무 어려워요.

언제 성공할까요?

다음에는 모자를 주문할 거예요.

Translation

I ordered a skirt on the Internet. This time was also a failure. The skirt is too small. Shopping online is too difficult. When will I succeed? Next time, I will order a hat.

Match each Korean word to its English translation.

실패 · · to order

쇼핑 · · the Internet

어렵다 · · to be small

모자 · · to be difficult, to be hard

치마 · · success

인터넷 · · shopping

주문하다 · · next

다음 · · hat, cap

성공 · · skirt

작다 · · failure

Crossword Puzzle

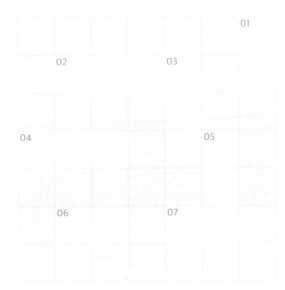

01 failure
02 to order
03 next
04 the Internet
05 to be difficult, to be hard
06 hat, cap
07 to be small

Fill in the blanks using one of the words that you learned in Day 31.
(Please refer to page 017 to review how to conjugate verbs/adjectives.)

1.   (   )으로 치마를 주문했어요.   I ordered a skirt on the Internet.

2.   인터넷으로 (   )를 주문했어요.   I ordered a skirt on the Internet.

3.   인터넷으로 치마를 (   ).   I ordered a skirt on the Internet.

4.   이번에도 (   )예요.   This time was also a failure.

5.   치마가 너무 (   ).   The skirt is too small.

6.   인터넷 (   )은 너무 어려워요.   Shopping online is too difficult.

7.   인터넷 쇼핑은 너무 (   ).   Shopping online is too difficult.

8.   언제 (   )할까요?   When will I succeed?

9.   (   )에는 모자를 주문할 거예요.   Next time, I will order a hat.

10. 다음에는 (   )를 주문할 거예요.   Next time, I will order a hat.

DAY 32

Check off the words
you already know. ↗

○ 약속 ○

○ 늦다 ○

○ 택시 ○

○ 오토바이 ○

○ 사고 ○

○ 경찰 ○

○ 문자 ○

○ 보내다 ○

○ 허리 ○

○ 조금 ○

↖
After you study these words, come back and
check off the ones you have memorized.

LET'S WARM UP!

Imagine the situation in the story below to help you
remember the ten Korean words in context.

약속   늦다

I had <u>plans</u> to meet a friend, but I was <u>late</u>.

택시

I took a <u>taxi</u>.

오토바이

But a <u>motorcycle</u> suddenly cut us off.

사고

So, we got into an <u>accident</u>.

경찰

The <u>police</u> came.

보내다 문자

I <u>sent</u> a   <u>text message</u> to my friend.

허리   조금

I think I hurt my <u>lower back</u> <u>a little</u>.

LET'S KEEP THE BALL ROLLING!

Word	Meaning	Related Words	Meaning
약속 *yak-ssok*	promise, plan, appointment	약속이 있다 *yak-sso-gi it-tta*	to have an appointment
		약속 시간 *yak-ssok si-gan*	appointment time
		약속 장소 *yak-ssok jang-so*	appointment place
		약속하다 *yak-sso-ka-da*	to promise
늦다 *neut-tta*	to be late	많이 늦다 *ma-ni neut-tta*	to be very late
		늦은 점심 *neu-jeun jeom-sim*	late lunch
		늦게 오다 *neut-kke o-da*	to come late
		지각 *ji-gak*	being late
택시 *taek-ssi*	taxi, cab	택시를 타다 *taek-ssi-reul ta-da*	to ride in a taxi
		택시를 잡다 *taek-ssi-reul jap-tta*	to catch a taxi
		택시 한 대 *taek-ssi han dae*	one taxi
		택시 기사 *taek-ssi gi-sa*	taxi driver

오토바이
o-to-ba-i

motorcycle

오토바이를 타다
o-to-ba-i-reul ta-da

to ride a motorcycle

오토바이 두 대
o-to-ba-i du dae

two motorcycles

헬멧
hel-met

helmet

사고
sa-go

accident

큰 사고
keun sa-go

big accident

자동차 사고
ja-dong-cha sa-go

car accident

사고가 나다
sa-go-ga na-da

to have an accident

사고를 당하다
sa-go-reul dang-ha-da

to get into an accident

경찰
gyeong-chal

police

경찰관
gyeong-chal-gwan

police officer

경찰이 오다
gyeong-cha-ri o-da

the police come

경찰에 신고하다
gyeong-cha-re sin-go-ha-da

to report to the police

경찰차
gyeong-chal-cha

police car

문자	text message	문자 메시지	text message
mun-jja		*mun-jja me-ssi-ji*	
		문자를 보내다	to send a text message
		mun-jja-reul bo-nae-da	
		문자를 받다	to receive a text message
		mun-jja-reul bat-tta	
		답장하다	to reply
		dap-jjang-ha-da	

보내다	to send, to spend	편지를 보내다	to send a letter
bo-nae-da		*pyeon-ji-reul bo-nae-da*	
		답장을 보내다	to send a reply
		dap-jjang-eul bo-nae-da	
		시간을 보내다	to spend time
		si-ga-neul bo-nae-da	

허리	lower back, waist, the small of one's back	허리를 다치다	to hurt one's lower back
heo-ri		*heo-ri-reul da-chi-da*	
		허리가 아프다	one's lower back hurts
		heo-ri-ga a-peu-da	
		날씬한 허리	slim waist
		nal-ssi-nan heo-ri	

조금	a little, a bit	조금 늦다	to be a little late
jo-geum		*jo-geum neut-tta*	
		조금씩	little by little
		jo-geum-ssik	
		조금밖에 없다	to only have a little
		jo-geum-ba-kke eop-tta	

LET'S REVIEW!

Read the story again, but this time in Korean!

친구와 **약속**이 있는데 **늦었어요.**

택시를 탔어요.

그런데 **오토바이**가 갑자기 끼어들었어요.

그래서 **사고**가 났어요. **경찰**이 왔어요.

친구한테 **문자**를 보냈어요.

허리를 **조금** 다친 것 같아요.

Translation

I had plans to meet a friend, but I was late. I took a taxi.
But a motorcycle suddenly cut us off. So, we got into an accident.
The police came. I sent a text message to my friend.
I think I hurt my lower back a little.

Match each Korean word to its English translation.

허리 · · police

문자 · · to be late

늦다 · · accident

경찰 · · text message

보내다 · · promise, plan, appointment

약속 · · motorcycle

조금 · · lower back, waist

택시 · · to send, to spend

사고 · · taxi

오토바이 · · a little, a bit

Crossword Puzzle

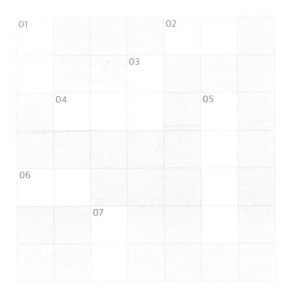

01 accident
02 text message
03 to be late
04 to send, to spend
05 motorcycle
06 a little, a bit
07 promise, plan

Fill in the blanks using one of the words that you learned in Day 32.
(Please refer to page 017 to review how to conjugate verbs/adjectives.)

1. 친구와 (）이 있는데 늦었어요.   I had plans to meet a friend, but I was late.

2. 친구와 약속이 있는데 (   ).   I had plans to meet a friend, but I was late.

3. (）를 탔어요.   I took a taxi.

4. 그런데 (）가 갑자기 끼어들었어요.   But a motorcycle suddenly cut us off.

5. 그래서 (）가 났어요.   So, we got into an accident.

6. (）이 왔어요.   The police came.

7. 친구한테 (）를 보냈어요.   I sent a text message to my friend.

8. 친구한테 문자를 (   ).   I sent a text message to my friend.

9. (）를 조금 다친 것 같아요.   I think I hurt my lower back a little.

10. 허리를 (   ) 다친 것 같아요.   I think I hurt my lower back a little.

DAY 33

Check off the words you already know.

○ 가수 ○

○ 인기 ○

○ 나라 ○

○ 한국어 ○

○ 필요하다 ○

○ 단어 ○

○ 귀 ○

○ 지도 ○

○ 주소 ○

○ 궁금하다 ○

After you study these words, come back and check off the ones you have memorized.

LET'S WARM UP!

Imagine the situation in the story below to help you
remember the ten Korean words in context.

가수 인기
These days, Korean singers are popular.

나라
They are more popular than singers from other countries.

한국어 필요하다
Studying Korean is   necessary in order to listen to Korean songs.

귀   단어
I pay close attention and listen to the pronunciation of the words.

지도
I look up Korea on a map.

궁금하다 주소
I am curious to know the address of the company of the singer that I like.

LET'S KEEP THE BALL ROLLING!

Word	Meaning	Related Words	Meaning
가수 *ga-su*	singer	**인기 있는 가수** *in-kki in-neun ga-su*	popular singer
		가수가 되다 *ga-su-ga doe-da*	to become a singer
		가수들 *ga-su-deul*	singers
		노래 *no-rae*	song
인기 *in-kki*	popularity	**인기가 많다** *in-kki-ga man-ta*	to be popular
		인기가 있다 *in-kki-ga it-tta*	to be popular
		인기 가요 *in-kki ga-yo*	popular pop song
		인기 상품 *in-kki sang-pum*	popular product
나라 *na-ra*	country, nation	**우리나라** *u-ri-na-ra*	our country, my country
		다른 나라 *da-reun na-ra*	other country, foreign country
		어느 나라 *eo-neu na-ra*	which country

한국어	Korean (language)	한국어 공부	Korean studies
han-gu-geo		han-gu-geo gong-bu	
		한국어 선생님	Korean teacher
		han-gu-geo seon-saeng-nim	
		한국어 시험	Korean test
		han-gu-geo si-heom	

필요하다	to need, to be necessary	나에게 필요하다	to be necessary to me
pi-ryo-ha-da		na-e-ge pi-ryo-ha-da	
		돈이 필요하다	to need money
		do-ni pi-ryo-ha-da	
		필요한 것	necessary things
		pi-ryo-han geot	

단어	word	영어 단어	English word
da-neo		yeong-eo da-neo	
		단어를 외우다	to memorize words
		da-neo-reul oe-u-da	
		단어를 찾다	to look up a word
		da-neo-reul chat-tta	
		사전	dictionary
		sa-jeon	

귀	ear	귀를 막다	to block one's ears
gwi		gwi-reul mak-tta	
		귀 기울이다	to pay attention to
		gwi gi-u-ri-da	
		귀가 잘 안 들리다	can't hear well
		gwi-ga jal an deul-li-da	
		귀가 아프다	one's ear hurts
		gwi-ga a-peu-da	

지도	map	서울 지도	Seoul map
ji-do		*seo-ul ji-do*	
		세계 지도	world map
		se-gye ji-do	
		지도를 보다	to see on a map
		ji-do-reul bo-da	
		지도에서 찾다	to look up on a map
		ji-do-e-seo chat-tta	

주소	address	집 주소	home address
ju-so		*jip ju-so*	
		주소가 잘못되다	the address is wrong
		ju-so-ga jal-mot-ttoe-da	
		틀린 주소	wrong address
		teul-lin ju-so	
		주소를 쓰다	to write down an address
		ju-so-reul sseu-da	

궁금하다	to be curious	이유가 궁금하다	to be curious about the reason
gung-geu-ma-da		*i-yu-ga gung-geu-ma-da*	
		궁금한 것	something that one is curious about
		gung-geu-man geot	
		궁금해하다	to feel curious
		gung-geu-mae-ha-da	
		물어보다	to ask
		mu-reo-bo-da	

LET'S REVIEW!

요즘 한국 **가수**들이 **인기**가 많아요.

다른 **나라** 가수들보다 인기가 많아요.

한국 노래를 듣기 위해서 **한국어** 공부가 **필요해요.**

단어 발음을 **귀** 기울여 들어요.

지도에서 한국을 찾아 봐요.

제가 좋아하는 가수 회사 **주소**가 **궁금해요.**

Translation

These days, Korean singers are popular. They are more popular than singers from other countries. Studying Korean is necessary in order to listen to Korean songs. I pay close attention and listen to the pronunciation of the words. I look up Korea on a map. I am curious to know the address of the company of the singer that I like.

Match each Korean word to its English translation.

나라   ·

가수   ·

지도   ·

궁금하다   ·

단어   ·

인기   ·

필요하다   ·

귀   ·

주소   ·

한국어   ·

· popularity

· map

· singer

· to need, to be necessary

· ear

· Korean (language)

· address

· to be curious

· country, nation

· word

Crossword Puzzle

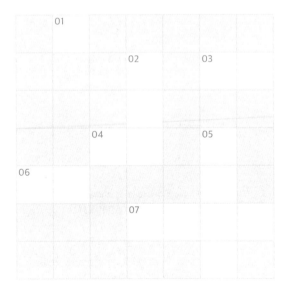

01   ear
02   Korean (language)
03   country, nation
04   word
05   to need, to be necessary
06   popularity
07   to be curious

Fill in the blanks using one of the words that you learned in Day 33.
(Please refer to page 017 to review how to conjugate verbs/adjectives.)

1. 요즘 한국 (   )들이 인기가 많아요.   These days, Korean singers are popular.

2. 요즘 한국 가수들이 (   )가 많아요.   These days, Korean singers are popular.

3. 다른 (   ) 가수들보다 인기가 많아요.   They are more popular than singers from
                                                            other countries.

4. 한국 노래를 듣기 위해서 (   ) 공부가   Studying Korean is necessary in order to
   필요해요.   listen to Korean songs.

5. 한국 노래를 듣기 위해서   Studying Korean is necessary in order to
   한국어 공부가 (   ).   listen to Korean songs.

6. (   ) 발음을 귀 기울여 들어요.   I pay close attention and listen to the
                                                         pronunciation of the words.

7. 단어 발음을 (   ) 기울여 들어요.   I pay close attention and listen to the
                                                           pronunciation of the words.

8. (   )에서 한국을 찾아 봐요.   I look up Korea on a map.

9. 제가 좋아하는 가수 회사 (   )가   I am curious to know the address of the
   궁금해요.   company of the singer that I like.

10. 제가 좋아하는 가수 회사   I am curious to know the address of the
    주소가 (   ).   company of the singer that I like.

DAY 34

Check off the words you already know.

○ 문

○ 열다

○ 감기

○ 열

○ 코

○ 나오다

○ 약국

○ 약

○ 차

○ 건강

After you study these words, come back and check off the ones you have memorized.

Day 34

Imagine the situation in the story below to help you
remember the ten Korean words in context.

열다 문

Yesterday I slept with the <u>door</u> <u>open</u>.

감기   열

So, I caught a <u>cold</u>. I had a <u>fever</u>.

나오다 코

I had a <u>runny</u> <u>nose</u>.

약국   약

I went to the <u>pharmacy</u> and bought <u>medicine</u>.

차

I will drink hot <u>tea</u> and rest at home.

건강

I think <u>health</u> is really important.

LET'S KEEP THE BALL ROLLING!

Word	Meaning	Related Words	Meaning
문 *mun*	door	문을 열다 *mu-neul yeol-da*	to open the door
		문을 닫다 *mu-neul dat-tta*	to close the door
		문을 잠그다 *mu-neul jam-geu-da*	to lock the door
열다 *yeol-da*	to open	뚜껑을 열다 *ttu-kkeong-eul yeol-da*	to open the lid, to lift the cover
		창문을 열다 *chang-mu-neul yeol-da*	to open the window
		열리다 *yeol-li-da*	to be opened, to get opened
		닫다 *dat-tta*	to close
감기 *gam-gi*	cold	감기에 걸리다 *gam-gi-e geol-li-da*	to catch a cold
		감기가 낫다 *gam-gi-ga nat-tta*	to recover from a cold
		감기약 *gam-gi-yak*	cold medicine

열 *yeol*	fever	**열이 나다** *yeo-ri na-da*	to have a fever
		열이 있다 *yeo-ri it-tta*	to have a fever
		열이 내려가다 *yeo-ri nae-ryeo-ga-da*	a fever breaks, a fever subsides
코 *ko*	nose	**콧물** *kon-mul*	nasal discharge, snot
		코가 막히다 *ko-ga ma-ki-da*	one's nose is stuffy
		코가 높다 *ko-ga nop-tta*	to have a high nose, to have high standards
		코가 낮다 *ko-ga nat-tta*	to have a low nose
나오다 *na-o-da*	to come out	**밖에 나오다** *ba-kke na-o-da*	to come outside
		물이 나오다 *mu-ri na-o-da*	the water comes out, the water runs (from the tap)
약국 *yak-kkuk*	pharmacy	**약국에 가다** *yak-kku-ge ga-da*	to go to the pharmacy
		약사 *yak-ssa*	pharmacist
		병원 *byeong-won*	hospital

약 *yak*	medicine	약을 먹다 *ya-geul meok-tta*	to take medicine
		약이 쓰다 *ya-gi sseu-da*	the medicine is bitter
		약을 바르다 *ya-geul ba-reu-da*	to apply medicine, to apply ointment
차 *cha*	tea	차를 마시다 *cha-reul ma-si-da*	to drink tea
		녹차 *nok-cha*	green tea
		홍차 *hong-cha*	black tea
건강 *geon-gang*	health	건강하다 *geon-gang-ha-da*	to be healthy
		건강에 좋다 *geong-gang-e jo-ta*	to be good for health
		건강이 안 좋다 *geon-gang-i an jo-ta*	to not be healthy

LET'S REVIEW!

Read the story again, but this time in Korean!

어제 **문**을 **열고** 잤어요.

그래서 **감기**에 걸렸어요. **열**이 났어요.

코에서 콧물이 **나왔어요.**

약국에 가서 **약**을 샀어요.

따뜻한 **차**를 마시고 집에서 푹 쉴 거예요.

건강은 정말 중요한 것 같아요.

Translation

Yesterday I slept with the door open. So, I caught a cold. I had a fever. I had a runny nose. I went to the pharmacy and bought medicine. I will drink hot tea and rest at home. I think health is really important.

Match each Korean word to its English translation.

Korean			English
열	·	·	to come out
열다	·	·	pharmacy
약국	·	·	nose
건강	·	·	to open
문	·	·	cold
차	·	·	door
약	·	·	fever
감기	·	·	medicine
나오다	·	·	tea
코	·	·	health

Crossword Puzzle

01 tea
02 door
03 to open
04 health
05 to come out
06 pharmacy
07 cold

Fill in the blanks using one of the words that you learned in Day 34.
(Please refer to page 017 to review how to conjugate verbs/adjectives.)

1.   어제 (   )을 열고 잤어요.   Yesterday I slept with the door open.

2.   어제 문을 (   ) 잤어요.   Yesterday I slept with the door open.

3.   그래서 (   )에 걸렸어요.   So, I caught a cold.

4.   (   )이 났어요.   I had a fever.

5.   (   )에서 콧물이 나왔어요.   I had a runny nose.

6.   코에서 콧물이 (   ).   I had a runny nose.

7.   (   )에 가서 약을 샀어요.   I went to the pharmacy and bought
                                                      medicine.

8.   약국에 가서 (   )을 샀어요.   I went to the pharmacy and bought
                                                      medicine.

9.   따뜻한 (   )를 마시고 집에서   I will drink hot tea and rest at home.
     푹 쉴 거예요.

10. (   )은 정말 중요한 것 같아요.   I think health is really important.

DAY 35

Check off the words you already know.

○ 사과 ○

○ 바나나 ○

○ 일하다 ○

○ 오이 ○

○ 토마토 ○

○ 배 ○

○ 마음 ○

○ 약하다 ○

○ 몸무게 ○

○ 절대 ○

After you study these words, come back and check off the ones you have memorized.

Day 35

LET'S WARM UP!

Imagine the situation in the story below to help you
remember the ten Korean words in context.

I am on a diet these days.

사과 바나나

This morning, I ate an <u>apple</u>,   <u>banana</u> and some potatoes.

일하다   오이   토마토

I <u>worked</u> hard. At lunch, I ate a <u>cucumber</u> and a <u>tomato</u>.

배   약하다 마음

In the evening, I became so <u>hungry</u> and <u>weak-</u>   <u>hearted</u>.

So, I ate a lot for dinner.

몸무게

I weighed myself. I gained <u>weight</u>.

절대

I will <u>never</u> be weak-hearted again.

LET'S KEEP THE BALL ROLLING!

Word	Meaning	Related Words	Meaning
사과 *sa-gwa*	apple	**사과를 깎다** *sa-gwa-reul kkak-tta*	to peel an apple
		빨간 사과 *ppal-gan sa-gwa*	red apple
		사과 나무 *sa-gwa na-mu*	apple tree
		과일 *gwa-il*	fruit
바나나 *ba-na-na*	banana	**바나나 한 송이** *ba-na-na han song-i*	one bunch of bananas
		바나나를 먹다 *ba-na-na-reul meok-tta*	to eat a banana
일하다 *i-ra-da*	to work	**열심히 일하다** *yeol-ssi-mi i-ra-da*	to work hard
		일하는 날 *i-ra-neun nal*	working day
		일 *il*	work
		쉬다 *swi-da*	to rest

오이 *o-i*	cucumber	오이 한 개 *o-i han gae*	one cucumber
		오이를 먹다 *o-i-reul meok-tta*	to eat a cucumber
		오이를 썰다 *o-i-reul sseol-da*	to chop a cucumber
토마토 *to-ma-to*	tomato	방울토마토 *bang-ul-to-ma-to*	cherry tomato
		토마토 소스 *to-ma-to sso-sseu*	tomato sauce
		토마토 스파게티 *to-ma-to seu-pa-ge-ti*	tomato spaghetti
배 *bae*	belly, stomach	배가 고프다 *bae-ga go-peu-da*	to be hungry
		배가 아프다 *bae-ga a-peu-da*	to have a stomachache
		배가 나오다 *bae-ga na-o-da*	to have a fat belly
		배꼽 *bae-kkop*	belly button
마음 *ma-eum*	mind, heart	마음에 들다 *ma-eu-me deul-da*	to like
		마음대로 *ma-eum-dae-ro*	as one pleases, as one wants
		마음껏 *ma-eum-kkeot*	as much as one wants
		속마음 *song-ma-eum*	true feeling, honest feeling

약하다 *ya-ka-da*	to be weak	힘이 약하다 *hi-mi ya-ka-da*	to be weak, to be feeble
		몸이 약하다 *mo-mi ya-ka-da*	to have a weak body
		약한 마음 *ya-kan ma-eum*	weak-hearted
		약해지다 *ya-kae-ji-da*	to become weak
몸무게 *mom-mu-ge*	body weight, one's weight	몸무게를 재다 *mom-mu-ge-reul jae-da*	to measure one's weight
		몸무게가 늘다 *mom-mu-ge-ga neul-da*	to gain weight
		몸무게가 줄다 *mom-mu-ge-ga jul-da*	to lose weight
		체중계 *che-jung-gye*	scale
절대 *jeol-ttae*	absolutely	절대로 *jeol-ttae-ro*	absolutely (not)
		절대 안 되다 *jeol-ttae an doe-da*	absolutely cannot happen

LET'S REVIEW!

Read the story again, but this time in Korean!

요즘 다이어트를 하고 있어요.

오늘 아침에는 **사과**랑 **바나나**랑 감자를 먹었어요.

그리고 열심히 **일했어요.**

점심에는 **오이**랑 **토마토**를 먹었어요.

저녁에는 너무 **배**가 고파서 **마음**이 **약해졌어요.**

그래서 저녁을 많이 먹었어요. 몸무게를 쟀어요. **몸무게**가

늘었어요. **절대**로 다시는 마음 약해지지 않을 거예요.

Translation

I am on a diet these days. This morning, I ate an apple, banana
and some potatoes. I worked hard. At lunch, I ate a cucumber and
a tomato. In the evening, I became so hungry and weak-hearted.
So, I ate a lot for dinner. I weighed myself. I gained weight.
I will never be weak-hearted again.

Match each Korean word to its English translation.

오이   ·   · to work

마음   ·   · apple

바나나 ·   · belly, stomach

절대   ·   · absolutely

사과   ·   · mind, heart

몸무게 ·   · banana

토마토 ·   · body weight, one's weight

일하다 ·   · to be weak

약하다 ·   · tomato

배   ·   · cucumber

Crossword Puzzle

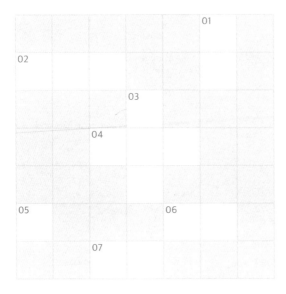

01 apple
02 banana
03 to work
04 to be weak
05 belly, stomach
06 absolutely
07 mind, heart

Fill in the blanks using one of the words that you learned in Day 35.
(Please refer to page 017 to review how to conjugate verbs/adjectives.)

1. 오늘 아침에는 (   )랑 바나나랑
    감자를 먹었어요.

    This morning, I ate an apple, banana and some potatoes.

2. 오늘 아침에는 사과랑 (   )랑
    감자를 먹었어요.

    This morning, I ate an apple, banana and some potatoes.

3. 그리고 열심히 (   ).

    I worked hard.

4. 점심에는 (   )랑 토마토를 먹었어요.

    At lunch, I ate a cucumber and a tomato.

5. 점심에는 오이랑 (   )를 먹었어요.

    At lunch, I ate a cucumber and a tomato.

6. 저녁에는 너무 (   )가 고파서 마음이
    약해졌어요.

    In the evening, I became so hungry and weak-hearted.

7. 저녁에는 너무 배가 고파서 (   )이
    약해졌어요.

    In the evening, I became so hungry and weak-hearted.

8. 저녁에는 너무 배가 고파서 마음이
    (   ).

    In the evening, I became so hungry and weak-hearted.

9. (   )가 늘었어요.

    I gained weight.

10. (   )로 다시는 마음 약해지지
    않을 거예요.

    I will never be weak-hearted again.

DAY 36

Check off the words you already know.

○ 어제 ○

○ 운동 ○

○ 넘어지다 ○

○ 손 ○

○ 다치다 ○

○ 아프다 ○

○ 병원 ○

○ 의사 ○

○ 쉬다 ○

○ 힘들다 ○

After you study these words, come back and
check off the ones you have memorized.

LET'S WARM UP!

Imagine the situation in the story below to help you
remember the ten Korean words in context.

넘어지다 운동   어제

I fell down while   working out yesterday.

다치다 손

I hurt my   hand.

아프다

It hurt so much.

병원

I went to the hospital.

의사

I received medical treatment from the doctor.

쉬다

I laid on the bed and rested.

힘들다

Because I hurt my hand, it is so hard to eat.

LET'S KEEP THE BALL ROLLING!

Word	Meaning	Related Words	Meaning
어제 *eo-je*	yesterday	어젯밤 *eo-jet-ppam*	last night
		어제 아침 *eo-je a-chim*	yesterday morning
		그제 *geu-je*	the day before yesterday
		전날 *jeon-nal*	the previous day
운동 *un-dong*	exercise	운동하다 *un-dong-ha-da*	to exercise
		운동장 *un-dong-jang*	field, playing field
		운동선수 *un-dong-seon-su*	athlete
넘어지다 *neo-meo-ji-da*	to fall down	뒤로 넘어지다 *dwi-ro neo-meo-ji-da*	to fall backwards
		미끄러지다 *mi-kkeu-reo-ji-da*	to slip

손 *son*	hand	손을 들다 *so-neul deul-da*	to raise one's hand
		손을 잡다 *so-neul jap-tta*	to hold someone's hand
		손가락 *son-kka-rak*	finger
		악수하다 *ak-ssu-ha-da*	to shake hands
다치다 *da-chi-da*	to get hurt	크게 다치다 *keu-ge da-chi-da*	to get seriously hurt
		많이 다치다 *ma-ni da-chi-da*	to get hurt a lot
		허리를 다치다 *heo-ri-reul da-chi-da*	to hurt one's back
		상처 *sang-cheo*	wound
아프다 *a-peu-da*	to be sick, to hurt	배가 아프다 *bae-ga a-peu-da*	to have a stomachache
		마음이 아프다 *ma-eu-mi a-peu-da*	to feel sad, to be heartbroken
		머리가 아프다 *meo-ri-ga a-peu-da*	to have a headache
병원 *byeong-won*	hospital	병원에 가다 *byeong-wo-ne ga-da*	to go to the hospital, to go see a doctor
		동물 병원 *dong-mul byeong-won*	animal hospital, vet, veterinary clinic
		주사 *ju-sa*	shot, injection

의사	doctor	의사 선생님 *ui-sa seon-saeng-nim*	doctor
ui-sa		치과 의사 *chi-kkwa ui-sa*	dentist
		간호사 *ga-no-sa*	nurse

쉬다	to rest	푹 쉬다 *puk swi-da*	to rest up, to rest a lot
swi-da		집에서 쉬다 *ji-be-seo swi-da*	to rest at home
		쉬는 날 *swi-neun nal*	day off
		쉬는 시간 *swi-neun si-gan*	break, recess, break time

힘들다	to be difficult, to be tiring, to be hard	먹기 힘들다 *meok-kki him-deul-da*	to be hard to eat
him-deul-da		일이 힘들다 *i-ri him-deul-da*	the work is hard
		힘든 *him-deun*	hard, difficult, tiring
		힘들게 *him-deul-ge*	in a difficult manner, in a tiring manner

Read the story again, but this time in Korean!

어제 운동을 하다가 **넘어졌어요.**

손을 **다쳤어요.** 너무 **아팠어요.**

병원에 갔어요.

의사 선생님에게 진료를 받았어요.

침대에 누워서 **쉬었어요.**

손을 다쳐서 밥 먹기가 너무 **힘들어요.**

Translation

I fell down while working out yesterday. I hurt my hand. It hurt so much. I went to the hospital. I received medical treatment from the doctor. I laid on the bed and rested. Because I hurt my hand, it is so hard to eat.

Match each Korean word to its English translation.

의사 ·   · to get hurt

아프다 ·   · to rest

힘들다 ·   · hospital

어제 ·   · exercise

병원 ·   · yesterday

운동 ·   · doctor

손 ·   · to fall down

쉬다 ·   · to be difficult, to be tiring

다치다 ·   · to be sick, to hurt

넘어지다 ·   · hand

Crossword Puzzle

01 to get hurt
02 to fall down
03 to be difficult, to be hard
04 to rest
05 hand
06 yesterday
07 hospital

Fill in the blanks using one of the words that you learned in Day 36.
(Please refer to page 017 to review how to conjugate verbs/adjectives.)

1. (   ) 운동을 하다가 넘어졌어요.   I fell down while working out yesterday.

2. 어제 (   )을 하다가 넘어졌어요.   I fell down while working out yesterday.

3. 어제 운동을 하다가 (   ).   I fell down while working out yesterday.

4. (   )을 다쳤어요.   I hurt my hand.

5. 손을 (   ).   I hurt my hand.

6. 너무 (   ).   It hurt so much.

7. (   )에 갔어요.   I went to the hospital.

8. (   ) 선생님에게 진료를 받았어요.   I received medical treatment from the doctor.

9. 침대에 누워서 (   ).   I laid on the bed and rested.

10. 손을 다쳐서 밥 먹기가 너무 (   ).   Because I hurt my hand, it is so hard to eat.

DAY 37

Check off the words you already know.

- ○ 학생 ○
- ○ 자전거 ○
- ○ 다니다 ○
- ○ 비 ○
- ○ 우산 ○
- ○ 없다 ○
- ○ 신발 ○
- ○ 벗다 ○
- ○ 발 ○
- ○ 목욕 ○

After you study these words, come back and check off the ones you have memorized.

Day 37

LET'S WARM UP!

Imagine the situation in the story below to help you
remember the ten Korean words in context.

학생 다니다   자전거

I am a student. I go to school on my bike.

비

Today on my way home, it rained.

없다   우산

I did not have an umbrella.

Therefore, my clothes got wet in the rain.

신발

My shoes got wet, too.

벗다

As soon as I came home, I took off my shoes.

발   목욕

My feet smelled. So, I took a bath.

LET'S KEEP THE BALL ROLLING!

Word	Meaning	Related Words	Meaning
학생 *hak-ssaeng*	student	**초등학생** *cho-deung-hak-ssaeng*	elementary school student
		중학생 *jung-hak-ssaeng*	middle school student
		고등학생 *go-deung-hak-ssaeng*	high school student
		학생들 *hak-ssaeng-deul*	students
자전거 *ja-jeon-geo*	bicycle	**자전거를 타다** *ja-jeon-geo-reul ta-da*	to ride a bicycle
		자전거를 타고 가다 *ja-jeon-geo-reul ta-go ga-da*	to go by bicycle
		자전거 바퀴 *ja-jeon-geo ba-kwi*	bicycle wheel
		자전거 한 대 *ja-jeon-geo han dae*	one bicycle
다니다 *da-ni-da*	to attend, to go to (regularly)	**학교에 다니다** *hak-kkyo-e da-ni-da*	to go to school
		병원에 다니다 *byeong-wo-ne da-ni-da*	to go to the hospital (regularly)
		가지고 다니다 *ga-ji-go da-ni-da*	to carry with
		타고 다니다 *ta-go da-ni-da*	to go around (in a vehicle)

비	rain	비를 맞다	to get rained on
bi		*bi-reul mat-tta*	
		비가 내리다	it rains, to rain
		bi-ga nae-ri-da	
		비가 오다	it rains, to rain
		bi-ga o-da	
		비에 젖다	to get wet in the rain
		bi-e jeot-tta	

우산	umbrella	우산을 쓰다	to use an umbrella
u-san		*u-sa-neul sseu-da*	
		우산을 펴다	to open an umbrella
		u-sa-neul pyeo-da	
		우산을 접다	to fold up an umbrella
		u-sa-neul jeop-tta	

없다	to not have, to not be, to not exist	아무도 없다	there is no one
eop-tta		*a-mu-do eop-tta*	
		여기 없다	to not be here
		yeo-gi eop-tta	
		없어지다	to disappear, to not be anymore
		eop-sseo-ji-da	
		있다	to be, to have, to exist
		it-tta	

신발 *sin-bal*	shoe	신발을 신다 *sin-ba-reul sin-tta*	to put on shoes, to wear shoes
		새 신발 *sae sin-bal*	new shoes
		신발장 *sin-bal-jjang*	shoe rack
		신발 끈 *sin-bal kkeun*	shoestring, shoe lace
벗다 *beot-tta*	to take off (clothing)	신발을 벗다 *sin-ba-reul beot-tta*	to take off one's shoes
		옷을 벗다 *o-seul beot-tta*	to take off one's clothes
발 *bal*	foot	발이 크다 *ba-ri keu-da*	to have big feet
		발 냄새 *bal naem-sae*	foot smell
		발바닥 *bal-ppa-dak*	sole of one's foot
		손 *son*	hand
목욕 *mo-gyok*	bath	목욕하다 *mo-gyo-ka-da*	to take a bath, to bathe
		목욕탕 *mo-gyok-tang*	bathhouse
		욕조 *yok-jjo*	bathtub

LET'S REVIEW!

Read the story again, but this time in Korean!

저는 **학생**이에요. 학교에 **자전거**를 타고 **다녀요.**

오늘 집에 가는데 **비**가 왔어요.

우산이 **없었어요.**

그래서 옷이 비에 젖었어요. **신발**도 젖었어요.

집에 오자마자 신발을 **벗었어요.**

발에서 냄새가 났어요. 그래서 **목욕**을 했어요.

Translation

I am a student. I go to school on my bike. Today on my way home, it rained. I did not have an umbrella. Therefore, my clothes got wet in the rain. My shoes got wet, too. As soon as I came home, I took off my shoes. My feet smelled. So, I took a bath.

Match each Korean word to its English translation.

다니다 ·   · umbrella

비 ·   · to take off (clothing)

우산 ·   · student

목욕 ·   · shoe

학생 ·   · bath

벗다 ·   · rain

자전거 ·   · foot

발 ·   · bicycle

신발 ·   · to not have, to not be, to not exist

없다 ·   · to attend, to go to (regularly)

Crossword Puzzle

				01	
02					
		03			
	04				
				05	
	06	07			

01 bicycle
02 foot
03 to take off (clothing)
04 to attend, to go to (regularly)
05 rain
06 umbrella
07 bath

Fill in the blanks using one of the words that you learned in Day 37.
(Please refer to page 017 to review how to conjugate verbs/adjectives.)

1. 저는 (   )이에요.   I am a student.

2. 학교에 (   )를 타고 다녀요.   I go to school on my bike.

3. 학교에 자전거를 타고 (   ).   I go to school on my bike.

4. 오늘 집에 가는데 (   )가 왔어요.   Today on my way home, it rained.

5. (   )이 없었어요.   I did not have an umbrella.

6. 우산이 (   ).   I did not have an umbrella.

7. (   )도 젖었어요.   My shoes got wet, too.

8. 집에 오자마자 신발을 (   ).   As soon as I came home, I took off my shoes.

9. (   )에서 냄새가 났어요.   My feet smelled.

10. 그래서 (   )을 했어요.   So, I took a bath.

DAY 38

Check off the words you already know.

○ 오빠 ○

○ 가끔 ○

○ 거짓말 ○

○ 짜증 ○

○ 오전 ○

○ 머리 ○

○ 벌레 ○

○ 놀라다 ○

○ 싫다 ○

○ 이상하다 ○

After you study these words, come back and check off the ones you have memorized.

Day 38

Imagine the situation in the story below to help you
remember the ten Korean words in context.

오빠   가끔   거짓말
My older brother sometimes lies.

짜증
So, it's very irritating.

오전   벌레 머리
This morning, he said that there was a bug on my head.

놀라다
I was really surprised.

싫다
I hate bugs so much.

이상하다
My brother is really weird.

LET'S KEEP THE BALL ROLLING!

Word	Meaning	Related Words	Meaning
오빠 *o-ppa*	older brother (for a girl)	친오빠 *chi-no-ppa*	real brother, biological brother
		아는 오빠 *a-neun o-ppa*	older man a girl knows
		첫째 오빠 *cheot-jjae o-ppa*	eldest brother (for a girl)
가끔 *ga-kkeum*	sometimes	가끔 만나다 *ga-kkeum man-na-da*	to meet sometimes
		가끔 생각하다 *ga-kkeum saeng-ga-ka-da*	to think of something sometimes
		항상 *hang-sang*	always
거짓말 *geo-jin-mal*	lie	거짓말을 하다 *geo-jin-ma-reul ha-da*	to lie, to tell a lie
		거짓말쟁이 *geo-jin-mal-jaeng-i*	liar
짜증 *jja-jeung*	frustration, anger, irritation	짜증이 나다 *jja-jeung-i na-da*	to be irritated, to be angry
		짜증을 내다 *jja-jeung-eul nae-da*	to show one's irritation, to show one's frustration

오전
o-jeon

morning,
before noon

오전에
o-jeo-ne
in the morning

오전 10시
o-jeon yeol-ssi
10 o'clock in the morning,
10 a.m.

오후
o-hu
afternoon

머리
meo-ri

head, hair

머리가 아프다
meo-ri-ga a-peu-da
to have a headache,
one's head hurts

머리가 좋다
meo-ri-ga jo-ta
to be smart

긴 머리
gin meo-ri
long hair

머리카락
meo-ri-ka-rak
hair

벌레
beol-le

bug, worm

벌레 한 마리
beol-le han ma-ri
one bug, one worm

징그럽다
jing-geu-reop-tta
to be gross

벌레를 잡다
beol-le-reul jap-tta
to catch a bug,
to catch a worm

기어가다
gi-eo-ga-da
to crawl

놀라다
nol-la-da

to be surprised

깜짝 놀라다
kkam-jjak nol-la-da
to be surprised,
to be startled

놀라게 하다
nol-la-ge ha-da
to surprise

놀란 얼굴
nol-lan eol-gul
surprised look on one's
face

싫다
sil-ta

to hate, to dislike,
to be displeasing

너무 싫다
neo-mu sil-ta

to really hate

싫은 사람
si-reun sa-ram

someone that one hates,
a hated person

싫지 않다
sil-chi an-ta

to not be averse to,
to not be displeasing,
to be alright

싫어하다
si-reo-ha-da

to hate

이상하다
i-sang-ha-da

to be strange,
to be weird

목소리가 이상하다
mok-sso-ri-ga i-sang-ha-da

one's voice is strange, to
have a strange voice

성격이 이상하다
seong-kkyeo-gi i-sang-ha-da

one's personality is
strange, to have a strange
personality

이상한 사람
i-sang-han sa-ram

strange person

LET'S REVIEW!

Read the story again, but this time in Korean!

오빠가 가끔 거짓말을 해요.

그래서 너무 짜증이 나요.

오늘 오전에는 제 머리에 벌레가 있다고 했어요.

정말 깜짝 놀랐어요.

저는 벌레가 너무 싫어요.

오빠는 정말 이상해요.

Translation

My older brother sometimes lies. So, it's very irritating. This morning, he said that there was a bug on my head. I was really surprised. I hate bugs so much. My brother is really weird.

Match each Korean word to its English translation.

오전 ·   · lie

놀라다 ·   · frustration, anger, irritation

이상하다 ·   · sometimes

거짓말 ·   · older brother (for a girl)

오빠 ·   · to be strange, to be weird

가끔 ·   · head, hair

벌레 ·   · morning, before noon

짜증 ·   · to hate, to dislike

싫다 ·   · to be surprised

머리 ·   · bug, worm

Crossword Puzzle

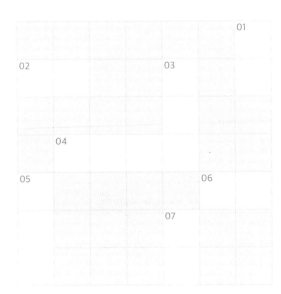

01 sometimes
02 frustration, anger
03 to be surprised
04 to be strange, to be weird
05 lie
06 bug, worm
07 head, hair

....

Fill in the blanks using one of the words that you learned in Day 38.
(Please refer to page 017 to review how to conjugate verbs/adjectives.)

1. (   )가 가끔 거짓말을 해요.   My older brother sometimes lies.

2. 오빠가 (   ) 거짓말을 해요.   My older brother sometimes lies.

3. 오빠가 가끔 (   )을 해요.   My older brother sometimes lies.

4. 그래서 너무 (   )이 나요.   So, it's very irritating.

5. 오늘 (   )에는 제 머리에 벌레가   This morning, he said that there was a bug
    있다고 했어요.   on my head.

6. 오늘 오전에는 제 (   )에 벌레가   This morning, he said that there was a bug
    있다고 했어요.   on my head.

7. 오늘 오전에는 제 머리에 (   )가   This morning, he said that there was a bug
    있다고 했어요.   on my head.

8. 정말 깜짝 (   ).   I was really surprised.

9. 저는 벌레가 너무 (   ).   I hate bugs so much.

10. 오빠는 정말 (   ).   My brother is really weird.

DAY 39

Check off the words you already know.

○ 저녁 ○
○ 엄마 ○
○ 마트 ○
○ 고기 ○
○ 사다 ○
○ 생선 ○
○ 채소 ○
○ 말하다 ○
○ 달걀 ○
○ 요리 ○

After you study these words, come back and check off the ones you have memorized.

Day 39

Imagine the situation in the story below to help you
remember the ten Korean words in context.

마트   엄마   저녁
I went to the <u>supermarket</u> with my <u>mom</u> in the <u>evening</u>.

사다   고기
Mom <u>bought</u> some <u>meat</u>. I really like meat.

생선 채소
We also bought <u>fish</u> and   <u>vegetables</u>.

I don't eat vegetables.

말하다
Mom <u>said</u> that I must also eat vegetables.

달걀
We also bought <u>eggs</u>. As for eggs, I like eating them.

요리
Mom will cook a delicious <u>dish</u> for me.

LET'S KEEP THE BALL ROLLING!

Word	Meaning	Related Words	Meaning
저녁 *jeo-nyeok*	evening	**저녁에** *jeo-nyeo-ge*	in the evening
		저녁 식사 *jeo-nyeok sik-ssa*	supper, dinner
		저녁때 *jeo-nyeok-ttae*	at dinner, in the evening
		저녁을 먹다 *jeo-nyeo-geul meok-tta*	to have dinner
엄마 *eom-ma*	mom	**우리 엄마** *u-ri eom-ma*	my mom
		새엄마 *sae-eom-ma*	stepmom
		부모 *bu-mo*	parents
마트 *ma-teu*	supermarket	**마트에 가다** *ma-teu-e ga-da*	to go to the supermarket
		대형 마트 *dae-hyeong ma-teu*	big supermarket
		장을 보다 *jang-eul bo-da*	to go grocery shopping

고기 *go-gi*	meat	돼지고기 *dwae-ji-go-gi*	pork
		소고기 *so-go-gi*	beef
		닭고기 *dak-kko-gi*	chicken

사다 *sa-da*	to buy	밥을 사다 *ba-beul sa-da*	to buy someone a meal
		선물을 사다 *seon-mu-reul sa-da*	to buy a present
		싸게 사다 *ssa-ge sa-da*	to buy at a low price
		팔다 *pal-da*	to sell

생선 *saeng-seon*	fish	생선 두 마리 *saeng-seon du ma-ri*	two fish
		생선 요리 *saeng-seon yo-ri*	fish dish
		물고기 *mul-kko-gi*	live fish

채소 *chae-so*	vegetable	채소를 기르다 *chae-so-reul gi-reu-da*	to grow vegetables
		채소를 먹다 *chae-so-reul meok-tta*	to eat vegetables
		녹색 채소 *nok-ssaek chae-so*	green vegetables

말하다 *ma-ra-da*	to talk, to speak	천천히 말하다 *cheon-cheo-ni ma-ra-da*	to talk slowly
		빨리 말하다 *ppal-li ma-ra-da*	to talk quickly
		말 *mal*	words, language
		이야기하다 *i-ya-gi-ha-da*	to talk, to chat
달걀 *dal-gyal*	egg	달걀을 깨다 *dal-gya-reul kkae-da*	to break an egg
		삶은 달걀 *sal-meun dal-gyal*	boiled egg
		계란 *gye-ran*	egg
요리 *yo-ri*	cooking, food, dish	요리사 *yo-ri-sa*	cook, chef
		요리하다 *yo-ri-ha-da*	to cook
		음식 *eum-sik*	dish, food

LET'S REVIEW!

Read the story again, but this time in Korean!

저녁에 엄마랑 마트에 갔어요.

엄마는 고기를 샀어요. 저는 고기를 정말 좋아해요.

그리고 생선이랑 채소도 샀어요. 저는 채소를 안 먹어요.

엄마는 채소도 꼭 먹어야 한다고 말했어요.

그리고 달걀도 샀어요. 저는 달걀은 잘 먹어요.

엄마가 맛있는 요리를 해 줄 거예요.

Translation

I went to the supermarket with my mom in the evening.
Mom bought some meat. I really like meat. We also bought fish
and vegetables. I don't eat vegetables. Mom said that I must also
eat vegetables. We also bought eggs. As for eggs, I like eating them.
Mom will cook a delicious dish for me.

Match each Korean word to its English translation.

마트 · · to buy

생선 · · meat

저녁 · · fish

채소 · · to talk, to speak

달걀 · · cooking, food, dish

요리 · · vegetable

엄마 · · supermarket

말하다 · · evening

사다 · · egg

고기 · · mom

Crossword Puzzle

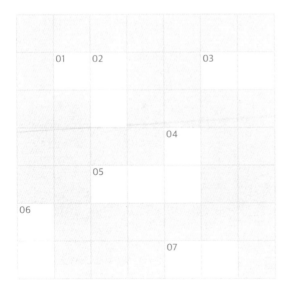

01 mom
02 supermarket
03 egg
04 to buy
05 to talk, to speak
06 evening
07 fish

Fill in the blanks using one of the words that you learned in Day 39.
(Please refer to page 017 to review how to conjugate verbs/adjectives.)

1. (   )에 엄마랑 마트에 갔어요.　　I went to the supermarket with my mom in the evening.

2. 저녁에 (   )랑 마트에 갔어요.　　I went to the supermarket with my mom in the evening.

3. 저녁에 엄마랑 (   )에 갔어요.　　I went to the supermarket with my mom in the evening.

4. 엄마는 (   )를 샀어요.　　Mom bought some meat.

5. 엄마는 고기를 (   ).　　Mom bought some meat.

6. 그리고 (   )이랑 채소도 샀어요.　　We also bought fish and vegetables.

7. 그리고 생선이랑 (   )도 샀어요.　　We also bought fish and vegetables.

8. 엄마는 채소도 꼭 먹어야 한다고 (
).　　Mom said that I must also eat vegetables.

9. 그리고 (   )도 샀어요.　　We also bought eggs.

10. 엄마가 맛있는 (   )를 해 줄 거예요.　　Mom will cook a delicious dish for me.

DAY 40

Check off the words you already know.

- 할아버지
- 산
- 올라가다
- 믿다
- 사람
- 새
- 나무
- 냄새
- 몸
- 움직이다

After you study these words, come back and check off the ones you have memorized.

Day 40

....

Imagine the situation in the story below to help you remember the ten Korean words in context.

할아버지 올라가다 산

My <u>grandfather</u>   <u>goes up</u> the   <u>mountain</u> every day.

믿다

He <u>believes</u> that he will become healthy if he hikes up the

mountain every day. I sometimes go with him, too.

사람

When we go to the mountain, there are a lot of <u>people</u>.

새   냄새 나무

There are a lot of <u>birds</u>, too. I like the <u>smell</u> of <u>trees</u>.

움직이다 몸

I also like <u>moving</u> my   <u>body</u> a lot.

So, I also like hiking up the mountain.

LET'S KEEP THE BALL ROLLING!

Word	Meaning	Related Words	Meaning
할아버지 *ha-ra-beo-ji*	grandfather, old man	**외할아버지** *oe-ha-ra-beo-ji*	maternal grandfather
		친할아버지 *chi-na-ra-beo-ji*	paternal grandfather
		할머니 *hal-meo-ni*	grandmother
산 *san*	mountain	**산이 낮다** *sa-ni nat-tta*	the mountain is low
		높은 산 *no-peun san*	high mountain
		등산 *deung-san*	mountain hiking
올라가다 *ol-la-ga-da*	to go up	**산에 올라가다** *sa-ne ol-la-ga-da*	to go up a mountain
		옥상에 올라가다 *ok-ssang-e ol-la-ga-da*	to go up to the roof
믿다 *mit-tta*	to trust, to believe	**이야기를 믿다** *i-ya-gi-reul mit-tta*	to believe a story
		사람을 믿다 *sa-ra-meul mit-tta*	to believe a person, to trust a person
		믿음 *mi-deum*	belief, trust

사람	person, people	미국 사람	a person from the United States
sa-ram		mi-guk sa-ram	
		아는 사람	someone that one knows
		a-neun sa-ram	
		모르는 사람	someone that one doesn't know, a stranger
		mo-reu-neun sa-ram	
		사람들	people
		sa-ram-deul	

새	bird	새가 날다	a bird flies
sae		sae-ga nal-da	
		새 한 마리	one bird
		sae han ma-ri	

나무	tree, wood	나무 세 그루	three trees
na-mu		na-mu se geu-ru	
		나무를 심다	to plant a tree
		na-mu-reul sim-tta	
		나무 의자	wooden chair
		na-mu ui-ja	

냄새	smell	냄새가 나다	to smell (lit. a smell grows/sprouts/happens)
naem-sae		naem-sae-ga na-da	
		냄새가 좋다	to smell good
		naem-sae-ga jo-ta	
		이상한 냄새	strange smell
		i-sang-han naem-sae	
		향기	scent, fragrance
		hyang-gi	

몸	body	건강한 몸	healthy body
mom		*geon-gang-han mom*	
		몸이 아프다	to be sick
		mo-mi a-peu-da	
		몸이 힘들다	to be tired
		mo-mi him-deul-da	
		몸에 좋다	to be good for one's body, to be good for health
		mo-me jo-ta	

움직이다	to move	천천히 움직이다	to move slowly
um-ji-gi-da		*cheon-cheo-ni um-ji-gi-da*	
		몸을 움직이다	to move one's body
		mo-meul um-ji-gi-da	

Read the story again, but this time in Korean!

저희 **할아버지**는 매일 **산**에 **올라가요.**

매일 산에 올라가면 건강해진다고 **믿어요.**

저도 가끔 같이 올라가요. 산에 가면 **사람**들이 많아요.

새들도 많아요. 저는 **나무 냄새**를 좋아해요.

몸을 많이 **움직이는** 것도 좋아해요.

그래서 저도 산에 올라가는 것을 좋아해요.

Translation

My grandfather goes up the mountain every day. He believes that he will become healthy if he hikes up the mountain every day. I sometimes go with him, too. When we go to the mountain, there are a lot of people. There are a lot of birds, too. I like the smell of trees. I also like moving my body a lot. So, I also like hiking up the mountain.

Match each Korean word to its English translation.

믿다 ·   · bird

냄새 ·   · tree, wood

새 ·   · mountain

산 ·   · to move

몸 ·   · to go up

움직이다 ·   · smell

나무 ·   · grandfather, old man

할아버지 ·   · person, people

올라가다 ·   · to trust, to believe

사람 ·   · body

Crossword Puzzle

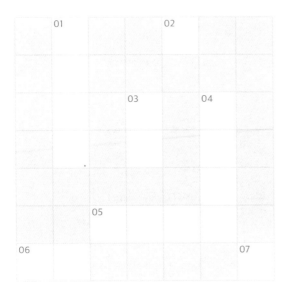

01 grandfather, old man
02 mountain
03 tree, wood
04 to go up
05 to move
06 person, people
07 bird

Fill in the blanks using one of the words that you learned in Day 40.
(Please refer to page 017 to review how to conjugate verbs/adjectives.)

1. 저희 (   )는 매일 산에
   올라가요.

   My grandfather goes up the mountain every day.

2. 저희 할아버지는 매일 (   )에
   올라가요.

   My grandfather goes up the mountain every day.

3. 저희 할아버지는 매일
   산에 (   ).

   My grandfather goes up the mountain every day.

4. 매일 산에 올라가면
   건강해진다고 (   ).

   He believes that he will become healthy if he hikes up the mountain every day.

5. 산에 가면 (   )들이 많아요.

   When we go to the mountain, there are a lot of people.

6. (   )들도 많아요.

   There are a lot of birds, too.

7. 저는 (   ) 냄새를 좋아해요.

   I like the smell of trees.

8. 저는 나무 (   )를 좋아해요.

   I like the smell of trees.

9. (   )을 많이 움직이는 것도 좋아해요.

   I also like moving my body a lot.

10. 몸을 많이 (   ) 것도 좋아해요.

    I also like moving my body a lot.

01 Choose the term that is an edible item.

    a. 인기   b. 사과   c. 지도   d. 주소

02 Where do you go to buy medicine?

    a. 약국   b. 나라   c. 가수   d. 발

03 Which one is **NOT** a mode of transportation?

    a. 택시   b. 건강   c. 오토바이   d. 자전거

04 Which body part is 허리?

    a. wrist   b. ankle   c. neck   d. waist

05 Choose the term that is **NOT** a loanword from English.

    a. 오이   b. 토마토   c. 바나나   d. 인터넷

06 Choose the word that is **NOT** a body part.

   a. 배   b. 코   c. 손   d. 약

07 How do you address your father's father in Korean?

   a. 할아버지   b. 할아버니   c. 할머니   d. 할머버지

08 Choose the item that you **CANNOT** wear.

   a. 신발   b. 치마   c. 감기   d. 모자

09 Where can you go 쇼핑?

   a. 마트   b. 달걀   c. 어제   d. 택시

10 Who do you most likely see when you go to the 병원?

   a. 엄마   b. 경찰   c. 의사   d. 학생

11 Which of the following is something you can drink?

   a. 고기   b. 생선   c. 차   d. 저녁

12 Which one syllable word means **"door"**?

a. 귀   b. 산   c. 비   d. 문

13 Which of the following means **"mind, heart"**?

a. 마음   b. 사고   c. 단어   d. 조금

14 How do you say **"to send a text message"** in Korean?

a. 약속을 보내다   b. 문자를 보내다
c. 문자를 주문하다   d. 약속을 주문하다

15 Which one of the following words is **NOT** related to time?

a. 어제   b. 머리   c. 오전   d. 가끔

16 Which of the following does **NOT** become a verb if you attach -하다?

a. 성공   b. 운동   c. 목욕   d. 벌레

17 What is the Korean word for the item in the picture?

a. 오빠

b. 요리

c. 우산

d. 채소

18 Which word is not related to the others?

a. 넘어지다   b. 다치다   c. 아프다   d. 필요하다

19 Choose the noun that refers to something you **CANNOT** see.

a. 새   b. 냄새   c. 나무   d. 사람

20 Choose the term that refers to the size of something.

a. 벗다   b. 이상하다   c. 작다   d. 늦다

QUIZ

DAY 41

Check off the words you already know.

○ 공항 ○
○ 넓다 ○
○ 길 ○
○ 잃어버리다 ○
○ 여기 ○
○ 어디 ○
○ 서점 ○
○ 들어가다 ○
○ 물어보다 ○
○ 찾다 ○

After you study these words, come back and check off the ones you have memorized.

Day 41

LET'S WARM UP!

Imagine the situation in the story below to help you remember the ten Korean words in context.

공항 넓다 잃어버리다 길
The <u>airport</u> is so <u>big</u> that I <u>lost</u> my <u>way</u>.

어디 여기
I don't know <u>where</u> <u>this place</u> is.

들어가다 서점
I <u>went into</u> the <u>bookstore</u>.

물어보다
I <u>asked</u> for directions.

찾다
Fortunately, I <u>found</u> my way.

LET'S KEEP THE BALL ROLLING!

Word	Meaning	Related Words	Meaning
공항 *gong-hang*	airport	공항버스 *gong-hang-ppeo-sseu*	airport shuttle bus
		비행기 *bi-haeng-gi*	airplane
		공항에 가다 *gong-hang-e ga-da*	to go to the airport
넓다 *neol-tta*	to be spacious, to be wide	공항이 넓다 *gong-hang-i neol-tta*	the airport is big
		넓은 집 *neol-beun jip*	spacious house
		좁다 *jop-tta*	to be narrow, to be small (in space)
길 *gil*	road, street	길가 *gil-kka*	roadside
		골목길 *gol-mok-kkil*	alley
		길이 막히다 *gi-ri ma-ki-da*	to be jammed with traffic
잃어버리다 *i-reo-beo-ri-da*	to lose, to misplace	길을 잃어버리다 *gi-reul i-reo-beo-ri-da*	to get lost
		돈을 잃어버리다 *do-neul i-reo-beo-ri-da*	to lose money
		잃어버린 지갑 *i-reo-beo-rin ji-gap*	lost wallet, misplaced wallet

여기 *yeo-gi*	here	여기에서 *yeo-gi-e-seo*	from here
		여기까지 *yeo-gi-kka-ji*	to here, up to here
		여기저기 *yeo-gi-jeo-gi*	here and there

어디 *eo-di*	where	어디에서 *eo-di-e-seo*	from where
		어디로 *eo-di-ro*	to where
		어디인지 모르다 *eo-di-in-ji mo-reu-da*	to not know where

서점 *seo-jeom*	bookstore	책방 *chaek-ppang*	bookstore
		책 *chaek*	book
		동네 서점 *dong-ne seo-jeom*	local bookstore, bookstore in the neighborhood
		대형 서점 *dae-hyeong seo-jeom*	large-scale bookstore
		도서관 *do-seo-gwan*	library

들어가다
deu-reo-ga-da

to enter

서점에 들어가다
seo-jeo-me deu-reo-ga-da

to go into a bookstore

교실로 들어가다
gyo-sil-lo deu-reo-ga-da

to go into a classroom

들어오다
deu-reo-o-da

to come in

나가다
na-ga-da

to go out

물어보다
mu-reo-bo-da

to ask

길을 물어보다
gi-reul mu-reo-bo-da

to ask for directions

전화로 물어보다
jeo-nwa-ro mu-reo-bo-da

to ask over the phone

대답하다
dae-da-pa-da

to answer

찾다
chat-tta

to find

길을 찾다
gi-reul chat-tta

to find one's way

답을 찾다
da-beul chat-tta

to find the answer

보물을 찾다
bo-mu-reul chat-tta

to find a treasure

LET'S REVIEW!

Read the story again, but this time in Korean!

공항이 너무 넓어서 길을 잃어버렸어요.

여기가 어디인지 모르겠어요.

서점에 들어갔어요.

길을 물어봤어요.

다행히 길을 찾았어요.

Translation

The airport is so big that I lost my way. I don't know where
this place is. I went into the bookstore. I asked for directions.
Fortunately, I found my way.

Match each Korean word to its English translation.

잃어버리다 ·   · to be spacious, to be wide

들어가다 ·   · bookstore

넓다 ·   · airport

어디 ·   · to ask

찾다 ·   · here

공항 ·   · to find

물어보다 ·   · to enter

길 ·   · where

서점 ·   · to lose, to misplace

여기 ·   · road, street

Crossword Puzzle

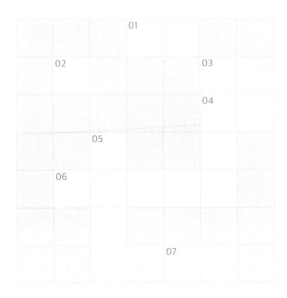

01 airport
02 road, street
03 to ask
04 where
05 to lose, to misplace
06 to enter
07 here

....

Fill in the blanks using one of the words that you learned in Day 41.
(Please refer to page 017 to review how to conjugate verbs/adjectives.)

1. (   )이 너무 넓어서 길을   The airport is so big that I lost my way.
   잃어버렸어요.

2. 공항이 너무 (   ) 길을 잃어버렸어요.   The airport is so big that I lost my way.

3. 공항이 너무 넓어서 (   )을   The airport is so big that I lost my way.
   잃어버렸어요.

4. 공항이 너무 넓어서 길을 (   ).   The airport is so big that I lost my way.

5. (   )가 어디인지 모르겠어요.   I don't know where this place is.

6. 여기가 (   )인지 모르겠어요.   I don't know where this place is.

7. (   )에 들어갔어요.   I went into the bookstore.

8. 서점에 (   ).   I went into the bookstore.

9. 길을 (   ).   I asked for directions.

10. 다행히 길을 (   ).   Fortunately, I found my way.

DAY 42

Check off the words you already know.

- ○ 대학교 ○
- ○ 역 ○
- ○ 가깝다 ○
- ○ 오른쪽 ○
- ○ 은행 ○
- ○ 왼쪽 ○
- ○ 편의점 ○
- ○ 앞 ○
- ○ 건너다 ○
- ○ 다시 ○

After you study these words, come back and
check off the ones you have memorized.

LET'S WARM UP!

Imagine the situation in the story below to help you remember the ten Korean words in context.

대학교   가깝다   역
My <u>university</u> is very <u>close</u> to Sinchon <u>station</u>.

Come out from Exit 2 at Sinchon station.

오른쪽   은행   왼쪽
On your <u>right</u>, there is a <u>bank</u>, and on your <u>left</u>,

편의점
there is a <u>convenience store</u>.

앞   건너다
Walk <u>straight</u>. <u>Cross</u> the road.

다시
Go straight <u>again</u>. You will see the university soon.

LET'S KEEP THE BALL ROLLING!

Word	Meaning	Related Words	Meaning
대학교 *dae-hak-kkyo*	university, college	대학교 1학년 *dae-hak-kkyo i-rang-nyeon*	freshman, first year of university
		대학생 *dae-hak-ssaeng*	university student
		전공 *jeon-gong*	major
역 *yeok*	station	기차역 *gi-cha-yeok*	train station
		지하철역 *ji-ha-cheol yeok*	subway station
		신촌 역 *sin-chon yeok*	Sinchon station (name of a place in Seoul)
가깝다 *ga-kkap-tta*	to be close	아주 가깝다 *a-ju ga-kkap-tta*	to be very close
		더 가깝다 *deo ga-kkap-tta*	to be closer
		가까운 곳 *ga-kka-un got*	close place
		멀다 *meol-da*	to be far

오른쪽 *o-reun-jjok*	right side, right-hand side	오른쪽으로 가다 *o-reun-jjo-geu-ro ga-da*	to go to the right
		오른쪽 길 *o-reun-jjok gil*	path on the right-hand side
		오른 *o-reun*	right, right-sided
은행 *eu-naeng*	bank	은행 이자 *eu-naeng i-ja*	bank interest
		통장 *tong-jang*	bank book, account book
		저금하다 *jeo-geu-ma-da*	to save money, to deposit money
왼쪽 *oen-jjok*	left side, left-hand side	왼쪽에 있다 *oen-jjo-ge it-tta*	to be on the left-hand side
		왼쪽 다리 *oen-jjok da-ri*	left leg
		왼 *oen*	left, left-sided
편의점 *pyeo-nui-jeom*	convenience store	편의점에 가다 *pyeo-nui-jeo-me ga-da*	to go to the convenience store
		편의점에서 사다 *pyeo-nui-jeo-me-seo sa-da*	to buy (something) at a convenience store
		편의점이 열려 있다 *pyeo-nui-jeo-mi yeol-lyeo it-tta*	the convenience store is open

| 앞
ap | front | 앞에
a-pe | in front |
| | | 앞으로
a-peu-ro | forward |

건너다 *geon-neo-da*	to cross	길을 건너다 *gi-reul geon-neo-da*	to cross the road
		다리를 건너다 *da-ri-reul geon-neo-da*	to cross the bridge
		횡단보도 *hoeng-dan-bo-do*	crosswalk

| 다시
da-si | again | 다시 하다
da-si ha-da | to do again |
| | | 또
tto | again |

Read the story again, but this time in Korean!

저희 **대학교**는 신촌 **역**에서 아주 **가까워요.**

신촌 역 2번 출구로 나와요.

오른쪽에 **은행**이 있고, **왼쪽**에 **편의점**이 있어요.

앞으로 걸어가요. 길을 **건너요.**

다시 앞으로 걸어가요.

곧 대학교가 보여요.

Translation

My university is very close to Sinchon station. Come out from Exit 2 at Sinchon station. On your right, there is a bank, and on your left, there is a convenience store. Walk straight. Cross the road.
Go straight again. You will see the university soon.

Match each Korean word to its English translation.

가깝다 ·   · university, college

은행 ·   · convenience store

역 ·   · right side, right-hand side

편의점 ·   · to cross

다시 ·   · station

대학교 ·   · to be close

앞 ·   · left side, left-hand side

건너다 ·   · front

왼쪽 ·   · again

오른쪽 ·   · bank

Crossword Puzzle

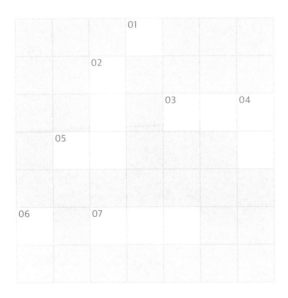

01 front
02 right side, right-hand side
03 to cross
04 again
05 left side, left-hand side
06 station
07 university, college

Fill in the blanks using one of the words that you learned in Day 42.
(Please refer to page 017 to review how to conjugate verbs/adjectives.)

1. 저희 (   )는 신촌 역에서 아주
   가까워요.

   My university is very close to Sinchon station.

2. 저희 대학교는 신촌 (   )에서 아주
   가까워요.

   My university is very close to Sinchon station.

3. 저희 대학교는 신촌 역에서
   아주 (   ).

   My university is very close to Sinchon station.

4. (   )에 은행이 있고, 왼쪽에 편의점이
   있어요.

   On your right, there is a bank, and on your left, there is a convenience store.

5. 오른쪽에 (   )이 있고, 왼쪽에 편의점
   이 있어요.

   On your right, there is a bank, and on your left, there is a convenience store.

6. 오른쪽에 은행이 있고, (   )에 편의점
   이 있어요.

   On your right, there is a bank, and on your left, there is a convenience store.

7. 오른쪽에 은행이 있고, 왼쪽에 (   )이
   있어요.

   On your right, there is a bank, and on your left, there is a convenience store.

8. (   )으로 걸어가요.

   Walk straight.

9. 길을 (   ).

   Cross the road.

10. (   ) 앞으로 걸어가요.

    Go straight again.

DAY 43

Check off the words you already know.

○ 색깔 ○

○ 검은색 ○

○ 지갑 ○

○ 자동차 ○

○ 가방 ○

○ 언제 ○

○ 모르다 ○

○ 형 ○

○ 하얀색 ○

○ 다르다 ○

After you study these words, come back and check off the ones you have memorized.

Day 43

Imagine the situation in the story below to help you remember the ten Korean words in context.

색깔 검은색
My favorite <u>color</u> is   <u>black</u>.

지갑
I have many things that are black, such as a black <u>wallet</u>,

자동차 가방
a black <u>car</u>, a black   <u>bag</u>, and so on.

모르다 언제
I <u>don't know</u>   <u>when</u> I started liking the color black.

형   하얀색
But my <u>older brother</u> likes the color <u>white</u>.

다르다
My personality and my brother's personality are very <u>different</u>.

Word	Meaning	Related Words	Meaning
색깔 *saek-kkal*	color	**색** *saek*	color
		좋아하는 색깔 *jo-a-ha-neun saek-kkal*	color that one likes
		무슨 색깔 *mu-seun saek-kkal*	what color, which color
검은색 *geo-meun-saek*	black	**검은색 자동차** *geo-meun-saek ja-dong-cha*	black car
		검은색 구두 *geo-meun-saek gu-du*	black shoes
		검정 *geom-jeong*	black
지갑 *ji-gap*	wallet	**동전 지갑** *dong-jeon ji-gap*	coin wallet
		지갑을 열다 *ji-ga-beul yeol-da*	to open one's wallet
		지갑을 잃어버리다 *ji-ga-beul i-reo-beo-ri-da*	to lose one's wallet
자동차 *ja-dong-cha*	car	**차** *cha*	car
		자동차 한 대 *ja-dong-cha han dae*	one car
		자동차를 타다 *ja-dong-cha-reul ta-da*	to ride in a car, to get in a car

가방	bag	가방이 무겁다	the bag is heavy
ga-bang		*ga-bang-i mu-geop-tta*	
		가방을 메다	to carry a bag over one's
		ga-bang-eul me-da	shoulder
		책가방	book bag
		chaek-kka-bang	
		여행 가방	suitcase, travel bag,
		yeo-haeng ga-bang	luggage

언제	when	언제부터	since when, from when
eon-je		*eon-je-bu-teo*	
		몇 시	what time
		myeot si	
		날짜	date
		nal-jja	
		며칠	what date,
		myeo-chil	how many days

모르다	to not know	아직 모르다	to still not know
mo-reu-da		*a-jik mo-reu-da*	
		아무도 모르다	nobody knows
		a-mu-do mo-reu-da	
		모르는 사람	a stranger, someone one
		mo-reu-neun sa-ram	doesn't know
		알다	to know
		al-da	

형 *hyeong*	older brother (for a boy)	우리 형 *u-ri hyeong*	my older brother (for a boy)
		첫째 형 *cheot-jjae hyeong*	oldest brother (for a boy)
		사촌 형 *sa-chon hyeong*	older male cousin (for a boy)

하얀색 *ha-yan-saek*	white	흰색 *huin-saek*	white
		하얗다 *ha-ya-ta*	to be white
		하얀 *ha-yan*	white (adjective)
		하얀색 운동화 *ha-yan-saek un-dong-hwa*	white tennis shoes

다르다 *da-reu-da*	to be different	성격이 다르다 *seong-kkyeo-gi da-reu-da*	to have different personalities
		많이 다르다 *ma-ni da-reu-da*	to be very different
		다른 점 *da-reun jeom*	different point, difference
		달라지다 *dal-la-ji-da*	to become different
		같다 *gat-tta*	to be the same

LET'S REVIEW!

Read the story again, but this time in Korean!

제가 좋아하는 **색깔**은 **검은색**이에요.

검은색 **지갑**, 검은색 **자동차**, 검은색 **가방** 등등

검은색 물건이 많아요.

언제부터 검은색을 좋아했는지는 **몰라요.**

그런데 저희 **형**은 하얀색을 좋아해요.

저랑 저희 형은 성격이 많이 **달라요.**

Translation

My favorite color is black. I have many things that are black, such as a black wallet, a black car, a black bag, and so on. I don't know when I started liking the color black. But my older brother likes the color white. My personality and my brother's personality are very different.

Match each Korean word to its English translation.

검은색   ·

가방   ·

모르다   ·

형   ·

색깔   ·

다르다   ·

자동차   ·

하얀색   ·

지갑   ·

언제   ·

· when

· older brother (for a boy)

· to be different

· black

· wallet

· white

· color

· to not know

· bag

· car

Crossword Puzzle

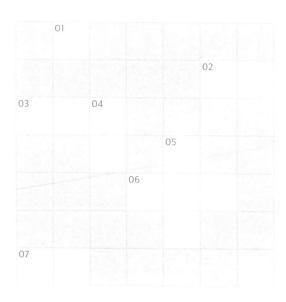

01 older brother (for a boy)
02 bag
03 black
04 color
05 to not know
06 to be different
07 when

Fill in the blanks using one of the words that you learned in Day 43.
(Please refer to page 017 to review how to conjugate verbs/adjectives.)

1. 제가 좋아하는 (   )은 검은색이에요.   My favorite color is black.

2. 제가 좋아하는 색깔은 (   )이에요.   My favorite color is black.

3. 검은색 (   ), 검은색 자동차,
   검은색 가방 등등 검은색 물건이 많아요.   I have many things that are black, such as a black wallet, a black car, a black bag, and so on.

4. 검은색 지갑, 검은색 (   ),
   검은색 가방 등등 검은색 물건이 많아요.   I have many things that are black, such as a black wallet, a black car, a black bag, and so on.

5. 검은색 지갑, 검은색 자동차, 검은색
   (   ) 등등 검은색 물건이 많아요.   I have many things that are black, such as a black wallet, a black car, a black bag, and so on.

6. (   )부터 검은색을 좋아했는지는
   몰라요.   I don't know when I started liking the color black.

7. 언제부터 검은색을 좋아했는지는
   (   ).   I don't know when I started liking the color black.

8. 그런데 저희 (   )은 하얀색을
   좋아해요.   But my older brother likes the color white.

9. 그런데 저희 형은 (   )을 좋아해요.   But my older brother likes the color white.

10. 저랑 저희 형은 성격이 많이 (   ).   My personality and my brother's personality are very different.

DAY 44

Check off the words
you already know.

- ○ 착하다 ○
- ○ 문제 ○
- ○ 연필 ○
- ○ 빌려주다 ○
- ○ 펜 ○
- ○ 또 ○
- ○ 이유 ○
- ○ 미치다 ○
- ○ 나쁘다 ○
- ○ 아니다 ○

After you study these words, come back and
check off the ones you have memorized.

LET'S WARM UP!

Imagine the situation in the story below to help you remember the ten Korean words in context.

착하다
My friend is very <u>kind-hearted</u>.

문제
But there is one <u>matter</u>.

빌려주다 연필
When I <u>lend</u> him a   <u>pencil</u>, he always loses them.

펜   또
Yesterday, I lent him a <u>pen</u>. He lost it <u>again</u>.

이유   미치다
I don't know <u>why</u>. It's driving me <u>crazy</u>.

아니다 나쁘다
He is <u>not</u> a   <u>bad</u> person.

LET'S KEEP THE BALL ROLLING!

Word	Meaning	Related Words	Meaning
착하다 *cha-ka-da*	to be nice, to be kind-hearted	마음이 착하다 *ma-eu-mi cha-ka-da*	to be kind-hearted
		착한 일 *cha-kan il*	nice deed
		착한 사람 *cha-kan sa-ram*	nice person, kind-hearted person
문제 *mun-je*	problem, matter	문제가 있다 *mun-je-ga it-tta*	to have a problem
		문제가 생기다 *mun-je-ga saeng-gi-da*	a problem occurs, a problem happens
		중요한 문제 *jung-yo-han mun-je*	important problem, important matter
		문제없다 *mun-je-eop-tta*	to have no problem
연필 *yeon-pil*	pencil	연필 한 자루 *yeon-pil han ja-ru*	one pencil
		연필로 쓰다 *yeon-pil-lo sseu-da*	to write with a pencil
		연필을 깎다 *yeon-pi-reul kkak-tta*	to sharpen a pencil

빌려주다	to lend	펜을 빌려주다	to lend a pen
bil-lyeo-ju-da		pe-neul bil-lyeo-ju-da	
		빌려준 돈	money that one has lent
		bil-lyeo-jun don	
		돌려주다	to return
		dol-lyeo-ju-da	
		갚다	to pay back
		gap-tta	

펜	pen	펜이 잘 나오다	the pen doesn't work well
pen		pe-ni jal na-o-da	
		펜이 안 나오다	the pen doesn't work
		pe-ni an na-o-da	
		펜을 다 쓰다	to use up a pen
		pe-neul da sseu-da	
		검은색 펜	black pen
		geo-meun-saek pen	

또	again	또 잃어버리다	to lose again
tto		tto i-reo-beo-ri-da	
		또 있다	to have another
		tto it-tta	
		다시	again
		da-si	

이유	reason	이유를 모르다	to not know the reason
i-yu		i-yu-reul mo-reu-da	
		이유가 없다	to have no reason
		i-yu-ga eop-tta	
		이유를 물어보다	to ask the reason
		i-yu-reul mu-reo-bo-da	

미치다 *mi-chi-da*	to be crazy, to go crazy	미치겠다 *mi-chi-get-tta*	something is driving me crazy
		미친 사람 *mi-chin sa-ram*	crazy person
		미친 듯이 *mi-chin deu-si*	like crazy
나쁘다 *na-ppeu-da*	to be bad	나쁜 사람 *na-ppeun sa-ram*	bad person
		기분이 나쁘다 *gi-bu-ni na-ppeu-da*	to feel offended
		나쁘게 *na-ppeu-ge*	badly
아니다 *a-ni-da*	to not be	사실이 아니다 *sa-si-ri a-ni-da*	to not be true
		사람이 아니다 *sa-ra-mi a-ni-da*	to not be human

Read the story again, but this time in Korean!

제 친구는 정말 **착해요.**

그런데 한 가지 **문제**가 있어요.

제가 **연필**을 **빌려주면** 항상 잃어버려요.

어제는 **펜**을 빌려줬어요. **또** 잃어버렸어요.

이유를 모르겠어요. **미치겠어요.**

나쁜 아이는 **아니에요.**

Translation

My friend is very kind-hearted. But there is one matter.
When I lend him a pencil, he always loses them.
Yesterday, I lent him a pen. He lost it again. I don't know why.
It's driving me crazy. He is not a bad person.

Match each Korean word to its English translation.

연필 ·   · pen

펜 ·   · to be bad

이유 ·   · pencil

문제 ·   · to lend

아니다 ·   · to be nice, to be kind-hearted

빌려주다 ·   · to be crazy, to go crazy

착하다 ·   · problem, matter

나쁘다 ·   · reason

미치다 ·   · to not be

또 ·   · again

Crossword Puzzle

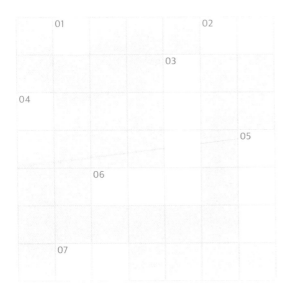

01 again
02 reason
03 to lend
04 pen
05 to be bad
06 to not be
07 problem, matter

Fill in the blanks using one of the words that you learned in Day 44.
(Please refer to page 017 to review how to conjugate verbs/adjectives.)

1. 제 친구는 정말 (   ).   My friend is very kind-hearted.

2. 그런데 한 가지 (   )가 있어요.   But there is one matter.

3. 제가 (   )을 빌려주면 항상   When I lend him a pencil, he always loses
    잃어버려요.   them.

4. 제가 연필을 (   ) 항상   When I lend him a pencil, he always loses
    잃어버려요.   them.

5. 어제는 (   )을 빌려줬어요.   Yesterday, I lent him a pen.

6. (   ) 잃어버렸어요.   He lost it again.

7. (   )를 모르겠어요.   I don't know why.

8. (   ).   It's driving me crazy.

9. (   ) 아이는 아니에요.   He is not a bad person.

10. 나쁜 아이는 (   ).   He is not a bad person.

DAY 45

Check off the words
you already know.

- ○ 결혼 ○
- ○ 식물 ○
- ○ 카드 ○
- ○ 정하다 ○
- ○ 싸다 ○
- ○ 끓이다 ○
- ○ 달다 ○
- ○ 쓰다 03 ○
- ○ 실망 ○
- ○ 계획 ○

After you study these words, come back and
check off the ones you have memorized.

Day 45

LET'S WARM UP!

Imagine the situation in the story below to help you remember the ten Korean words in context.

결혼   식물
I changed a lot after <u>getting married</u>. I grow <u>plants</u> at home.

정하다   카드
I <u>decided</u> not to use credit <u>cards</u> and use cash (instead).

싸다
I go to the market where they sell stuff for <u>cheap</u>.

끓이다
I <u>boil</u> soup and cook rice.

But I am still not good at making other foods.

달다   쓰다 ⁰³
Some dishes are too <u>sweet</u>. Some dishes are too <u>bitter</u>.

실망   계획
But I don't get <u>disappointed</u>. I <u>plan</u> to practice more.

LET'S KEEP THE BALL ROLLING!

Word	Meaning	Related Words	Meaning
결혼 *gyeo-ron*	marriage, wedding	**결혼하다** *gyeo-ro-na-da*	to get married
		결혼식 *gyeo-ron-sik*	wedding ceremony
		결혼 생활 *gyeo-ron saeng-hwal*	married life
식물 *sing-mul*	plant	**식물을 기르다** *sing-mu-reul gi-reu-da*	to grow a plant
		식물이 자라다 *sing-mu-ri ja-ra-da*	a plant grows
		동물 *dong-mul*	animal
카드 *ka-deu*	card	**신용 카드** *si-nyong ka-deu*	credit card
		생일 카드 *saeng-il ka-deu*	birthday card
		카드를 쓰다 *ka-deu-reul sseu-da*	to use a card, to write a card

정하다
jeong-ha-da

to decide, to choose

하기로 정하다
ha-gi-ro jeong-ha-da

to decide to do

장소를 정하다
jang-so-reul jeong-ha-da

to decide on a place

정해지다
jeong-hae-ji-da

to be decided

정한 날짜
jeong-han nal-jja

date that has been chosen

싸다
ssa-da

to be cheap,
to be inexpensive

과일이 싸다
gwa-i-ri ssa-da

fruit is cheap

싼 물건
ssan mul-geon

cheap things

싸게 팔다
ssa-ge pal-da

to sell inexpensively

비싸다
bi-ssa-da

to be expensive

끓이다
kkeu-ri-da

to boil

끓다
kkeul-ta

to boil

국을 끓이다
gu-geul kkeu-ri-da

to boil soup

차를 끓이다
cha-reul kkeu-ri-da

to boil tea

끓여 먹다
kkeu-ryeo meok-tta

to boil and eat

달다 *dal-da*	to be sweet	초콜릿이 달다 *cho-kol-li-si dal-da*	chocolate is sweet
		단 음식 *dan eum-sik*	sweet food
		단맛 *dan-mat*	sweet taste
쓰다 [03] *sseu-da*	to be bitter	커피가 쓰다 *keo-pi-ga sseu-da*	coffee is bitter
		쓴 약 *sseun yak*	bitter medicine
		쓴맛 *sseun-mat*	bitter taste
실망 *sil-mang*	disappointment	실망하다 *sil-mang-ha-da*	to be disappointed
		실망이 크다 *sil-mang-i keu-da*	to be greatly disappointed
계획 *gye-hoek*	plan	계획이 있다 *gye-hoe-gi it-tta*	to have a plan
		계획을 짜다 *gye-hoe-geul jja-da*	to make a plan
		할 계획이다 *hal gye-hoe-gi-da*	to be planning to
		계획하다 *gye-hoe-ka-da*	to plan

LET'S REVIEW!

Read the story again, but this time in Korean!

저는 **결혼**한 다음에 많이 달라졌어요. 집에서 **식물**을 길러요.

카드를 안 쓰고 현금을 쓰기로 **정했어요.**

물건을 **싸게** 파는 시장에 가요. 국을 **끓이고** 밥을 해요.

하지만 다른 음식은 아직 잘 못 해요.

어떤 음식은 너무 **달아요.** 어떤 음식은 너무 **써요.**

그래도 **실망**하지 않아요. 더 연습할 **계획**이에요.

Translation

I changed a lot after getting married. I grow plants at home.
I decided not to use credit cards and use cash (instead). I go to the
market where they sell stuff for cheap. I boil soup and cook rice.
But I am still not good at making other foods. Some dishes are too
sweet. Some dishes are too bitter. But I don't get disappointed.
I plan to practice more.

Match each Korean word to its English translation.

카드 ·   · to decide, to choose

달다 ·   · disappointment

계획 ·   · plant

결혼 ·   · to be bitter

실망 ·   · marriage, wedding

끓이다 ·   · card

식물 ·   · to boil

정하다 ·   · to be cheap, to be inexpensive

쓰다 03 ·   · to be sweet

싸다 ·   · plan

Crossword Puzzle

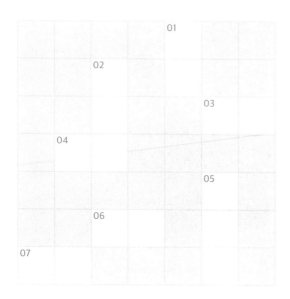

01 plant
02 to decide, to choose
03 disappointment
04 to be cheap, to be inexpensive
05 to boil
06 plan
07 card

Fill in the blanks using one of the words that you learned in Day 45.
(Please refer to page 017 to review how to conjugate verbs/adjectives.)

1. 저는 ( )한 다음에 많이 달라졌어요. I changed a lot after getting married.

2. 집에서 ( )을 길러요. I grow plants at home.

3. ( )를 안 쓰고 현금을 쓰기로 I decided not to use credit cards and use
   정했어요. cash (instead).

4. 카드를 안 쓰고 현금을 I decided not to use credit cards and use
   쓰기로 ( ). cash (instead).

5. 물건을 ( ) 파는 시장에 가요. I go to the market where they sell stuff for cheap.

6. 국을 ( ) 밥을 해요. I boil soup and cook rice.

7. 어떤 음식은 너무 ( ). Some dishes are too sweet.

8. 어떤 음식은 너무 ( ). Some dishes are too bitter.

9. 그래도 ( )하지 않아요. But I don't get disappointed.

10. 더 연습할 ( )이에요. I plan to practice more.

Check off the words
you already know.

○ 팔다

○ 털

○ 반지

○ 짧다

○ 때

○ 라디오

○ 유리

○ 신문

○ 종이

○ 인사

After you study these words, come back and
check off the ones you have memorized.

Day 46

LET'S WARM UP!

Imagine the situation in the story below to help you remember the ten Korean words in context.

팔다

I run a clothing store. I <u>sell</u> women's clothes and men's clothes.

털   반지

In winter, I even sell <u>woolen</u> hats. I also sell <u>rings</u> and necklaces.

짧다

These days, <u>short</u> skirts sell well.

때   라디오

<u>When</u> there are no customers, I listen to the <u>radio</u>.

유리

I also wipe down the <u>glass</u> windows of the store.

신문   종이

I normally wipe the glass windows with <u>newspaper</u> or <u>paper</u>.

인사

When a customer comes, I <u>greet</u> them cheerfully.

LET'S KEEP THE BALL ROLLING!

Word	Meaning	Related Words	Meaning
팔다 pal-da	to sell	**옷을 팔다** o-seul pal-da	to sell clothes
		파는 물건 pa-neun mul-geon	stuff that one sells
		팔리다 pal-li-da	to be sold, to get sold
		사다 sa-da	to buy
털 teol	fur, hair	**털이 많다** teo-ri man-ta	to be furry, to have a lot of hair/fur
		털이 부드럽다 teo-ri bu-deu-reop-tta	the fur is soft
		털모자 teol-mo-ja	woolen hat
반지 ban-ji	ring	**반지를 끼다** ban-ji-reul kki-da	to put on a ring
		반지를 빼다 ban-ji-reul ppae-da	to take off a ring
		금반지 geum-ban-ji	gold ring
		커플 반지 keo-peul ban-ji	couple ring (for boyfriends and girlfriends)

짧다 *jjal-tta*	to be short	다리가 짧다 *da-ri-ga jjal-tta*	one's legs are short
		밤이 짧다 *ba-mi jjal-tta*	the night is short
		짧은 치마 *jjal-beun chi-ma*	short skirt
		짧은 머리 *jjal-beun meo-ri*	short hair
때 *ttae*	time, when	때와 장소 *ttae-wa jang-so*	time and place
		손님이 없을 때 *son-ni-mi eop-sseul ttae*	when there are no customers
		방학 때 *bang-hak ttae*	during school break
		점심때 *jeom-sim-ttae*	at lunch
라디오 *ra-di-o*	radio	라디오를 듣다 *ra-di-o-reul deut-tta*	to listen to the radio
		라디오에 출연하다 *ra-di-o-e chu-ryeo-na-da*	to appear on the radio
		라디오 주파수 *ra-di-o ju-pa-su*	radio frequency
유리 *yu-ri*	glass	유리가 깨지다 *yu-ri-ga kkae-ji-da*	the glass breaks
		유리로 만들다 *yu-ri-ro man-deul-da*	to make (something) with glass
		유리창 *yu-ri-chang*	glass window
		유리컵 *yu-ri-keop*	glass cup

신문 *sin-mun*	newspaper	신문을 읽다 *sin-mu-neul ik-tta*	to read the newspaper
		신문에 나다 *sin-mu-ne na-da*	to be in the newspaper
		신문 기사 *sin-mun gi-sa*	newspaper article

종이 *jong-i*	paper	종이를 찢다 *jong-i-reul jjit-tta*	to tear paper
		종이에 적다 *jong-i-e jeok-tta*	to write down on paper
		종이 한 장 *jong-i han jang*	a piece of paper
		종이컵 *jong-i-keop*	paper cup

인사 *in-sa*	greeting	인사를 잘하다 *in-sa-reul ja-ra-da*	to greet people well, to be diligent in greeting people
		작별 인사 *jak-ppyeol in-sa*	farewell message, good-bye
		인사말 *in-sa-mal*	words of greeting
		인사하다 *in-sa-ha-da*	to greet

Read the story again, but this time in Korean!

저는 옷 가게를 해요. 여자 옷이랑 남자 옷을 **팔아요.**

겨울에는 **털**모자도 팔아요. **반지**랑 목걸이도 팔아요.

요즘에는 **짧은** 치마가 잘 팔려요.

손님이 없을 **때**는 **라디오**를 들어요.

가게 **유리**창을 닦기도 해요.

유리창은 보통 **신문**이나 **종이**로 닦아요.

손님이 오면 밝게 **인사**해요.

Translation

I run a clothing store. I sell women's clothes and men's clothes. In winter, I even sell woolen hats. I also sell rings and necklaces. These days, short skirts sell well. When there are no customers, I listen to the radio. I also wipe down the glass windows of the store. I normally wipe the glass windows with newspaper or paper. When a customer comes, I greet them cheerfully.

Match each Korean word to its English translation.

때 ·   · greeting

짧다 ·   · to sell

인사 ·   · fur, hair

종이 ·   · ring

팔다 ·   · radio

신문 ·   · glass

털 ·   · to be short

유리 ·   · time, when

반지 ·   · paper

라디오 ·   · newspaper

Crossword Puzzle

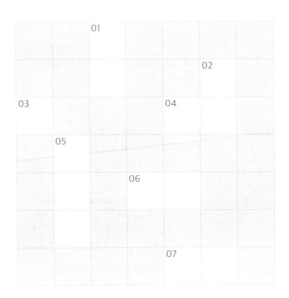

01 greeting
02 to be short
03 time, when
04 to sell
05 radio
06 newspaper
07 paper

Fill in the blanks using one of the words that you learned in Day 46.
(Please refer to page 017 to review how to conjugate verbs/adjectives.)

1. 여자 옷이랑 남자 옷을 (   ).

   I sell women's clothes and men's clothes.

2. 겨울에는 (   )모자도 팔아요.

   In winter, I even sell woolen hats.

3. (   )랑 목걸이도 팔아요.

   I also sell rings and necklaces.

4. 요즘에는 (   ) 치마가 잘 팔려요.

   These days, short skirts sell well.

5. 손님이 없을 (   )는 라디오를
   들어요.

   When there are no customers, I listen to the radio.

6. 손님이 없을 때는 (   )를 들어요.

   When there are no customers, I listen to the radio.

7. 가게 (   )창을 닦기도 해요.

   I also wipe down the glass windows of the store.

8. 유리창은 보통 (   )이나 종이로
   닦아요.

   I normally wipe the glass windows with newspaper or paper.

9. 유리창은 보통 신문이나 (   )로
   닦아요.

   I normally wipe the glass windows with newspaper or paper.

10. 손님이 오면 밝게 (   )해요.

    When a customer comes, I greet them cheerfully.

DAY 47

Check off the words you already know.

- ○ 쌍둥이 ○
- ○ 어리다 ○
- ○ 비슷하다 ○
- ○ 생각하다 ○
- ○ 쉽다 ○
- ○ 안경 ○
- ○ 입 ○
- ○ 멀다 ○
- ○ 뒤 ○
- ○ 실수 ○

After you study these words, come back and check off the ones you have memorized.

Day 47

LET'S WARM UP!

....

Imagine the situation in the story below to help you remember the ten Korean words in context.

쌍둥이   어리다

There are <u>twin</u> brothers at our school. When they were <u>little</u>, they

비슷하다

were very much the same. Now, they just look <u>similar</u>.

생각하다   쉽다

They <u>think</u> similarly, too. But you can <u>easily</u> distinguish them.

안경

The older brother wears <u>glasses</u>. The younger brother has a mole

입   멀다

next to his <u>mouth</u>. But, if you look from <u>afar</u>, you can't easily tell.

뒤

If you also look from <u>behind</u>, you can't know for sure.

실수

You might make a <u>mistake</u>.

LET'S KEEP THE BALL ROLLING!

Word	Meaning	Related Words	Meaning
쌍둥이 *ssang-dung-i*	twin	쌍둥이 형제 *ssang-dung-i hyeong-je*	twin brother
		쌍둥이를 낳다 *ssang-dung-i-reul na-ta*	to give birth to twins
		세쌍둥이 *se-ssang-dung-i*	triplets
어리다 *eo-ri-da*	to be young	나이가 어리다 *na-i-ga eo-ri-da*	to be young
		세 살 어리다 *se sal eo-ri-da*	to be three years younger
		어렸을 때 *eo-ryeo-sseul ttae*	when one was young
		어린 시절 *eo-rin si-jeol*	one's childhood
비슷하다 *bi-seu-ta-da*	to be similar	많이 비슷하다 *ma-ni bi-seu-ta-da*	to be quite similar
		친구랑 비슷하다 *chin-gu-rang bi-seu-ta-da*	to be similar to a friend
		비슷한 노래 *bi-seu-tan no-rae*	similar song
		비슷하게 생기다 *bi-seu-ta-ge saeng-gi-da*	to look similar

생각하다 saeng-ga-ka-da	to think	쉽게 생각하다 swip-kke saeng-ga-ka-da	to think easily, to think lightly of something
		잘 생각하다 jal saeng-ga-ka-da	to think well
		생각 saeng-gak	thought
		생각 중이다 saeng-gak jung-i-da	to be thinking
쉽다 swip-tta	to be easy	시험이 쉽다 si-heo-mi swip-tta	the exam is easy
		쉬운 문제 swi-un mun-je	easy question
		쉽게 구별하다 swip-kke gu-byeo-ra-da	to easily distinguish
안경 an-gyeong	glasses	안경을 쓰다 an-gyeong-eul sseu-da	to put on one's glasses
		안경을 벗다 an-gyeong-eul beot-tta	to take off one's glasses
		안경테 an-gyeong-te	eyeglass frames
		동그란 안경 dong-geu-ran an-gyeong	round glasses
입 ip	mouth	입을 벌리다 i-beul beol-li-da	to open one's mouth
		입을 다물다 i-beul da-mul-da	to close one's mouth
		입 냄새 ip naem-sae	breath smell
		입술 ip-ssul	lips

멀다 *meol-da*	to be far	집이 멀다 *ji-bi meol-da*	one's house is far away
		거리가 멀다 *geo-ri-ga meol-da*	the distance is far
		멀리 *meol-li*	far away
		멀리서 보다 *meol-li-seo bo-da*	to see from far away
뒤 *dwi*	behind, after	뒤에 있다 *dwi-e it-tta*	to be behind
		뒤에서 보다 *dwi-e-seo bo-da*	to look from behind
		며칠 뒤 *myeo-chil dwi*	a few days after
		앞 *ap*	front
실수 *sil-ssu*	mistake	작은 실수 *ja-geun sil-ssu*	small mistake
		말실수 *mal-sil-ssu*	slip of the tongue
		실수하다 *sil-ssu-ha-da*	to make a mistake
		실수로 *sil-ssu-ro*	by mistake

LET'S REVIEW!

Read the story again, but this time in Korean!

저희 학교에는 **쌍둥이** 형제가 있어요.

어렸을 때는 아주 똑같았어요. 지금은 **비슷하게** 생겼어요.

생각하는 것도 비슷해요. 하지만 **쉽게** 구별할 수 있어요.

형은 **안경**을 썼어요. 동생은 **입** 옆에 점이 있어요.

그런데 **멀리서** 보면 잘 몰라요. **뒤**에서 봐도 잘 몰라요.

실수할 수도 있어요.

Translation

There are twin brothers at our school. When they were little, they were very much the same. Now, they just look similar. They think similarly, too. But you can easily distinguish them. The older brother wears glasses. The younger brother has a mole next to his mouth. But, if you look from afar, you can't easily tell. If you also look from behind, you can't know for sure. You might make a mistake.

Match each Korean word to its English translation.

비슷하다 ·   · to be far

입 ·   · glasses

실수 ·   · to think

쌍둥이 · · to be young

뒤 · · twin

쉽다 · · mistake

멀다 · · behind, after

어리다 · · to be similar

안경 · · to be easy

생각하다 · · mouth

Crossword Puzzle

01 behind, after
02 mistake
03 mouth
04 to be similar
05 twin
06 to be young
07 to be easy

....

Fill in the blanks using one of the words that you learned in Day 47.
(Please refer to page 017 to review how to conjugate verbs/adjectives.)

1. 저희 학교에는 (   ) 형제가 있어요.　　There are twin brothers at our school.

2. (   ) 때는 아주 똑같았어요.　　When they were little, they were very much the same.

3. 지금은 (   ) 생겼어요.　　Now, they just look similar.

4. (   ) 것도 비슷해요.　　They think similarly, too.

5. 하지만 (   ) 구별할 수 있어요.　　But you can easily distinguish them.

6. 형은 (   )을 썼어요.　　The older brother wears glasses.

7. 동생은 (   ) 옆에 점이 있어요.　　The younger brother has a mole next to his mouth.

8. 그런데 (   ) 보면 잘 몰라요.　　But, if you look from afar, you can't easily tell.

9. (   )에서 봐도 잘 몰라요.　　If you also look from behind, you can't know for sure.

10. (   )할 수도 있어요.　　You might make a mistake.

DAY 48

Check off the words you already know.

○ 축구 ○

○ 농구 ○

○ 야구 ○

○ 지나다 ○

○ 이기다 ○

○ 팔 ○

○ 비밀 ○

○ 발가락 ○

○ 영어 ○

○ 사전 ○

After you study these words, come back and check off the ones you have memorized.

LET'S WARM UP!

Imagine the situation in the story below to help you remember the ten Korean words in context.

축구 농구 야구
I like all kinds of sports. I like <u>soccer</u>, <u>basketball</u>, <u>baseball</u>,

지나다   이기다
all of them! I played basketball <u>last</u> weekend. My team <u>won</u>.

팔   비밀
But I hurt my <u>arm</u>. I kept it a <u>secret</u> from my mom.

발가락
When I was little, I liked playing soccer, but I hurt my <u>toes</u> often.

So, my mom didn't like me playing sports.

영어
My mom likes it the most when I study <u>English</u>.

사전
I received an English <u>dictionary</u> as my birthday present.

LET'S KEEP THE BALL ROLLING!

Word	Meaning	Related Words	Meaning
축구 *chuk-kku*	soccer	**축구를 하다** *chuk-kku-reul ha-da*	to play soccer
		축구 선수 *chuk-kku seon-su*	soccer player
		축구팀 *chuk-kku-tim*	soccer team
농구 *nong-gu*	basketball	**농구를 하다** *nong-gu-reul ha-da*	to play basketball
		농구공 *nong-gu-gong*	basketball ball
		농구장 *nong-gu-jang*	basketball court
야구 *ya-gu*	baseball	**야구를 하다** *ya-gu-reul ha-da*	to play baseball
		야구 경기 *ya-gu gyeong-gi*	baseball game
		야구 시즌 *ya-gu si-jeun*	baseball season
		프로 야구 *peu-ro ya-gu*	professional baseball

지나다	to pass	시간이 지나다	time passes
ji-na-da		si-ga-ni ji-na-da	
		날짜가 지나다	dates pass
		nal-jja-ga ji-na-da	
		지난 주말	past weekend
		ji-nan ju-mal	
		지난달	past month
		ji-nan-dal	
		지난주	past week
		ji-nan-ju	

이기다	to win	쉽게 이기다	to win easily
i-gi-da		swip-kke i-gi-da	
		겨우 이기다	to barely manage to win
		gyeo-u i-gi-da	
		이긴 팀	winning team, team that won
		i-gin tim	
		지다	to lose
		ji-da	

팔	arm	팔을 다치다	to hurt one's arm
pal		pa-reul da-chi-da	
		왼팔	left arm
		oen-pal	
		오른팔	right arm
		o-reun-pal	
		팔꿈치	elbow
		pal-kkum-chi	

비밀 *bi-mil*	secret	비밀번호 *bi-mil-beo-no*	password
		비밀 이야기 *bi-mil i-ya-gi*	secret, secret story
		비밀을 지키다 *bi-mi-reul ji-ki-da*	to keep a secret
		비밀로 하다 *bi-mil-lo ha-da*	to keep as a secret

| 발가락
bal-kka-rak | toe | 엄지 발가락
eom-ji bal-kka-rak | big toe |
| | | 발가락을 다치다
bal-kka-ra-geul da-chi-da | to hurt one's toe |

영어 *yeong-eo*	English (language)	영어를 배우다 *yeong-eo-reul bae-u-da*	to learn English
		영어를 잘하다 *yeong-eo-reul ja-ra-da*	to be good at English
		영어로 말하다 *yeong-eo-ro ma-ra-da*	to speak in English
		영어 사전 *yeong-eo sa-jeon*	English dictionary

사전 *sa-jeon*	dictionary	사전에서 찾다 *sa-jeo-ne-seo chat-tta*	to look up in a dictionary
		한영사전 *ha-nyeong-sa-jeon*	Korean-English dictionary
		전자사전 *jeon-ja-sa-jeon*	electronic dictionary

Read the story again, but this time in Korean!

저는 운동을 좋아해요. **축구, 농구, 야구** 다 좋아해요.

지난 주말에 농구를 했어요. 저희 팀이 **이겼어요.**

하지만 **팔**을 다쳤어요. 엄마한테는 **비밀**이에요.

어렸을 때는 축구를 좋아해서 **발가락**을 자주 다쳤어요.

그래서 엄마는 제가 운동하는 것을 싫어해요.

엄마는 제가 **영어** 공부하는 것을 제일 좋아해요.

엄마한테 생일 선물로 영어 **사전**을 받았어요.

Translation

I like all kinds of sports. I like soccer, basketball, baseball, all of them! I played basketball last weekend. My team won. But I hurt my arm. I kept it a secret from my mom. When I was little, I liked playing soccer, but I hurt my toes often. So, my mom didn't like me playing sports. My mom likes it the most when I study English. I received an English dictionary as my birthday present.

Match each Korean word to its English translation.

이기다 ·   · toe

지나다 ·   · secret

사전 ·   · arm

축구 ·   · basketball

영어 ·   · dictionary

발가락 ·   · baseball

비밀 ·   · to pass

농구 ·   · English (language)

야구 ·   · soccer

팔 ·   · to win

Crossword Puzzle

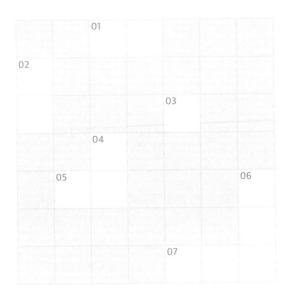

01 secret
02 dictionary
03 arm
04 baseball
05 soccer
06 to pass
07 to win

Fill in the blanks using one of the words that you learned in Day 48.
(Please refer to page 017 to review how to conjugate verbs/adjectives.)

1. (   ), 농구, 야구 다 좋아해요.   I like soccer, basketball, baseball, all of them!

2. 축구, (   ), 야구 다 좋아해요.   I like soccer, basketball, baseball, all of them!

3. 축구, 농구, (   ) 다 좋아해요.   I like soccer, basketball, baseball, all of them!

4. (   ) 주말에 농구를 했어요.   I played basketball last weekend.

5. 저희 팀이 (   ).   My team won.

6. 하지만 (   )을 다쳤어요.   But I hurt my arm.

7. 엄마한테는 (   )이에요.   I kept it a secret from my mom.

8. 어렸을 때는 축구를 좋아해서 (   )을 자주 다쳤어요.   When I was little, I liked playing soccer, but I hurt my toes often.

9. 엄마는 제가 (   ) 공부하는 것을 제일 좋아해요.   My mom likes it the most when I study English.

10. 엄마한테 생일 선물로 영어 (   )을 받았어요.   I received an English dictionary as my birthday present.

DAY 49

Check off the words you already know.

○ 주차장 ○

○ 고르다 ○

○ 표 ○

○ 세다 ○

○ 불 ○

○ 날다 ○

○ 지구 ○

○ 우주 ○

○ 알아듣다 ○

○ 바꾸다 ○

After you study these words, come back and check off the ones you have memorized.

Day 49

Imagine the situation in the story below to help you remember the ten Korean words in context.

주차장

I got out of the car in the <u>parking lot</u> of the movie theater. I went

고르다　　　표

up to the ticket counter and <u>chose</u> a movie. I bought a <u>ticket</u>.

세다

I went inside. There were not that many people. I <u>counted</u> the

불

number of people. There were ten people. The <u>lights</u> went out and

날다

the movie started. The main character <u>flew</u> around the sky. He left

지구　　우주

<u>Earth</u> and went to <u>space</u>. But the person next to me was loud, so

알아듣다 바꾸다

it was hard to <u>understand</u>. So, I <u>changed</u> seats.

LET'S KEEP THE BALL ROLLING!

Word	Meaning	Related Words	Meaning
주차장 *ju-cha-jang*	parking lot	주차장이 넓다 *ju-cha-jang-i neol-tta*	the parking lot is big
		무료 주차장 *mu-ryo ju-cha-jang*	free parking lot
		유료 주차장 *yu-ryo ju-cha-jang*	paid parking lot
		지하 주차장 *ji-ha ju-cha-jang*	underground parking lot
고르다 *go-reu-da*	to pick, to choose	세 개 중에서 고르다 *se gae jung-e-seo go-reu-da*	to choose out of three
		하나를 고르다 *ha-na-reul go-reu-da*	to choose one
		고르기 어렵다 *go-reu-gi eo-ryeop-tta*	to be hard to pick
표 *pyo*	ticket	표를 사다 *pyo-reul sa-da*	to buy a ticket
		표가 다 팔리다 *pyo-ga da pal-li-da*	the tickets are sold out
		표 두 장 *pyo du jang*	two tickets

세다
se-da

to count

숫자를 세다
sut-jja-reul se-da

to count numbers

돈을 세다
do-neul se-da

to count money

사람 수를 세다
sa-ram su-reul se-da

to count the number of people

세어 보다
se-eo bo-da

to count

불
bul

fire, light

불을 켜다
bu-reul kyeo-da

to turn on the light

불을 끄다
bu-reul kkeu-da

to turn off the light

산불
san-ppul

forest fire, wildfire

뜨거운 불
tteu-geo-un bul

hot fire

날다
nal-da

to fly

하늘을 날다
ha-neu-reul nal-da

to fly in the sky

새가 날다
sae-ga nal-da

a bird flies

날아가다
na-ra-ga-da

to fly somewhere

날개
nal-gae

wing

지구	Earth	지구에 살다	to live on Earth
ji-gu		*ji-gu-e sal-da*	
		지구가 돌다	the Earth rotates
		ji-gu-ga dol-da	
		태양	the Sun
		tae-yang	

우주	cosmos, universe, space	우주에 가다	to go to space
u-ju		*u-ju-e ga-da*	
		우주여행	space travel
		u-ju-yeo-haeng	
		우주선	spaceship
		u-ju-seon	

알아듣다	to understand	알아들을 수 없다	to not be able to understand
a-ra-deut-tta		*a-ra-deu-reul su eop-tta*	
		못 알아듣다	to not understand
		mot a-ra-deut-tta	
		잘 알아듣다	to understand well
		jal a-ra-deut-tta	
		알아듣기 힘들다	to be hard to understand
		a-ra-deut-kki him-deul-da	

바꾸다	to change	표를 바꾸다	to change tickets
ba-kku-da		*pyo-reul ba-kku-da*	
		이름을 바꾸다	to change one's name
		i-reu-meul ba-kku-da	
		바꾼 자리	seats that have been switched
		ba-kkun ja-ri	

LET'S REVIEW!

Read the story again, but this time in Korean!

영화관 **주차장**에 내렸어요.

매표소로 올라가서 영화를 **골랐어요.**

표를 샀어요. 안으로 들어갔어요. 사람들이 별로 없었어요.

사람 수를 **세어** 봤어요. 열 명 있었어요.

불이 꺼지고 영화가 시작됐어요. 주인공이 하늘을 **날았어요.**

지구를 떠나서 **우주**로 갔어요. 그런데 옆 사람이 시끄러워서

알아듣기 힘들었어요. 그래서 자리를 **바꿨어요.**

Translation

I got out of the car in the parking lot of the movie theater. I went up to the ticket counter and chose a movie. I bought a ticket. I went inside. There were not that many people. I counted the number of people. There were ten people. The lights went out and the movie started. The main character flew around the sky. He left Earth and went to space. But the person next to me was loud, so it was hard to understand. So, I changed seats.

Match each Korean word to its English translation.

불 ·	· to count
날다 ·	· to understand
바꾸다 ·	· cosmos, universe, space
우주 ·	· parking lot
주차장 ·	· to pick, to choose
세다 ·	· Earth
알아듣다 ·	· fire, light
고르다 ·	· ticket
지구 ·	· to fly
표 ·	· to change

Crossword Puzzle

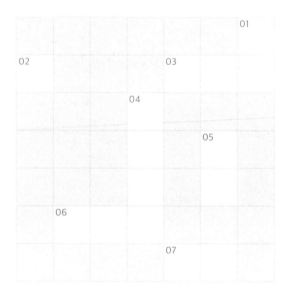

01 to count
02 ticket
03 to pick, to choose
04 to understand
05 Earth
06 to change
07 cosmos, universe, space

Fill in the blanks using one of the words that you learned in Day 49.
(Please refer to page 017 to review how to conjugate verbs/adjectives.)

1. 영화관 (   )에 내렸어요.   I got out of the car in the parking lot of the movie theater.

2. 매표소로 올라가서 영화를 (   ).   I went up to the ticket counter and chose a movie.

3. (   )를 샀어요.   I bought a ticket.

4. 사람 수를 (   ) 봤어요.   I counted the number of people.

5. (   )이 꺼지고 영화가 시작됐어요.   The lights went out and the movie started.

6. 주인공이 하늘을 (   ).   The main character flew around the sky.

7. (   )를 떠나서 우주로 갔어요.   He left Earth and went to space.

8. 지구를 떠나서 (   )로 갔어요.   He left Earth and went to space.

9. 그런데 옆 사람이 시끄러워서
    (   ) 힘들었어요.   But the person next to me was loud, so it was hard to understand.

10. 그래서 자리를 (   ).   So, I changed seats.

DAY 50

Check off the words
you already know.

○ 운전 ○

○ 느리다 ○

○ 내리다 ○

○ 열쇠 ○

○ 잡다 ○

○ 그것 ○

○ 가볍다 ○

○ 휴지 ○

○ 맞다 ○

○ 서다 ○

After you study these words, come back and
check off the ones you have memorized.

LET'S WARM UP!

Imagine the situation in the story below to help you remember the ten Korean words in context.

운전
I drove to the supermarket.

느리다 내리다
I slowly parked and got out of the car.

열쇠
I dropped my key. The key went under the car.

잡다
I reached down and grabbed the key.

그것 가볍다 휴지
But, it (what I picked up) was too light. It was trash.

맞다
I reached down again. This time, it was a key. It was indeed a key.

서다
People who were standing around were looking at me.

LET'S KEEP THE BALL ROLLING!

Word	Meaning	Related Words	Meaning
운전 *un-jeon*	driving	운전을 배우다 *un-jeo-neul bae-u-da*	to learn to drive
		운전하다 *un-jeo-na-da*	to drive
		차를 운전하다 *cha-reul un-jeo-na-da*	to drive a car
		운전면허 *un-jeon-myeo-neo*	driver's license
느리다 *neu-ri-da*	to be slow	말이 느리다 *ma-ri neu-ri-da*	to speak slowly
		시계가 느리다 *si-gye-ga neu-ri-da*	the clock is slow
		느리게 *neu-ri-ge*	slowly
		느리게 기어가다 *neu-ri-ge gi-eo-ga-da*	to crawl slowly
내리다 *nae-ri-da*	to get off/out of (a vehicle)	차에서 내리다 *cha-e-seo nae-ri-da*	to get out of a car
		서울에 내리다 *seo-u-re nae-ri-da*	to get off in Seoul
		타다 *ta-da*	to ride, to get in a vehicle

열쇠	key	열쇠를 잃어버리다	to lose a key
yeol-ssoe		*yeol-ssoe-reul i-reo-beo-ri-da*	
		열쇠를 떨어뜨리다	to drop a key
		yeol-ssoe-reul tteo-reo-tteu-ri-da	
		집 열쇠	house key
		jip yeol-ssoe	
		열쇠고리	keychain
		yeol-ssoe-go-ri	

잡다	to grab, to hold	손을 잡다	to hold someone's hand
jap-tta		*so-neul jap-tta*	
		손잡이를 잡다	to hold a handle/knob
		son-ja-bi-reul jap-tta	
		꼭 잡다	to hold firmly
		kkok jap-tta	
		놓다	to let go
		no-ta	

그것	it, that	그거	that, that thing
geu-geot		*geu-geo*	
		그게	that is
		geu-ge	
		그	the, that
		geu	
		이것	this thing
		i-geot	
		저것	that thing
		jeo-geot	

가볍다 ga-byeop-tta	to be light	가방이 가볍다 ga-bang-i ga-byeop-tta	the bag is light
		몸이 가볍다 mo-mi ga-byeop-tta	one's body is light
		가벼운 짐 ga-byeo-un jim	light luggage
		무겁다 mu-geop-tta	to be heavy

휴지 hyu-ji	tissue, toilet paper, trash	휴지 한 장 hyu-ji han jang	one tissue
		휴지통 hyu-ji-tong	trash can, rubbish bin
		화장실 hwa-jang-sil	bathroom

맞다 mat-tta	to be correct, to be right	답이 맞다 da-bi mat-tta	the answer is correct
		맞는 말 man-neun mal	words that are right/true
		틀리다 teul-li-da	to be wrong

서다 seo-da	to stand	서 있다 seo it-tta	to be standing
		일어서다 i-reo-seo-da	to stand up
		앉다 an-tta	to sit

Read the story again, but this time in Korean!

운전을 해서 마트에 갔어요.

느리게 주차를 하고 차에서 **내렸어요.**

열쇠를 떨어뜨렸어요. 열쇠가 차 아래로 들어갔어요.

손을 넣어서 열쇠를 **잡았어요.**

그런데 **그것**은 너무 **가벼웠어요.**

휴지였어요. 다시 손을 넣었어요. 이번에는 무거웠어요.

열쇠가 **맞았어요. 서** 있는 사람들이 저를 쳐다봤어요.

Translation

I drove to the supermarket. I slowly parked and got out of the car. I dropped my key. The key went under the car. I reached down and grabbed the key. But, it (what I picked up) was too light. It was trash. I reached down again. This time, it was a key. It was indeed a key. People who were standing around were looking at me.

Match each Korean word to its English translation.

열쇠 · · to be correct, to be right

서다 · · to be light

가볍다 · · to get off/out of (a vehicle)

운전 · · it, that

맞다 · · key

느리다 · · driving

그것 · · to stand

내리다 · · to grab, to hold

휴지 · · to be slow

잡다 · · tissue, toilet paper, trash

Crossword Puzzle

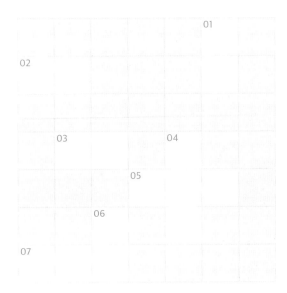

01 tissue, toilet paper, trash

02 it, that

03 key

04 to get off/out of (a vehicle)

05 to be slow

06 to grab, to hold

07 to be light

Fill in the blanks using one of the words that you learned in Day 50.
(Please refer to page 017 to review how to conjugate verbs/adjectives.)

1. ( )을 해서 마트에 갔어요.   I drove to the supermarket.

2. ( ) 주차를 하고 차에서 내렸어요.   I slowly parked and got out of the car.

3. 느리게 주차를 하고
   차에서 ( ).   I slowly parked and got out of the car.

4. ( )를 떨어뜨렸어요.   I dropped my key.

5. 손을 넣어서 열쇠를 ( ).   I reached down and grabbed the key.

6. 그런데 ( )은 너무 가벼웠어요.   But, it (what I picked up) was too light.

7. 그런데 그것은 너무 ( ).   But, it (what I picked up) was too light.

8. ( )였어요.   It was trash.

9. 열쇠가 ( ).   It was indeed a key.

10. ( ) 있는 사람들이 저를 쳐다봤어요.   People who were standing around were looking at me.

01 What is **"airport"** in Korean?

a. 궁항   b. 공항   c. 공헝   d. 공향

02 What does 대학교 mean in Korean?

a. high school   b. elementary school

c. university   d. middle school

03 What is the antonym of 가깝다?

a. 말다   b. 멀다   c. 몰다   d. 물다

04 How do you say **"English (language)"** in Korean?

a. 영어   b. 식물   c. 안경   d. 이유

05 Which of the following words is a place?

a. 비밀   b. 실수   c. 결혼   d. 편의점

06 Which word is most related to age?

    a. 아니다   b. 고르다   c. 어리다   d. 모르다

07 Besides "to write" or "to use", what other meaning does 쓰다 have?

    a. to be easy   b. to be cheap

    c. to be bitter   d. to be sweet

08 Choose the item that refers to a direction.

    a. 은행   b. 왼쪽   c. 지갑   d. 짧다

09 Choose the word that best replaces O.

> 축O = soccer   농O = basketball   야O = baseball

    a. 구   b. 고   c. 그   d. 가

10 Choose the word that best replaces O.

> 기차O = train station   지하철O = subway station

    a. 뒤   b. 또   c. 역   d. 털

11 "[something] boils" is 끓다 in Korean. What is **"to boil [something]"** in Korean?

a. 끓히다   b. 끓이다   c. 끓리다   d. 끓기다

12 Choose the term that is **NOT** a loanword from English.

a. 팔   b. 펜   c. 라디오   d. 카드

13 How do Korean boys address an older brother?

a. 입   b. 표   c. 불   d. 형

14 What is 신문 made of?

a. 가방   b. 종이   c. 열쇠   d. 반지

15 Which of the following does **NOT** refer to an action?

a. 들어가다   b. 내리다   c. 건너다   d. 나쁘다

16 Where do you park your car?

a. 오른쪽   b. 서점   c. 주차장   d. 발가락

17 Which of the following terms becomes a noun and keeps the same meaning if you dettach 하다?

    a. 생각하다   b. 비슷하다   c. 정하다   d. 착하다

18 Which of the following does **NOT** become a verb if you attach ‑하다?

    a. 운전   b. 실망   c. 계획   d. 연필

19 What does 길을 잃어버리다 mean in English?

    a. to find the way   b. to throw away
    c. to lose money   d. to get lost

20 What 색깔 is the 자동차 in the picture?

    a. 검은색
    b. 하얀색
    c. 빨간색
    d. none of the above

QUIZ
DAY 41-50

Answers : b c b a d / c c b a c / b a d b d / c a d d a

ANTONYMS ◈

ANSWERS ◈

INDEX ◈

ANTONYMS

Here is a compilation of words that have the opposite meaning from one another. All of these words appear in this book.

I, me	나	↔	너	you
busy	바쁘다	↔	한가하다	to be free, to not be busy
weekend	주말	↔	평일	weekday
to wear, to put on	입다	↔	벗다	to take off clothes
to be dirty	더럽다	↔	깨끗하다	to be clean
up	위	↔	아래	down
to be hungry	배고프다	↔	배부르다	to be full
to give	주다	↔	받다	to receive
teacher	선생님	↔	학생	student
to be a lot	많다	↔	적다	to be few, to be little
winter	겨울	↔	여름	summer
grandmother	할머니	↔	할아버지	grandfather
to go	가다	↔	오다	to come
to ride, to get on/in (a vehicle)	타다	↔	내리다	to get off/out of (a vehicle)
man	남자	↔	여자	woman
to fight, to argue	싸우다	↔	화해하다	to make up (with), to reconcile (with)

to lose	지다	↔	이기다	to win
to close	닫다	↔	열다	to open
to listen, to hear	듣다	↔	말하다	to talk, to tell
to exist, to have, to be	있다	↔	없다	to not have, to not be, to not exist
to live	살다	↔	죽다	to die
to be sad	슬프다	↔	기쁘다	to be glad, to be happy
younger brother/sister	동생	↔	형	older brother (for a boy)
to cry	울다	↔	웃다	to laugh, to smile
to borrow, to rent	빌리다	↔	빌려주다	to lend
to be cold	차갑다	↔	뜨겁다	to be hot
to teach	가르치다	↔	배우다	to learn
to write	쓰다	↔	지우다	to erase
to be good	좋다	↔	나쁘다	to be bad
to like	좋다	↔	싫다	to hate, to dislike, to be displeasing
to be fun	재미있다	↔	재미없다	to be boring
dad	아빠	↔	엄마	mom
to be delicious	맛있다	↔	맛없다	to be not tasty
to dislike, to hate	싫어하다	↔	좋아하다	to like

to be hot (temperature)	덥다	↔	춥다	to be cold
outside	밖	↔	안	inside
to go out	나가다	↔	들어오다	to come in
to turn on	켜다	↔	끄다	to turn off
to be cool (temperature)	시원하다	↔	따뜻하다	to be warm
night	밤	↔	낮	day, daytime
to lie down	눕다	↔	일어나다	to get up
afternoon	오후	↔	오전	morning
arrival	도착	↔	출발	departure
daughter	딸	↔	아들	son
to be the same	같다	↔	다르다	to be different
morning	아침	↔	저녁	evening
to forget	잊어버리다	↔	기억하다	to remember
to depart	출발하다	↔	도착하다	to arrive
countryside	시골	↔	도시	city
to be noisy	시끄럽다	↔	조용하다	to be quiet
to be high	높다	↔	낮다	to be low
to be dark	어둡다	↔	밝다	to be bright
to go down	내려가다	↔	올라가다	to go up

to be big	크다	↔	작다	to be small
to be long	길다	↔	짧다	to be short
to sit	앉다	↔	서다	to stand
to be heavy	무겁다	↔	가볍다	to be light
to put in	넣다	↔	빼다	to take out, to pull out
to be narrow	좁다	↔	넓다	to be wide
to be comfortable	편하다	↔	힘들다	to be difficult, to be tiring, to be hard
to be expensive	비싸다	↔	싸다	to be cheap
spring (season)	봄	↔	가을	fall, autumn
to know	알다	↔	모르다	to not know
to do well, to be good at	잘하다	↔	못하다	to not do well, to be bad at
failure	실패	↔	성공	success
to be difficult, to be hard	어렵다	↔	쉽다	to be easy
to send	보내다	↔	받다	to receive
to come out	나오다	↔	들어가다	to go in, to enter
to work	일하다	↔	쉬다	to rest
hand	손	↔	발	foot
to be difficult, to be tiring, to be hard	힘들다	↔	쉽다	to be easy

to buy	**사다**	↔	**팔다**	to sell
to lose, to misplace	**잃어버리다**	↔	**찾다**	to find
to ask	**물어보다**	↔	**대답하다**	to answer
to be close	**가깝다**	↔	**멀다**	to be far
right side, right-hand side	**오른쪽**	↔	**왼쪽**	left side, left-hand side
front	**앞**	↔	**뒤**	behind, after
black	**검은색**	↔	**하얀색**	white
to be sweet	**달다**	↔	**쓰다**	to be bitter
to be slow	**느리다**	↔	**빠르다**	to be quick
to grab, to hold	**잡다**	↔	**놓다**	to let go
to be correct, to be right	**맞다**	↔	**틀리다**	to be wrong

ANSWERS

Day 01 page 047

Match

주말 ──────── I, me
만나다 ──────── to meet
보통 ──────── movie
카페 ──────── to be busy
너무 ──────── café
바쁘다 ──────── we, our
나 ──────── usually, usual
회사원 ──────── weekend
영화 ──────── company employee
우리 ──────── too, very

Crossword Puzzle

		만		
		나		주 말
	바	쁘 다		
나				회
	우	리		사
				원
	보	통		

Fill in the blanks

01 제
02 회사원
03 너무
04 바빠요
05 저희
06 보통
07 주말
08 만나요
09 영화
10 카페

Day 02 page 055

Match

회사 ──────── make-up
물 ──────── to wear, to put on
일찍 ──────── clothes
세수 ──────── to drink
일어나다 ──────── water
마시다 ──────── every day
매일 ──────── company
옷 ──────── early
입다 ──────── to get up
화장 ──────── washing one's face

Crossword Puzzle

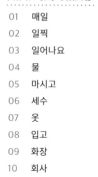

	물			입
		일 어 나 다		
화	장	찍		
			마	
	회	사	시	
			다	

Fill in the blanks

01 매일
02 일찍
03 일어나요
04 물
05 마시고
06 세수
07 옷
08 입고
09 화장
10 회사

Day 03   page 063

Match

공책 — notebook
더럽다 — to be dirty
청소 — cleaning
깨끗하다 — to be clean
시험 — text, exam
시작하다 — to begin, to start
필통 — pencil case
의자 — chair
책상 — desk
위 — up, top

pencil case
up, top
notebook
desk
to begin, to start
to be clean
text, exam
chair
to be dirty
cleaning

Crossword Puzzle

Fill in the blanks

01   시험
02   의자
03   책상
04   더러워요
05   위
06   청소
07   깨끗해요
08   공책
09   필통
10   시작해요

Day 04   page 071

Match

졸다 — to doze
무섭다 — to be scary
배고프다 — to be hungry
아까 — earlier
빵 — bread
선생님 — teacher
음료수 — beverage
주다 — to give
지금 — now
배부르다 — to be full

to be full
to doze
teacher
to be scary
to give
now
earlier
bread
beverage
to be hungry

Crossword Puzzle

Fill in the blanks

01   배고파요
02   아까
03   빵
04   음료수
05   줬어요
06   지금
07   배불러요
08   졸면
09   선생님
10   무서워요

Day 05   page 079

Match

어른 — adult, grown-up
공원 — park
아기 — baby
신기하다 — to be interesting
어떻게 — how
학교 — school
적다 — to be few, to be little
어린이 — child
가족 — family
많다 — to be a lot

to be a lot
adult, grown-up
child
to be few, to be little
park
family
baby
school
to be interesting
how

Crossword Puzzle

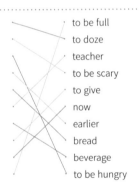

Fill in the blanks

01   어린이
02   학교
03   가족
04   공원
05   많았어요
06   어른
07   아기
08   적었어요
09   신기했어요
10   어떻게

Day 06 page 087

Match

동물	bus
가다	subway
겨울	to ride
타다	school vacation
놀다	winter
할머니	cat
방학	animal
지하철	to hang out
고양이	grandmother
버스	to go

Crossword Puzzle

					동	물
		놀				
	가	다				
지				할	머	니
하		방				
철		학		겨		
				울		

Fill in the blanks

01 겨울
02 방학
03 할머니
04 가요
05 버스
06 지하철
07 타요
08 고양이
09 동물
10 놀고

Day 07 page 095

Match

샴푸	underwear
티셔츠	socks
속옷	hairdryer
휴가	t-shirt
남자	vacation, leave
양말	pants
드라이기	man
바지	shampoo
린스	woman
여자	hair conditioner

Crossword Puzzle

				양	말
드	라	이	기		
					여
	린		남	자	
	스				
		티	셔	츠	
샴	푸				

Fill in the blanks

01 휴가
02 남자
03 여자
04 샴푸
05 린스
06 속옷
07 양말
08 드라이기
09 바지
10 티셔츠

Day 08 page 103

Match

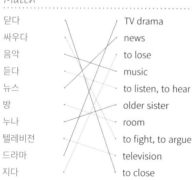

닫다	TV drama
싸우다	news
음악	to lose
듣다	music
뉴스	to listen, to hear
방	older sister
누나	room
텔레비전	to fight, to argue
드라마	television
지다	to close

Crossword Puzzle

		텔	레	비	전
	드				
	라	싸			
	마	우		누	나
		닫	다		
				듣	
			지	다	

Fill in the blanks

01 누나
02 텔레비전
03 드라마
04 뉴스
05 싸웠어요
06 져요
07 방
08 닫고
09 음악
10 들었어요

Day 09 page 111

Match

죽다
슬프다
동생
개
시간
있다
살다
이름
눈물
울다

· name
· time
· to live
· tear
· younger sibling
· dog
· to cry
· to exist, to have
· to be sad
· to die

Crossword Puzzle

Fill in the blanks

01 개
02 있었어요
03 이름
04 시간
05 살았어요
06 죽었어요
07 슬퍼요
08 동생
09 울었어요
10 눈물

Day 10 page 119

Match

수영
수건
차갑다
돈
어깨
빌리다
비누
가게
가르치다
힘

· store
· soap
· to teach
· strength, power
· swimming
· to be cold
· towel
· money
· shoulder
· to borrow, to rent

Crossword Puzzle

Fill in the blanks

01 수영
02 수건
03 가게
04 돈
05 빌렸어요
06 비누
07 차가웠어요
08 어깨
09 힘
10 가르쳐

Day 11 page 131

Match

쓰다 01
기쁘다
받다
무엇
목걸이
좋다
선물
친하다
귀고리
내일

· to receive
· to be good
· earrings
· necklace
· to write
· tomorrow
· to be close
· present, gift
· to be glad
· what

Crossword Puzzle

Fill in the blanks

01 내일
02 친한
03 쓸
04 받으면
05 기뻐할까요
06 선물
07 뭐
08 좋을까요
09 귀고리
10 목걸이

Day 12 page 139

Match

친구	to congratulate
축하하다	birthday
춤	friend
오늘	day, one day
먹다	song
생일	today
하루	classroom
재미있다	to eat
교실	dance
노래	to be fun

Crossword Puzzle

			오	늘		
먹						
다				축		
	노	래		하	루	
				하		
	재	미	있	다		친
						구

Fill in the blanks

01	오늘
02	생일
03	교실
04	먹었어요
05	친구
06	노래
07	춤
08	축하해
09	재미있는
10	하루

Day 13 page 147

Match

보다	restaurant
커피	to walk
음식	to see, to watch
식당	dad
아빠	to be happy
행복하다	sea, ocean
바다	coffee
별	to be delicious
맛있다	star
걷다	food

Crossword Puzzle

		커				
별		피			맛	
					있	
			행	복	하	다
	보					
바	다			음		
				식		

Fill in the blanks

01	아빠
02	바다
03	걸었어요
04	식당
05	맛있는
06	음식
07	커피
08	별
09	봤어요
10	행복했어요

Day 14 page 155

Match

집	to be hot
나가다	summer
얼음	to be cool
에어컨	to turn on
여름	to dislike, to hate
시원하다	outside
덥다	to go out
싫어하다	ice
켜다	house, home
밖	air conditioner

Crossword Puzzle

		싫				
		어			여	름
시	원	하	다			
		다				
	밖			켜		
		나	가	다		
	집					

Fill in the blanks

01	여름
02	싫어해요
03	더워요
04	밖
05	나가요
06	집
07	에어컨
08	켜요
09	시원한
10	얼음

Day 15 page 163

Match

눕다		bed
벌써		book
읽다		milk
냉장고		already
침대		bathroom
잠		to read
화장실		night
우유		to lie down
밤		sleep
책		refrigerator

Crossword Puzzle

		침			
냉		대		우	유
장					
고			밤		
	눕		화	장	실
읽	다				

Fill in the blanks

01 벌써
02 밤
03 침대
04 누워요
05 잠
06 화장실
07 책
08 읽어요
09 냉장고
10 우유

Day 16 page 171

Match

뜨겁다		computer
이메일		to charge
중요하다		to be hot
컵		e-mail
바르다		make-up product
컴퓨터		cup
충전하다		to be important
화장품		to apply, to put on
거울		laptop computer
노트북		mirror

Crossword Puzzle

거					
울		컵		충	
				전	
		중	요	하	다
		바		다	
		르			
뜨	겁	다		노	트	북

Fill in the blanks

01 컵
02 뜨거운
03 컴퓨터
04 이메일
05 노트북
06 충전해요
07 중요한
08 거울
09 화장품
10 발라요

Day 17 page 179

Match

부부		invitation
오후		arrival
딸		side, next to
같다		age
사이		kindergarten
옆		married couple
유치원		relationship
초대		afternoon
나이		daughter
도착		to be the same

Crossword Puzzle

	오	후			
				부	
		나		부	
		사	이		
딸			유		
			치		
	초	대	원		

Fill in the blanks

01 옆
02 부부
03 초대
04 오후
05 도착
06 딸
07 나이
08 같아요
09 유치원
10 사이

Day 18 page 187

Match

아침	game
점심	rice, food, meal
아들	to feel angry
화나다	morning
걱정	son
공부	why
밥	lunch
게임	study
왜	day of the week
요일	worry, concern

Crossword Puzzle

			밥	
	아	침		
	들			요
			화	일
걱	정		나	
			다	
				왜

Fill in the blanks

01 아들
02 게임
03 토요일
04 아침
05 점심
06 밥
07 화났어요
08 걱정
09 왜
10 공부

Day 19 page 195

Match

날짜	feeling
전화번호	calendar
빨리	to forget
느낌	shape
아래	date
출발하다	phone number
잊어버리다	reservation
달력	to depart
예약	fast, quickly
모양	down, below

Crossword Puzzle

아			모	양		
래		잊				
		어		달	력	
		버		느		
빨	리		낌			
	다					
			전	화	번	호

Fill in the blanks

01 느낌
02 달력
03 날짜
04 모양
05 아래
06 전화번호
07 잊어버렸어요
08 빨리
09 예약
10 출발해요

Day 20 page 203

Match

도시	to be quiet
등산	the sun
낮다	to be noisy
내려가다	to be high
어둡다	to go down
시골	hiking
시끄럽다	city
해	to be dark
높다	to be low
조용하다	countryside

Crossword Puzzle

		도			
내		시			해
려				시	
가				끄	
낮	다			럽	
	조	용	하	다	
등	산				

Fill in the blanks

01 시골
02 도시
03 시끄러워요
04 조용해요
05 등산
06 높은
07 낮은
08 해
09 어두워요
10 내려가요

Day 21 page 215

Match

키 — eye
얼굴 — to be big
웃다 — entertainer
귀엽다 — who
연예인 — one's height
눈 **01** — to be long
길다 — face
다리 — to laugh, to smile
크다 — to be cute
누구 — leg

Crossword Puzzle

Fill in the blanks

01 연예인
02 누구
03 키
04 커요
05 웃는
06 얼굴
07 귀여워요
08 눈
09 다리
10 길어요

Day 22 page 223

Match

비행기 — beginning
창문 — together
이따가 — to sit
구름 — later
앉다 — older sister
여행 — sky
언니 — travel
하늘 — cloud
처음 — window
같이 — airplane

Crossword Puzzle

Fill in the blanks

01 언니
02 같이
03 여행
04 비행기
05 처음
06 창문
07 앉았어요
08 이따가
09 하늘
10 구름

Day 23 page 231

Match

넣다 — to be heavy
엘리베이터 — to lift, to carry
무겁다 — to be narrow
빼다 — floor
들다 — contact
좁다 — to help
상자 — elevator
도와주다 — to put in
연락 — to take out
층 — box

Crossword Puzzle

Fill in the blanks

01 연락
02 도와줄
03 층
04 엘리베이터
05 무거운
06 상자
07 들고
08 넣어요
09 좁아요
10 빼요

Day 24   page 239

Match

거실 · · clock
그림 · · to be cool
혼자 · · wall
시계 · · alone
부엌 · · to make
쓰다 **02** · · moving
이사 · · living room
벽 · · painting, drawing
만들다 · · to use
멋있다 · · kitchen

Crossword Puzzle

			혼		
	만	자			
	들				
	쓰	다		벽	
					거
멋	있	다			실
		이	사		

Fill in the blanks

01 이사
02 혼자
03 멋있게
04 거실
05 벽
06 그림
07 시계
08 부엌
09 만들
10 쓸

Day 25   page 247

Match

부르다 · · to wash
편하다 · · all, every
버섯 · · to call
산책 · · mushroom
감사 · · gratitude
지우다 · · to be comfortable
씻다 · · to erase, to wash off
당근 · · walk
밝다 · · carrot
다 · · to be bright

Crossword Puzzle

			버	섯
		씻		
부	르	다	감	
			사	
				편
	당	근		하
			밝	다

Fill in the blanks

01 지워요
02 씻어요
03 버섯
04 당근
05 불러요
06 다
07 산책
08 밝아요
09 편해요
10 감사

Day 26   page 255

Match

사진 · · camera
비싸다 · · price
휴대폰 · · to be famous
연습하다 · · dream
유명하다 · · to learn
찍다 · · to be expensive
꿈 · · photo
가격 · · to practice
카메라 · · to take, to film
배우다 · · mobile phone

Crossword Puzzle

		유		가	격
꿈		명			
	연	습	하	다	
		다			
	카			찍	
	메	배	우	다	
	라				

Fill in the blanks

01 꿈
02 사진
03 배우고
04 카메라
05 가격
06 비싸요
07 휴대폰
08 찍어요
09 연습할
10 유명한

Day 27 page 263

Match

오다 · · weather
예쁘다 · · to be warm
딸기 · · flower
빨간색 · · to come
과일 · · strawberry
봄 · · to be pretty
날씨 · · red (color)
좋아하다 · · fruit
꽃 · · spring (season)
따뜻하다 · · to like

Crossword Puzzle

Fill in the blanks

01 봄
02 왔어요
03 날씨
04 따뜻해요
05 예쁜
06 꽃
07 딸기
08 빨간색
09 좋아하는
10 과일

Day 28 page 271

Match

눈 02 · · to be cold
자주 · · inside
전화하다 · · wind
목도리 · · to wait
장갑 · · scarf
기다리다 · · snow
알다 · · glove
바람 · · often
안 · · to know
춥다 · · to call

Crossword Puzzle

자 주
눈 기
다
리
알 다 춥
전 화 하 다
바 람

Fill in the blanks

01 기다리고
02 눈
03 바람
04 추워요
05 자주
06 안
07 전화했어요
08 알아요
09 장갑
10 목도리

Day 29 page 279

Match

못하다 · · potato
양파 · · knife
칼 · · to do well
썰다 · · taste
맛 · · love
배달 · · onion
잘하다 · · to not do well
손가락 · · delivery
감자 · · finger
사랑 · · to chop, to cut

Crossword Puzzle

Fill in the blanks

01 잘해요
02 맛
03 못해요
04 사랑
05 양파
06 감자
07 칼
08 썰었어요
09 손가락
10 배달

Day 30　　page 287

Match

베개 — pillow
쓰레기 — trash
준비하다 — to prepare
손님 — guest
빨래 — laundry
버리다 — to throw away
과자 — snack
설거지 — doing the dishes
이불 — blanket
시장 — market

laundry
doing the dishes
blanket
pillow
guest
trash
market
snack
to prepare
to throw away

Crossword Puzzle

	준			빨	래
	비				
	하				
버	리	다	베		
			개		설
	시	장			거
		과	자		지

Fill in the blanks

01 손님
02 빨래
03 설거지
04 이불
05 베개
06 쓰레기
07 버렸어요
08 시장
09 과자
10 준비할 거예요

Day 31　　page 299

Match

실패 — failure
쇼핑 — shopping
어렵다 — to be difficult
모자 — hat, cap
치마 — skirt
인터넷 — the Internet
주문하다 — to order
다음 — next
성공 — success
작다 — to be small

to order
the Internet
to be small
to be difficult
success
shopping
next
hat, cap
skirt
failure

Crossword Puzzle

					실
주	문	하	다		패
			음		
인	터	넷		어	
				렵	
모	자	작	다		

Fill in the blanks

01 인터넷
02 치마
03 주문했어요
04 실패
05 작아요
06 쇼핑
07 어려워요
08 성공
09 다음
10 모자

Day 32　　page 307

Match

허리 — lower back
문자 — text message
늦다 — to be late
경찰 — police
보내다 — to send, to spend
약속 — promise, plan
조금 — a little, a bit
택시 — taxi, cab
사고 — accident
오토바이 — motorcycle

police
to be late
accident
text message
promise, plan
motorcycle
lower back
to send, to spend
taxi, cab
a little, a bit

Crossword Puzzle

사			문	자
고		늦		
	보	내	다	오
				토
조	금			바
	약			이
	속			

Fill in the blanks

01 약속
02 늦었어요
03 택시
04 오토바이
05 사고
06 경찰
07 문자
08 보냈어요
09 허리
10 조금

Day 33　page 315

Match

나라 　　　　 popularity
가수 　　　　 map
지도 　　　　 singer
궁금하다 　　 to need
단어 　　　　 ear
인기 　　　　 Korean (language)
필요하다 　　 address
귀 　　　　　 to be curious
주소 　　　　 country, nation
한국어 　　　 word

Crossword Puzzle

	귀				
		한		나	라
		국			
		어		필	
인	기			요	
		궁	금	하	다
				다	

Fill in the blanks

01　가수
02　인기
03　나라
04　한국어
05　필요해요
06　단어
07　귀
08　지도
09　주소
10　궁금해요

Day 34　page 323

Match

열 　　　　 to come out
열다 　　　 pharmacy
약국 　　　 nose
건강 　　　 to open
문 　　　　 cold
차 　　　　 door
약 　　　　 fever
감기 　　　 medicine
나오다 　　 tea
코 　　　　 health

Crossword Puzzle

				차	
	문				
		열		건	강
	나	오	다		
			약		
감	기		국		

Fill in the blanks

01　문
02　열고
03　감기
04　열
05　코
06　나왔어요
07　약국
08　약
09　차
10　건강

Day 35　page 331

Match

오이 　　　 to work
마음 　　　 apple
바나나 　　 belly, stomach
절대 　　　 absolutely
사과 　　　 mind, heart
몸무게 　　 banana
토마토 　　 body weight
일하다 　　 to be weak
약하다 　　 tomato
배 　　　　 cucumber

Crossword Puzzle

				사	
바	나	나		과	
			일		
		약	하	다	
			다		
배			절	대	
		마	음		

Fill in the blanks

01　사과
02　바나나
03　일했어요
04　오이
05　토마토
06　배
07　마음
08　약해졌어요
09　몸무게
10　절대

Day 36 page 339

Match

의사	to get hurt
아프다	to rest
힘들다	hospital
어제	exercise
병원	yesterday
운동	doctor
손	to fall down
쉬다	to be difficult
다치다	to be sick, to hurt
넘어지다	hand

Crossword Puzzle

					다
넘				치	
어		힘	들	다	
지					
쉬	다	손		어	
				제	
병	원				

Fill in the blanks

01 어제
02 운동
03 넘어졌어요
04 손
05 다쳤어요
06 아팠어요
07 병원
08 의사
09 쉬었어요
10 힘들어요

Day 37 page 347

Match

다니다	umbrella
비	to take off
우산	student
목욕	shoe
학생	bath
벗다	rain
자전거	foot
발	bicycle
신발	to not have
없다	to attend

Crossword Puzzle

				자	
발				전	
		벗		거	
다	니	다			
					비
우		목	욕		
산					

Fill in the blanks

01 학생
02 자전거
03 다녀요
04 비
05 우산
06 없었어요
07 신발
08 벗었어요
09 발
10 목욕

Day 38 page 355

Match

오전	lie
놀라다	frustration, anger
이상하다	sometimes
거짓말	older brother
오빠	to be strange
가끔	head, hair
벌레	morning
짜증	to hate
싫다	to be surprised
머리	bug, worm

Crossword Puzzle

					가
짜	증		놀		끔
			라		
	이	상	하	다	
거				벌	레
짓			머		
말			리		

Fill in the blanks

01 오빠
02 가끔
03 거짓말
04 짜증
05 오전
06 머리
07 벌레
08 놀랐어요
09 싫어요
10 이상해요

Day 39 page 363

Match

마트 — to buy
생선 — meat
저녁 — fish
채소 — to talk, to speak
달걀 — cooking, food
요리 — vegetable
엄마 — supermarket
말하다 — evening
사다 — egg
고기 — mom

Crossword Puzzle

엄	마			달	걀
	트				
			사		
	말	하	다		
저					
녁			생	선	

Fill in the blanks

01 저녁
02 엄마
03 마트
04 고기
05 샀어요
06 생선
07 채소
08 말했어요
09 달걀
10 요리

Day 40 page 371

Match

믿다 — bird
냄새 — tree, wood
새 — mountain
산 — to move
몸 — to go up
움직이다 — smell
나무 — grandfather
할아버지 — person, people
올라가다 — to trust
사람 — body

Crossword Puzzle

할			산		
아					
버		나		올	
지		무		라	
				가	
	움	직	이	다	
사	람				새

Fill in the blanks

01 할아버지
02 산
03 올라가요
04 믿어요
05 사람
06 새
07 나무
08 냄새
09 몸
10 움직이는

Day 41 page 383

Match

잃어버리다 — to be spacious
들어가다 — bookstore
넓다 — airport
어디 — to ask
찾다 — here
공항 — to find
물어보다 — to enter
길 — where
서점 — to lose
여기 — road, street

Crossword Puzzle

		공	항		
길				물	
				어	디
		들		보	
잃	어	버	리	다	
		가			
		다		여	기

Fill in the blanks

01 공항
02 넓어서
03 길
04 잃어버렸어요
05 여기
06 어디
07 서점
08 들어갔어요
09 물어봤어요
10 찾았어요

Day 42 page 391

Match

가깝다 — university, college
은행 — convenience store
역 — right side
편의점 — to cross
다시 — station
대학교 — to be close
앞 — left side
건너다 — front
왼쪽 — again
오른쪽 — bank

Crossword Puzzle

Fill in the blanks

01 대학교
02 역
03 가까워요
04 오른쪽
05 은행
06 왼쪽
07 편의점
08 앞
09 건너요
10 다시

Day 43 page 399

Match

검은색 — when
가방 — older brother
모르다 — to be different
형 — black
색깔 — wallet
다르다 — white
자동차 — color
하얀색 — to not know
지갑 — bag
언제 — car

Crossword Puzzle

Fill in the blanks

01 색깔
02 검은색
03 지갑
04 자동차
05 가방
06 언제
07 몰라요
08 형
09 하얀색
10 달라요

Day 44 page 407

Match

연필 — pen
펜 — to be bad
이유 — pencil
문제 — to lend
아니다 — to be nice
빌려주다 — to be crazy
착하다 — problem
나쁘다 — reason
미치다 — to not be
또 — again

Crossword Puzzle

Fill in the blanks

01 착해요
02 문제
03 연필
04 빌려주면
05 펜
06 또
07 이유
08 미치겠어요
09 나쁜
10 아니에요

Day 45 page 415

Match

카드 — card
달다 — to be sweet
계획 — plan
결혼 — marriage, wedding
실망 — disappointment
끓이다 — to boil
식물 — plant
정하다 — to decide, to choose
쓰다 03 — to be bitter
싸다 — to be cheap

Crossword Puzzle

			식		
	정		물		
	하		실	망	
싸	다				
			끓		
	계	획	이		
카	드		다		

Fill in the blanks

01 결혼
02 식물
03 카드
04 정했어요
05 싸게
06 끓이고
07 달아요
08 써요
09 실망
10 계획

Day 46 page 423

Match

때 — time, when
짧다 — to be short
인사 — greeting
종이 — paper
팔다 — to sell
신문 — newspaper
털 — fur, hair
유리 — glass
반지 — ring
라디오 — radio

Crossword Puzzle

		인			
		사		짧	
때			팔	다	
	라				
	디		신	문	
	오				
			종	이	

Fill in the blanks

01 팔아요
02 털
03 반지
04 짧은
05 때
06 라디오
07 유리
08 신문
09 종이
10 인사

Day 47 page 431

Match

비슷하다 — to be similar
입 — mouth
실수 — mistake
쌍둥이 — twin
뒤 — behind, after
쉽다 — to be easy
멀다 — to be far
어리다 — to be young
안경 — glasses
생각하다 — to think

Crossword Puzzle

		뒤		실	
입				수	
				비	
	쌍	둥	이	슷	
				하	
			어	리	다
쉽	다				

Fill in the blanks

01 쌍둥이
02 어려울
03 비슷하게
04 생각하는
05 쉽게
06 안경
07 입
08 멀리서
09 뒤
10 실수

Day 48 page 439

Match

이기다   toe
지나다   secret
사전   arm
축구   basketball
영어   dictionary
발가락   baseball
비밀   to pass
농구   English
야구   soccer
팔   to win

Crossword Puzzle

		비	밀		
사					
전			팔		
		야			
	축	구			지
					나
			이	기	다

Fill in the blanks

01   축구
02   농구
03   야구
04   지난
05   이겼어요
06   팔
07   비밀
08   발가락
09   영어
10   사전

Day 49 page 447

Match

불   to count
날다   to understand
바꾸다   cosmos, universe
우주   parking lot
주차장   to pick, to choose
세다   Earth
알아듣다   fire, light
고르다   ticket
지구   to fly
표   to change

Crossword Puzzle

					세
표			고	르	다
		알			
		아		지	
		듣		구	
	바	꾸	다		
			우	주	

Fill in the blanks

01   주차장
02   골랐어요
03   표
04   세어
05   불
06   날았어요
07   지구
08   우주
09   알아듣기
10   바꿨어요

Day 50 page 455

Match

열쇠   to be correct
서다   to be light
가볍다   to get off/out of
운전   it, that
맞다   key
느리다   driving
그것   to stand
내리다   to grab, to hold
휴지   to be slow
잡다   tissue

Crossword Puzzle

				휴
그	것			지
	열	쇠	내	
		느	리	다
		잡	다	
가	볍	다		

Fill in the blanks

01   운전
02   느리게
03   내렸어요
04   열쇠
05   잡았어요
06   그것
07   가벼웠어요
08   휴지
09   맞았어요
10   서

INDEX listed in Korean dictionary order

MP3 audio files can be downloaded at
http://TalkToMeInKorean.com/audio